Praise for *The BreakBeat Poets*

"[T]he first definitive anthology of poems by poets who fuse together the aesthetic of hip-hop and the style of slam poetry with the written-word tradition… [a] dynamic, groundbreaking, genre-merging volume."

—Booklist

"A cool & diversified version of a mix tape. *The BreakBeat Poets* is a thorough and complete summation of Golden Era writers who continue to build the scene of literary and performance poetry."

—Chance The Rapper

"*The BreakBeat Poets* presents the struggle-born whispers, joyous shouts, and hopeful flows of a beautiful multitude four decades in the making. Here are the voices of a movement that just won't stop. For the urgent midnight roar of the people's poetry and the glimpses of freshly conjured dawns awaiting their own breaks—this book is nothing short of essential."

—Jeff Chang, author of *Who We Be: The Colorization of America*

"*The BreakBeat Poets* digs past simplified stereotypes and outdated narratives and opens us up to thoughtfully crafted work that positions hip hop not only as a culture, but also as a messenger of social context, a vehicle of political response, and a tangible solution."

—Lambda Literary

"One of the most diverse and important poetry anthologies of the last 25 years."

—Latino Rebels

"The success of hip-hop has radically reshaped many American art forms. This is particularly true of poetry… *The BreakBeat Poets* comes at an exciting time."

—Gawker

"*The BreakBeat Poets* is not concerned with proving that hip-hop is poetry but rather with documenting the positive impact this musical form has had on poetry. In addition to the diversity of writers and themes, there is a wonderful variety of forms and styles in *The BreakBeat Poets*."

—The Rumpus

The BreakBeat Poets

New American Poetry in the Age of Hip-Hop

Kevin Coval,
Quraysh Ali Lansana,
& Nate Marshall, editors

Haymarket Books

Haymarket Books
PO Box 180165
Chicago, IL 60618
773-583-7884
info@haymarketbooks.org
www.haymarketbooks.org

ISBN: 978-1-60846-395-4

Trade distribution:
In the US, through Consortium Book Sales and Distribution, www.cbsd.com
In the UK, Turnaround Publisher Services, www.turnaround-psl.com
All other countries, Publishers Group Worldwide, www.pgw.com

Special discounts are available for bulk purchases by organizations and
institutions. Please contact Haymarket Books for more information at
773-583-7884 or info@haymarketbooks.org.

This book was published with the generous support
of Lannan Foundation and the Wallace Action Fund.

Printed in Canada by union labor.

Library of Congress CIP data is available.

10 9 8 7 6

Cover art from *Untitled... Negro Mythos Series* by Hebru Brantley.

Contents

Ars Poeticas & Essays

Introduction

Ciphers rise together:

The Black Poets, edited by Dudley Randall

Black Fire, edited by Amiri Baraka and Larry Neal

The New American Poetry, edited by Donald Allen

"Scenario," by A Tribe Called Quest, featuring Leaders of the New School.

Posse Cuts, and the Rock Steady Crew. The Harlem Renaissance and the Native Tongues. The Black Arts Poets and the Good Life Cafe. Flavor Unit and the Beat Generation.

This is the first anthology of poems by and for the hip-hop generation. And it's about time. This book is this first of its kind. It includes more than four decades of poets and covers the birth to the now of hip-hop culture and music and style. This is the story of how generations of young people reared on hip-hop culture and aesthetics took to the page and poem and microphone to create a movement in american letters in the tradition of the Black Arts, Nuyorican, and Beat generations and add to it and innovate on top. We are in the tradition— and making one up. Hip-hop saves young people from voicelessness and art-less public educations. We came to writing in numerous ways, inside and outside of academia. We are dropouts and MFA degree holders, money folders and working folk. The story of how we got here, how I got here, is indicative of how many of my peers and colleagues came to the page, to the poem, and to this book.

Here we go:

At some point I was building on the phone with Idris Goodwin, rapper/ poet/essayist and hip-hop's August Wilson. A continuing conversation, trying to assess and theorize and practice what hip-hop generation writers are doing that's different from writers of other generations. How we flip it and make it fresh, our own, how it's similar attention to the syllabic breath unit paid by Gwendolyn Brooks, John Coltrane, and Lil Wayne, how it's some AFRICOBRA kool-aid color realist portraiture and also legible/illegible graffiti wildstyle and sometimes simultaneously Sun Ra futurism/future world/reclamation of history, on some Lerone Bennett Jr., Alice Walker, Toni Morrison, Howard Zinn–type shit.

It was the early '90s. Not too long after *The Miseducation of Lauryn Hill* and, after reading a magazine whose title I can't remember, I realized this particular magic was meant for me. In this magazine the words of Sekou Sundiata, Willie Perdomo, and Paul Beatty appeared. So did something about Poets, the Lower East Side, and New Africa. Something like that. That experience was similar to when I first read Sonia Sanchez, Jayne Cortez, Nikki Giovanni, Amiri Baraka, and Haki Madhubuti, of sitting cross-legged in the stacks of a public library completely engrossed in Dudley Randall's anthology, when I felt that finally *here* is poetry that is alive and relatable, a language of the working: all the horror and hope and humanity. And here, via Willie and Paul particularly, was, in my mind, how hip-hop might look and read and sing and break and holler on the page.

Reading these poets sent me to find the public cultural spaces of hip-hop praxis. The open-mic live spots and B-boy/B-girl jams that operate as aesthetic showcase and battleground and communal sanctuary. In Chicago, it was the Blue Groove Lounge, a Monday-night set run by DJ Jesse De La Pena and the Afro-centric oil and book shop Another Level at Lit-X's Saturday-night live open-mic spot. These were public cultural spaces where budding practitioners brought their kung-fu out in the open. Hip-hop's need and desire to connect to an audience, in the call and response, made manifest.

So Idris and I were talking, right… and conferring on the growing audience for this work, the tens of thousands of young people we are in front of on a yearly basis with this new poetic, who give it back tenfold in the growing hyper/multi-literate hip-hop–centric educational ciphers and spaces, informal and otherwise, in the organizations we build and build with: Youth Speaks in the Bay and the Brave New Voices network; Urban Word in NYC; the Neutral Zone in Ann Arbor, MI; the First Wave cohorts in Madison, WI; crews of young writers in Tulsa, OK; Dallas–Fort Worth, TX; Omaha, NE; DC-Maryland-Virginia; South Florida; Hamilton, Ontario; Boston; Nashville; Seattle; and of course the tens of thousands of young writers we have communed with around the word at Young Chicago Authors and the Louder Than A Bomb festivals blossoming around the country. Today, there are dozens of community-based organizations engaged in building and educating around this work. And we were talking about this new mass and growing movement and army, and we were on one and thinking about the whole thing and Idris said something crazy like, "Yeah man, you know, we are the BreakBeat Poets, our generation, this is what we do." And I was like... *excuse me?* And then I was silent for a minute and knew he was on to something and felt like some miracle break just happened and it took me back and I think my eyes watered and think I might've let a tear drop... maybe.

The BreakBeat Poets. Poets influenced by the breaks. The break down, polyrhythmic, funky sections of records extended by Kool Herc, Afrika Bambaataa, and Grandmaster Flash to lay a sonic foundation for the largest global youth culture in the history of the planet rock. The break where dancers, break boys and break girls (B-boys and B-girls), emerge on the floor to pop and lock and spin and defy the limitations of body and gravity. To break from the norm. The BreakBeat is the earth of hip-hop, what rappers began to rhyme couplets over. They extended those couplets to make verses and choruses and began to slant rhyme and enjam and extend the line and line break in odd, thrilling places. A break in time. A rupture in narrative. A signifying of something new. Fresh. Dope. Ill. A generation unto itself. Arrived and here. A break from the Beats, an extension of the Black Arts, a continuation of the Nuyorican crew on the Lower East Side, a pidgin and Nation language, to cite Kamau Brathwaite. Hybrid and mixed. The BreakBeat Poets blow up bullshit distinctions between high and low, academic and popular, rap and poetry, page and stage. A break from the wack. A break from the hidden and precious, the elite and esteemed. A break from pejorative notions about what constitutes art, who it's for and by and why. A break with the past. The bridge is over. The BreakBeat Poets and hip-hop culture are saving american poetry.

When I was in high school, and still in many in high schools now, poetry, and often art in general, is taught through the lens of a eurocentric, white supremacist, boring-ass canon. Poetry, perhaps more so than any other art, is not taught as a practice but only as a site of pseudo-criticism and reading comprehension. It seemed dead white dudes who got lost in the forest were the only ones to pick up a pen, and what they wrote had to be about horses or beechwood. I also thought all the poetry had already been written. All the books closed, all the poets dead (and white). I garnered this from the backward, destructive way teachers were/are taught to teach poetry. Perhaps it was when DJs put their hands on the records, something you were *never* supposed to do as a kid, that the idea of writing and contributing to a public rhythmic, civic discourse became so prevalent in the minds of a generation.

KRS-One called himself a poet (and teacher). Chuck D, Big Daddy Kane, MC Lyte, and Rakim are all poets. These are some of the first poets my generation fell in love with and whose prose and style we wanted to emulate. Rappers made poetry relevant and readable and likeable and popular and populist. They sent us into the libraries to read *The Autobiography of Malcolm X* and then find the other books in that section. In the stacks is where we found the Black Arts Poets and Gwendolyn Brooks, Howard Zinn, and Lerone Bennett Jr. In the cited samples on the back of an album or digging through our parents' record collections, we heard again and for the first time Gil Scott-Heron (Rest In Power), the Last Poets, and the Watts Prophets.

Hip-hop made poetry an everyday thing well before Billy Collins. We recited poetry out loud on trains and buses, on our walks to school, bumped poetry in the jeeps of our imaginations. We knew anthologies of new american letters by heart. Poems readable, listenable, relatable, and unfuckwitable. Descriptions of neighborhoods like or unlike our own were an invitation to record, to look out the window, into the streets, and put our surroundings down on paper.

Hip-hop made poetry relevant. It was no longer this dreadful, dead-white-male–centered, highly dull piece to sleep through in English class. It was very much alive and in our Walkmen and notebooks. Hip-hop wrote poetry about the block and aspirant, working-class hopes. It is a culture made by latchkey kids in the crack era, left to their own devices to experiment wildly and make language and art new and meaningful. A poetics designed to move the crowd, a poetics designed to relate to the crowd, to save the crowd. Hip-hop is participatory, radically democratic culture. Everyone is invited and asked to contribute, to get down, in their own way and on their own terms.

Hip-hop invited us to write. To do what Gwendolyn Brooks told thousands of young writers in Chicago and everywhere: tell the story that's in front of your nose. We began to document, to represent, to re-present the physical, metaphysical, and emotional spaces we inhabited and hoped to create. We became *magnetized by the mixing* to quote the g-d Rakim. Everyday language, slang, multisyllabic words we copped in a thesaurus, names of people we knew, blocks we ran, schools we went to, haircuts we got, all were viable pronoun particulars to put in the poem. If Mos Def was talking about Broadway and Myrtle Ave in

Brooklyn and Willie Perdomo was talking about 110th and Lexington Ave in Spanish Harlem, then we knew to talk about our block.

To paraphrase KRS-One, the poems in our anthology are not doing or about hip-hop (though some of them are indeed *about* the music and culture): these poems *are* hip-hop. They are engaged in the aesthetic, cultural, and often public practice of the art form. These poems are readable at multiple levels of accessibility. Some references will fly over the head of the reader not immersed in the culture or generation. Therefore the poems practice what graffiti art bequeathed the page, a legible/illegible read, the public and stealth aspects of style. The graffiti artist can write a legible handstyle that communicates with the largest possible audience; the same artist or writer can also create wildstyle letters only "readable" by practitioners or trained viewers. This happens again and again. The artist has multiple conversations in one moment. A viewer can see a piece of graffiti and perhaps recognize it as letters or someone's name, or maybe not read it at all but understand it as a mass of color, or just vandalism and criminal activity. A writer might be able to read the letters on the wall and also have a sense of what block they grew up on, what crews they ran with, whose style(s) they are mimicking or mastering.

In ways similar to how blues influenced the Harlem Renaissance or the ways jazz influenced the Black Arts Poets, the music and culture of hip-hop shape this moment of american letters and create a generation engaged in similar and variant aesthetic principles and experimentations. The BreakBeat Poets are not all strict hip-hop heads and some folks in the collection might not consider what they do to be hip-hop cultural practice at all. Word. Hip-hop is open and comprised of every culture and music, though it is rooted in and part of African diasporic cultural histories and practices. Hip-hop is Black, therefore hip-hop poetics are Black and are created in part as a response to the historic and currently maintained legacies and realities of white supremacy and institutional racism, the war of drugs, and the growing privatized prison-industrial complex and school-to-prison pipeline, a.k.a. the new Jim Crow, as Michelle Alexander calls it.

Like all diasporic cultures, hip-hop also values and pedestalizes the mix, has a fetish for the fresh. If it wasn't for the collision of uptown and downtown in the late '70s/early '80s on the Lower East Side in New York and the mixing of punk and late disco in Larry Levan's Paradise Garage or the house Frankie Knuckles and Ron Hardy built in Chicago, then we would not be in the same place and perhaps there would be no book or records or global youth culture that changed and are changing the world. The B-boy and B-girl are synthesizing martial arts, robotic flicking, gymnastics, capoeira, cartoon expressionism, uprock, salsa, African dance, and more in the same moment to create something in the tradition and altogether fresh. As a vocational high-school student in the South Bronx, Grandmaster Flash took the electric circuits of two turntables and placed a simple light switch between them: Hegelian synthesis. The mix was born, again, and opened a space-time diasporic continuum to usher in the miscegenated moment, a place firmly entrenched in the era and simultaneously beyond time. Magic. Aime and Suzanne Cesaire, Sun Ra Black Surreal Super-real, indigenous-future funk. The mix is what miscegenated the dance floors, what blended the records and languages, a pidgin bridge to the future world.

Hip-hop saved american poetry. Made it new, fresh, made it something anybody gave a fuck about. Hip-hop did this. Black and Brown and Asian writers made poetry a tool to communicate with an intentionally large audience and also went out in the streets and clubs and community centers to organize and build and find that audience. american poetry is growing in popularity because of hip-hop poetics, the public performances and widely diverse strategies of publishing poems: YouTube, mixtapes, chapbooks, constant gigs, readings, tours, crews, television shows, popular documentaries, school assemblies, slams, open mics, and online journals are all avenues to publish poems broadly. In addition, hip-hop generation writers are beginning to infiltrate ivory towers, their magazines and presses. Hip-hop saved poetry from becoming classical music. It dusted it off, brought it out the closet, put some Js on its feet, told it to speak with the people, *all the people*. Have a conversation, tell a story, rouse the spirit, spit the truth. Hip-hop is making poetry cool in schools across the country, changing the culture of literature and thereby the culture of education. Poets now walk high-school hallways like star athletes. Hip-hop did this.

There are a number of aesthetic innovations in hip-hop poetics/BreakBeat poetics that some of the authors in this collection will explore in the last section of the book, the Ars Poeticas & Essays section. One foundational principle of the poetic that binds us all is an overt and intentional participation in civic discourse. These poems are political and intensely human and arc toward justice and a new, fresher future world. Hip-hop culture reimagines the public sphere and claims agency in sites and systems of disenfranchisement. Hip-hop is a pastiched community at the margins of dominant discourse that uses the creative elements of dance, graffiti, turntablism, and oral and written poetics to insist on participation at the center of the american experience. Hip-hop and BreakBeat poetics is the desire to see and be seen, to paraphrase Denizen Kane, as is a tag on a street sign or the inclusion of a familiar horn stab sample, a robotic tic or Rerun uprock. Hip-hop and BreakBeat poetics use the familiar—food, family, and neighborhood—to connect to a vastly disparate audience in order to bring awareness to the sanctity and humanity of the people and places at the center of the poem. The South Bronx was abandoned by the country/city and hip-hop insisted it look and be heard. In this collection are stories and peoples and experiences systematically denied, whose experiences are untold or criminally underreported in the media and history class. Hip-hop/BreakBeat poetics sets the record straight or at least scratches it, pulls it back, makes it stop and alters it, cuts it, until it's fresher, until we re/member the parts the artist desires us to recall. Hip-hop and the BreakBeat generation(s) are the people who said no more columbus day, no more fuckery and denial and exclusion and exemption from whatever story or institution or art or sport or country/club white supremacists wished to keep restricted. Hip-hop generation artists and intellectuals and people, just people ultimately, bum rushed the show and changed the game and flipped the script and constantly are at war with a country and history that seeks to murder its young and Black and Brown and hip-hop is ultimately a weapon for life and against the wack, the white supremacist. Hip-hop has its shortcomings (I concede). Some of these shortcomings are well traversed in this collection as well as in other places. But hip-hop is a space where we are able to have incredibly honest and difficult and essential conversations about the issues of the day in order to push the crew and community forward.

The BreakBeat Poets has more than seventy writers in it. I wanted more, and more deserve to be here. There are some poets we reached out to who never got back. Some folks we couldn't get in touch with. Some have gone off the grid. There are a few I really wanted in whose absence I feel, and there are many, many more to come.

The poets in this collection were born between 1961 to 1999. There are established and highly decorated poets with several publications and there are poets whose first time appearing in print is this collection. All dope and equally relevant. Hip-hop cultural space practices a kind of meritocracy. If you have skills you can participate in the cipher. No bio or pedigree follows you in. Dope is dope. The poets cover much terrain both stylistically and creatively in terms of poem form and narrative content. Readers may notice different capitalization or hyphenation among the authors. We chose to keep these creative differences expressed in the poems and essays since poets purposefully play with (the aesthetics of) language. I am honored that such a giant crew of people dispersed throughout the country gave us the opportunity and honor to publish their work.

I want to note that my coeditors and colleagues are homies and men I admire. Nate is a former student and Quraysh someone I looked up to way before we met many years ago. Both stay teaching me shit about the word and the world and I am so grateful to them for their work and trust through this process.

I trust this book to be a piece of the growing discourse on how art can be used to create a fresher world, a useful tool to further and extend and generate conversations in classrooms and ciphers, on the corner, in living rooms, in institutions, and in the renegade spaces young people carve out for themselves despite state control. This is a call with the anticipation of the undoubted response. Hip-hop has connected more people on the planet than any culture in the history of ever. This is a prayer book and a shank, concrete realism and abstracted futurism.

Yet the work is far from finished cuz this is america and the world, and we have much to do and far to go. The work is somewhere in the mix, is in accounting for the beauty and freshness of each body, each culture and utterance, and seeing/hearing/not harming its essential dopeness and bringing that into the cipher, the radically democratic cultural space where hip-hop lives actually and as metaphor for how we might (re)organize our selves. "Have you forgotten why we buildin' in a cipher / Yo hear me kid, government is building in a pyramid," says KRS-One. And the work is in extending the cipher, the party/ jam is open to anyone willing to get down, and you can get down and "punks jump up to get beat down," Brand Nubian insists we remember. Remember, we, this country and culture, are at a breaking point. These poems are the work and will fuel the work. And the work is to make a fresher, more equitable world for all. And the work don't stop. Yes Yes Y'all / It Don't Stop.

Kevin Coval
12/22/14

an (i)witness say he still had the mike in his hand

at an archeological site in new york
but it could have been atlanta
then too   cali is not impervious
a male m.c. unearthed himself (at last) from the dirt
had been compressing the species down forever
annihilated it is believed   **not one real muthafucka** inhabits
america especially   has sought to exterminate
anything sagging or claiming to be   .&. .&. .&.
still on the rise   anthropologist say   the body
perfectly intact   a-check-one-a-check   two times
onlookers blinked at the rustic microphone
long suffering in its extinction   a conceit
the lecherous inability to transform
our initial state so often voted its death
even the posse ak-(there was none found)-a crew
all skeletoid offered introspections on capitalism
at the present   archivist are looking
on the good foot *James Brown is making a comeback*
is what they chant in the streets rejuvenating
a precarious species can disappear in a handclap.

Joel Dias-Porter
aka DJ Renegade (1962)

Turning the Tables
(for Eardrum)

First hold the needle
   like a lover's hand
Lower it slowly
   let it tongue
   the record's ear
Then cultivate
the sweet beats
   blooming in the valley
   of the groove
Laugh at folks
   that make requests
What chef would let
   the diners determine
Which entrees
   make up the menu?
Young boys
   think it's about
flashy flicks
   of the wrist
But it's about filling the floor
   with the manic
   language of dance
About knowing the beat
of every record
   like a mama knows
   her child's cries
Nobody cares
how fast you scratch
Cuz it ain't about
   soothing any itch
It's about how many hairstyles
   are still standing
At the end of the night.

Wednesday Poem

Joel Dias-Porter

I pass through the metal detector,
inside the front doors of Cardozo High,
with xeroxed poems and a lesson planned
to introduce my students to the wild iris.
After signing my name in the visitors' log,
I bop down two flights of steps.
Outside the classroom things are too quiet
and Mr. Bruno (who's Puerto Rican and writes poetry)
takes ten minutes to answer the door.
There's a student snapshot in his hand.
One of our kids got shot last night,
Remember Maurice? Maurice Caldwell.
He didn't come to school much.
A Crisis Response Team has the kids in a circle,
and I've never seen them sit so quietly.
Every computer in the classroom is dead.
A drawing of Maurice is taped to the board,
a bouquet of cards pinned under it,
Keisha (who writes funny poems in class)
says Maurice would help her with math,
she liked him but never told him.
The Crisis lady says *It's OK to cry.*
Keisha says she been ran out of tears.
Mr. Bruno tells me *Somebody called him*
from a parked Buick on Thomas Place NW.
When he walked up, they fired three times.
I freeze. That's a half block from my house.
There are four crackhouses on that block
and I never walk down that street.
I wonder why he approached the car,
was he hustling crack or weed?
Or did he recognize the dude and smile
before surprise blossomed across his face
and the truth rooted into his flesh.
His face flashes before my irises,
I see him horseplaying with Haneef,
his hair slicked back into a ponytail.
He wrote one poem this whole semester,

a battle rap between cartoon characters.
Mr. Bruno asks if I still want to teach.
I open my folder of nature poems,
then close the folder and slump in a chair.
What simile can seal a bullet wound?
Which student could these pistils protect,
here where it's natural to never see seventeen?

Thomas Sayers Ellis (1963)

An Excerpt from *Crank Shaped Notes*

[The Non Fictitious Sticks]

It was all practice (for something), so you just started hitting them, the books like they were drums and (later) the rototoms like they were books, right in their dark vowels, but first you covered them with towels or thin blankets to muffle the strokes of grammar—except for the one you hit once, which is how you got a son. Terrell. If there were roaches, and there were, then they heard you building a bridge but too young to cross it. Those years in college, college-hoping, bored, and calling home to find out how the shows went, how the culture was doing, but no one would tell you or could tell you, well, not to your satisfaction not even one of your best friends who could talk, lead talk, with his eyes closed but didn't read—which made you think "Where does the language in him come from? Is it all an act, a natural act?" Your new friends, though, could do both but knew nothing about you as a pair of sticks, one stick that did not behave like the other stick, so you missed a home that didn't miss you.

*

I am tired of the hyphen. It makes Go-Go stutter.

*

Hip Hop may break studio-dawn all night long but GoGo percussions the concert-sun till the lights come on.

*

Our inability to identify the stages of Cultural Revolution has tricked us into a belief that GoGo is non political and not a Resistance Movement. There are three branches of crank (groove, bucket, and bounce) and when they share "the floor," they move the people in the back, against the wall, up from the bottom of themselves.

*

Washington's famous humidity is not a result of the city being built on a swamp. The sweltering tension comes from the "hot chopped bar-b-que" between local and federal interests. They eat on a hill. We beat on a river.

*

Short rolls in the groove and long rolls to finish, but the best way to knock a bama Mayor (who ain't in the band and who ain't supposed to be on stage) off the stage is with the base of the mic stand. A base is what every local candidate needs to protect it from a synthesized Federal sting.

*

I'd rather be a an old, single, beaten cowbell addicted to the hardest drink at the bar than an entire, well-dressed set-list-dependent Grown and Sexy Band. There's nothing worse than pharmaceutical groove. Get those cheat sheets off the stage so the lead talker can work his two sheets to the wind.

*

You know "the pocket" is all about parenting and sexuality, yet another family discussion of percussion. That is why you never see the big congas without their juniors, the seeds they got from having their skins hit by the reproductive sounds and signs of hands.

*

Pure crank resists privilege. In fact its socio-percussive-political value reunions a frontline akin to a rare and highly contagious form of prolific-triflin'.

*

Like subject-verb agreement the physical grammar of a GoGo frontline used to be linear, a uniformed unit, but that was before "La Di Da Di," that's when natural speech, pure non-rhymed lead talk (in the pocket) began its first phase of dying.

I miss the days when the Hammond B3 was used to foreshadow a groove, the easing before entering, like an organic literary device. The pocket used to contain so much foreplay and the grooves were structured like lovemaking—touch, taste, togetherness. Your organ did not orgasm without a Leslie. Without fingers your keys did not please.

*

The loudest part of GoGo may be the beat but the loudest part of the beat is still poverty. Like it or not, those are poor hands in your pocket. Get in. Get out.

*

There is nothing or no one in the GoGo community, simultaneously, more old school and more new school than the drum. It goes to every school because its instructor, the human heart, is all schools.

*

What a groove feels like: A neck so sensitive it demands choke. Good itch-scratching, back and forth, like a hardness only flow can stroke.

*

The "flashy stuff" (like extra arm movements and spinning in circles, etc., while playing the congas) is just like the camera flash and truly only necessary when there is not enough available light or talent or when the lens is too slow to handle the amount of darkness onstage. Most of the stuff we attribute to skill is, perhaps, really just an expression of physical style. The real purpose of flash and flashiness, for some, may not be to illuminate but to evaporate.

*

A beat is just a beat but a beat followed by a beat and followed by another beat with a beat between the beat and a beat under the beat and a beat on top of the beat and a beat beside the beat is a beating, a continuous one, so regarding so-called battles and beefs between bands and band members, know this: percussion without drama is like GoGo without percussion, gen-tri-fried, and every GoGo percussionist (born and raised in the District) has two very non-Shakespearian pockets of behavior to choose from: (1) If you beat your kids now, they will beat their kids later and you will have bad ass grandkids and (2) If you don't beat your kids now, they will beat you later and you will still have bad ass grandkids. In other words: as does hitting, the beat goes on. We crank shaped. We get things twisted, bent, bent from all the dramatic beatings, the loving, the DC listening.

*

Grooving is getting along with folks but cranking is cussing somebody out. All curse words are percussive and all percussions like to be hit from the front and the back, back it on up.

*

The definition of Milton "GoGo Mickey" Freeman: the lawmaker of left-handed social order, the rare reality of classic essence, and he who grooved out of one helluva shadow to become its owner.

*

We knows what Sugar Bear keeps in his nose: everything he owns. And even if we discovered that all of his snot was cake, the icing on his face would still be a muscular bass.

*

Born in 1935 and known for his love of hats, the Godfather of GoGo was rarely seen in public without one, but did you know that Porky Pig made his debut in 1935 in a featurette titled *I Haven't Got A Hat*? Porky also used to burst (bust loose) through a bass drum at the end of cartoons with his trademark, "Th-Th-Th-That's all folks!" And years later Chuck Brown turned one of Porky's famous stutters into a brand new groove.

*

A GoGo is a form of gathering and being a form of gathering, it is also a form of community organizing even if it is only held together by the ritual of dancing and our need to enter the freak-a-deke zone. The moment you add community news (lead talking), an exchange between the band and the audience (call and response), and more than one talking drum (the pocket), the gathering becomes something with purpose, a political possibility, folk power!

*

A little lead talk, like salt, is good for you—especially your boogie body. It can make you sweat. The calcium in the pocket comes from milking the cowbell. The iron in the pocket comes from putting the foot pedal to the metal. There's nothing healthier or more chewable or more one-a-day vitamin, than hearing your name roll-called and tossed back at you, amplified, from one respiratory sound system to another. The walls we used to work, work us when we don't drink enough water.

*

They did not brand GoGo violent to stop us from hurting ourselves but to limit us to hurting and killing only ourselves and to prevent us from organizing our guns and fists into proper forms of community self offense and community self defense. DC exists (by federal design and unconstitutionally so) to provide Washington with workers, cheap labor, a lower class. That's how Capital and so-called Capitol cities work. DC is a damaged colony, a colony that contains real ruthless punching (poverty, disease, miss-education) and every pocket has become a flurry of mismanaged counter-punching. It makes sense that GoGo's full pockets would party and that GoGo's empty pockets would punch. The tension makes sense, but the ideal foot-fist must bravely march the wrong punch right out of town, and punch the wrong the march right out of town. A lot of percussion begins in confusion and a lot of confusion ends in percussion.

*

These crank shaped notes don't mean shit if our city remains their torn square. They tore it, blamed us, and now want to take credit for the fixins'. A drum-kit is like a sit-in, Bitch!

*

I have a feeling that if Bounce Beat declares itself separate from GoGo, Bounce, being more industrial, will eventually out-perform GoGo. I have a related feeling that if Southeast declares itself separate from Washington, Southeast, being more agricultural, will eventually out perform Washington. Maybe Bounce is GoGo and what we thought was GoGo was something else, a replica of R&B and Funk, slowly taking shape. Maybe Southeast is Washington and what we thought was Washington was something else, a replica of Paris and Rome, slowly taking shape. Perhaps GoGo is only as original as its maverick landowner, Washington, DC

*

The poetry of GoGo has nothing to do with words. In fact, it is limited by the packaging nature of words. The poetry of GoGo can hurt any poem that dares to steal its home: up in the air, ready for hands, in the spaces left by all the banging.

*

Our home is unique because it is the seat, the seat of government. The term "Government" is just a political, man-made name for drumming. It should be called Drummer-ment. The drum lets the drummer sit in the seat but the drum, not the drummer, is responsible for its own proper council in the streets, a coalition. A good coalition is like a good seamstress, making sure every pocket has at least three pairs of talking hands in it.

The term "Government" actually means drumming, Drummer-ment. The drum lets the drummer sit in the seat and the drum, not the drummer, is responsible for its own coalition and council.

*

You think this thing called GoGo cannot save you. You think it is just a another noise and unimportant but what if the most crank shaped thing in all of Washington is DC and the most crank shaped thing in all of DC is Anacostia, and what if Anacostia is GoGo's Bethlehem on the Potomac. Would that make Barry Farms a holy place, the most crank shaped thing in the world a newborn foot?

A crank note is the opposite of a car note.
A car note hurts the pocket.
A crank note locks it.

*

To destroy the content of Crank, trace the shape of the black body
with white chalk then call it art.

*

I don't have a dream but I do believe that crank awakens us.

*

The citizens (young and old) who gifted and continue to gift DC a
sound for the town, the sound of struggle, a cry we need and love,
are only half of the bright miracle that is GoGo. You out there, the
community audience, are equally responsible for this miracle because
when GoGo began, soul-ing and searching, you accepted the call to
the floor. You didn't need a seat, Senate or House, to be recognized or
heard, or to fill the room, Panorama or Maverick, with the birth of
our most lasting vote: Us!

Quraysh Ali Lansana (1964)

mascot
for zack. for mark.

I.

the red undertones that inform my melanin
were birthed in the black mountain foothills
near the tennessee-mississippi border.

my great-grandfather albert found freedom
just before the trail of tears migration
and hooked up with an ornery black
woman in westpoint, muddy waters' neighbor.

ms. cora mae, never one to hold anything
long but money, sent him to his horse
upon the news—she had things to do—my grandma
would join the family business in a while.

ms. cora mae carried three daughters and two sons
into post-reconstruction mississippi, sown
from different seeds. the women, their doors
always open, were sexy to kill for. the men
loyal enough to do the job—cooking shine and running
game.
    when the klan came calling the guns were loaded.
my father and uncles, all under ms. cora mae's command
led rebellion against attack on their cottage industry, left
red cotton to feed brittle soil, then scattered in four directions.

after three draft-dodging years in miami, daddy ended
up in oklahoma, where his sisters somehow landed
and his mama joined them after california.

II.

i am an okie. grew up on cherokee

as did zack, my first best friend,
who lived two blocks away and wore
the street in his skin. we liked basketball,
cars, and never watched westerns.
zack disappeared in high school after one year
in warpaint riding a spotted mare at pre-game.
he was gone before i had the chance
to tell him what i already knew.

grandma never claimed native and hated
anyone darker than a grocery bag. this is where
i begin, on cherokee, trying to find zack
to talk about this mascot issue.

III.

the beantown honkies
the johnson city jarheads
the washington senators
the oaktown wannabees
the cushing crackers
the tulsa rednecks
the old baltimore bigots
the chicago police department
the white city afrikaaners
the cook county overseers
the heritage foundation
the riverside peckerwoods
the german shepherds

IV.

> *How politically correct can we get? To me, the folks that
> make these decisions need to get out more often. I think
> they insult those people by telling them, "No. No. You're
> not smart enough to understand this. You should be feeling
> really horrible about it." It's ridiculous.*
>> Jeb Bush, governor of Florida, *St. Petersburg (FL)*
>> *Times*, August 10, 2005

V.

ms. brooks urged me to return to school
from the nervous backseat of my mustang
in 1994. but what triggered the movement
was an enid, oklahoma, drunken conversation
in a honky tonk with friends from high school,
all white and pseudo-liberal. we deliberated
level playing fields & jesse jackson
while the sad child of hank williams warbled
something loud about loneliness. just as twelve
years prior, i was cultural diversity at the table
and no longer comfortable. one man, maybe
my closest oklahomey in the bar, assured me
the residuals of chattel slavery no longer existed,
while leaning against the door of a 100-year-old
family business. i enrolled in african american
studies two months later. he will not remember
this exchange any more than he will recall the night
i was informed my blackness was a liability
in his pursuit of teenage pussy. history will tell on you.

crack house

Quraysh Ali Lansana

greeter

she hustles us in
eyes tired

shadows stutter
behind nervous trees

outer room

screen door grime
a porous portal

paneling drips
frantic carpet

living room

up early ricki lake
an endless loop

tv's wide blue mouth
the only thing moving

pantry

she fast food she
buy one get one free

kitchen

parched bones
silently akimbo

peel of burn
gray of skin

he sizzles
cooks

seventy-first & king drive

night smells catfish crispness
while sista girl works them curls
s's lounge buzz and slam
as brothas basehead
brothas boomin
basehead brothas boomin
bass boomin
boomin base
blowin the plastic in the used-to-be back window
a baby boppin in the backseat

jackie's restaurant is always open
well, in july, until 11:30 pm
urban queens with Newport lips
hardened softness serving biscuits of like texture
leo's flowers, a fading pastel
succumbs to evening's wings
chicken wings

wild irish the bouquet of the 'hood

Evie Shockley (1965)

duck, duck, redux

those who cannot remember the past are doomed to repeat it.
—george santayana

those who cannot forget the past are destined to remix it. —me

this is the way we wash our face, wash our face, wash our face, this is the way we wash our face, so early in the morning. this is the way we segregate our schools in 1896. this is the way we segregate our schools in 2007. *mary had a little lamb,* a bad, bad black sheep with three bags full of wool. *it followed her to school one day, work one day, wimbledon one day, it followed her to church one day, which was against the rule.* this is the way we patrol the roads in the antebellum south. this is the way we patrol the streets in our shiny new york. cue wedding bell. *oh bring back my sean-y to me.* this is the way we appropriate black culture in the post-reconstruction period. this is the way we appropriate black culture in the 21st century. *this little piggy went to market,* got mad bling for spittin wack rhymes and calling women hos, and still wound up crying *we, we, we, all the way home.* this is the way we use a noose in jim crow america. this is the way we use a noose in jena, louisiana. *little blues boy, come blow your horn.* i'm sorry to tell you, but his horn's done gone, and as for the boy who used to blow so sweet, he's under a mountain of debt, working for minimum wage. *this is the way we wash our hands of you historically, throw you into the atlantic, spray you with birmingham hoses, this is the way we wash our hands of you today, with jerry-rigged levees, so early, so so early in the millennium.*

post-white

my country tears of thee sparkling on a stiff gray bow tied against
cognitive dissonance getting a)head holding it together keeping it
really warm sweet land of basketball barbeque sweet potato pie and
cadillac liberty crowned lady with a torch in her voice of(f thee i
spring hopeful at last my love you've come a long way baby on the
stony road we trod through this land where my fathers and mothers
died on poplars in quarters under the lash and over the objections of
the vocal few singing freedom oh freedom over me and the authors
of declarations of independence finally appointed to positions of
authority phillis wheatley with pen in hand and internationally
recognized skill in diplomacy secretary of state frederick douglass who
won't dread scott's claim of citizenship chief justice of the supreme
court harriet jacobs master strategist speaker of the house music
moving mountains i'd let freedom ring with the harmonies of liberty
a work song hold it steady right there while i hit it reckon you oughta
get it a tisket a tasket we drop-kicked that old basket mama's got a
brand new bag and say it plain from that day forward we were all hip
hop you don't stop being american

Everything You Wanted to Know about Hip Hop But Were Afraid to Be Hipped for Fear of Being Hopped

Hip Hop Halitosis Hip Hop Hosiery Hip Hop Haberdashery
Hip Hop Hollandaise Sauce Hip Hop Alupent Inhaler Hip Hop
Hysterectomy Hip Hop Viagra Hip Hop Lamborghini Hip Hop
Chancletas Hip Hop Unemployment Hip Hop Fortune Cookie Hip
Hop Auction Block Hip Hop Umbrella Hip Hop Rocking Chair
Hip Hop Chandelier Hip Hop Hool-a-Hoop Hip Hop Hooray Hip
Hop Hurricane Hip Hop Quagmire Hip Hop Radial Tire Hip Hop
Earth Wind & Fire Hip Hop Muck & Mire Hip Hop Hotwire Hip
Hop Perspire Hip Hop Fire & Desire Hip Hop Murder for Hire Hip
Hop Liar Hip Hop Sire Hip Hop Retirement Plan Hip Hop and The
Man Hip Hop Hoolihan Hip Hop Bogey Man Hip Hop Sanitation
Truck Hip Hop Don't Give a Fuck Hip Hop Can You Spare a Buck
Hip Hop Desperation Hip Hop Inflation Hip Hop Hives Hip Hop
Urtication Hip Hop Meditation Hip Hop Medication Hip Hop
Tokyo Rose Hip Hop Potato Chips Hip Hop Stovetop Stuffing Hip
Hop Putrefaction Hip Hop Pepto Bismol Hip Hop Pundit Hip Hop
Fund It Hip Hop Brothel Hip Hop Silverware Hip Hop Crystal Stair
Hip Hop Buyer Beware Hip Hop Nuclear Scare Hip Hop Dental
Care Hip Hop Fred Astaire Hip Hop Flair Hip Hop Nightmare Hip
Hop Tupperware Hip Hop Hair Hip Hop Stare Hip Hop Chair
Hip Hop Bear Hip Hop Share Hip Hop Glare Hip Hop Air Hip
Hop Where Hip Hop Heir Hip Hop Dare Hip Hop Holocaust Hip
Hop Hucklebuck Hip Hop Helium Hip Hop Delirium Hip Hop
Landing Hip Hop Scanning Hip Hop Canning Hip Hop Fanning
Hip Hop Tanning Salon Hip Hop Rayon Hip Hop Ding Dong Hip
Hop Donkey Kong Hip Hop Churning Hip Hop Is Burning Hip
Hop Earning Hip Hop Learning Hip Hop Discerning Hip Hop
Ham Sandwich Hip Hop Pork Rinds Hip Hop Spare Ribs Hip Hop
Ham on Rye Hip Hop Lady Di Hip Hop High Five Hip Hop Hard
Drive Hip Hop Wanted Dead or Alive Hip Hop Beehive Hip Hop
Jive Hip Hop Sour Cream and Chives Hip Hop Dives Hip Hop
Wives Hip Hop Friendly Skies Hip Hop Handle Hip Hop Scandal
Hip Hop Cross Your Heart Bra Hip Hop Crossword Puzzle Hip

Hop Crossing Hip Hop Bossing Hip Hop Salad Tossing Hip Hop
Dental Floss Hip Hop Hobby Horse Hip Hop Mister Ed Hip Hop
Mr. Potato Head Hip Hop Freddy's Dead Hip Hop Pro Keds Hip
Hop Giving Head Hip Hop Lead Hip Hop Better Dead Than Red
Hip Hop Shed Hip Hop Dread Hip Hop Sled Hip Hop Feds Hip
Hop Rorschach Test Hip Hop Rutabaga Hip Hop Scapular Hip Hop
Spatula Hip Hop Ambiguity Hip Hop Anxiety Hip Hop Quadruped
Hip Hop Acumen Hip Hop Chihuahua Hip Hop Stockpile Hip
Hop Projectile Hip Hop Cake with File Hip Hop Gomer Pyle Hip
Hop Dream Weaver Hip Hop Dumb Beaver Hip Hop Back Alley
Hip Hop Rally Hip Hop White Trash Hip Hop Monster Mash Hip
Hop Moroccan Hash Hip Hop Pipes Hip Hop Swipes Hip Hop Baby
Wipes Hip Hop Snipes Hip Hop Gripes Hip Hop Stereotypes Hip
Hop Dukes of Hazzard Hip Hop Old Dirty Bastards Hip Hop Hotel
Hip Hop Motel Hip Hop Holiday Inn Hip Hop Constipation Hip
Hop Chia Pet Hip Hop Seeing Eye Dog Hip Hop Kermit the Frog
Hip Hop Closed Captions Hip Hop Subtitles Hip Hop Country
Club Hip Hop City Hip Hop Boo Boo Kitty Hip Hop Itty Bitty
Titty Committee Hip Hop Pity Hip Hop Diddy Hip Hop Eponymy
Hip Hop Economy Hip Hop Sunlight Hip Hop Ultra Bright Hip
Hop Out of Sight Hip Hop Fly By Night Hip Hop Fly a Kite Hip
Hop Despite Hip Hop Drawers Hip Hop Hog Maws Hip Hop
Tattoo Paws Hip Hop Broken Jaws Hip Hop Flaws Hip Hop Crawls
Hip Hop Shores Hip Hop Snores Hip Hop Bronchitis Hip Hop
Meningitis Hip Hop Gold Tooth Gingivitis Hip Hop Grammar
Book Hip Hop Graham Crackers Hip Hop Quarterback Sackers
Hip Hop Weed Whackers Hip Hop Dunkin' Donut Snackers Hip
Hop Crumb Snatchers Hip Hop Booty Smackers Hip Hop Asthma
Attack Hip Hop Comeback Hip Hop Hooligan Hip Hop Stool
Pigeon Hip Hop Incision Hip Hop Derision Hip Hop Precision Hip
Hop Aneurysm Hip Hop Harvey Wall Banger Hip Hop No More
Wire Hangers Hip Hop Apologia Hip Hop Mama Mia Hip Hop
Candy Yams Hip Hop Credit Card Scams Hip Hop Winnebago Hip
Hop Let My People Go Hip Hop Let Go My Eggo Hip Hop Shake
'N Bake Hip Hop Frosted Flakes Hip Hop Earthquakes Hip Hop
On a Plane with Snakes Hip Hop These Are the Breaks Hip Hop
Jewelry Fakes Hip Hop Wakes Hip Hop Makes Mistakes Hip Hop
Morphine Drip Hip Hop Liposuction Hip Hop Face Lift Hip Hop
Temper Tantrum Hip Hop Prenup Hip Hop D-Up Hip Hop Lay
Up Hip Hop Layoff Hip Hop Pink Slip Hip Hop Sinking Ship Hip
Hop Chocolate Chip Hip Hop Dip Hip Hop Trip Hip Hop Sip Hip

Hop Similac Hip Hop Stevedore Hip Hop I Adore Hip Hop Mi
Amor Hip Hop Fundamentalist Hip Hop Insanity Hip Hop Payola
Hip Hop Crayola Hip Hop Barbie Hip Hop Stretch Marks Hip
Hop Robitussin High Hip Hop Epidemic Hip Hop Epidural Hip
Hop Pandemic Hip Hop Pandora's Box Hip Hop Pancake Mix Hip
Hop Panic Button Hip Hop Pedantic Hip Hop Eye Tic Hip Hop
Puritanical Hip Hop Botanical Hip Hop Purist Hip Hop Fingerprints
Hip Hop Nation Hip Hop Escalation Hip Hop Exclamation Mark
Hip Hop After Dark Hip Hop Orthopedic Shoes Hip Hop Hebrews
Hip Hop EKG Machine Hip Hop Hydroplane Hip Hop Crash Test
Dummies Hip Hop Down the Drain

The Keepin' It Real Awards

Best Welfare Cheat
Best Empty Beer Can Collector
Best Ant & Roach Killer
Best Broke Back Mountain Rat Rider
Best Drive-by Shooting Victim
Best Crime Scene Tape Cordoner
Best Chalk-marked Silhouette Model
Best Stripper in a Turquoise Thong
Best Toilet Roll Holder
Best Projects Elevator Pisser
Best Jheri Curl Weave
Best Gold Toofus
Best Crack Attack Running Man Dancer
Breaking & Scraping Along the Concrete
    Until Your Limbs Bleed
Best Sisyphean Government Surplus Cheese Hauler
Best Mister Softee Chaser
Best Popsicle Stick Race Along the Curbside Fire Hydrant Stream
Best Lower Back Tattoo
Best Dry Hump Beneath a Staircase
Best Heroin-Induced Vomit Nod
Best Hip Hop Grimace
Best Pallbearer

Shit to Write About

The last time Kriptonite stopped me on Lexington Avenue was the night he had a bottle fight with his girlfriend. He asked me to write something sweet for her. He said it should be something like the poem I wrote for Spy's girl on Valentine's Day. He asked me to recite the poem. The poem went like this:

The longer I look
for something to say
the harder I search
for another way to
show you my love
I don't have a rose
or a box of chocolates
to send in place of
my heart
but I can start
with a bouquet of
I love you and I miss you
close your eyes and
feel me kiss you
If I could I would turn into
a greeting card
and send myself express
but all I have is this poem
to show that I love you
more than I love you less

Krip yelled, "Yeah, yeah, that's the shit I'm talking about! But I want mine to be better than that, you know what I'm sayin'?"

"Tell me what you miss about your girl, Krip," I said.

"You know how she puts me to sleep? She sings me lullabies while she writes her name in cursive on my bare back with the tips of her fingernails. She loves it when I tell her to sit in front of me so I can run a comb real soft through her hair. I miss my girl, yo," he said like he was lost for the first time.

It reminded me of the night we were standing in front of 1990 and Krip pointed to a cardboard shrine on the corner. And then he pointed to a row of Air Jordans hanging off the neck of a light post; the glow-in-the-dark rosaries hanging off red candles with eternal flames; untapped forties and unwrapped cigars; 'hood libations for our mans and them, who may they rest in peace as we leave "R.I.P." burning on the wall and visit their tombstones daily. And Krip said, "Now if you gotta write about something, that's some shit to write about."

Today he stopped me because his subject was life stories; unauthorized biographies about players who are reaching the end of their game.

"Yo, I been looking all over Lexington for you, man. I heard you was living in Brooklyn now. Coño, you getting fat, kid. Que Dios te bendiga, mano. Word up. Last time I saw you, you looked like you was smoking lovely. Not for nothin' but everybody thought you was down with the dead poets' society. Kenny Mac told me that you was getting paid to write your life story and like I been having these scrambling nights and hand-to-mouth baby crying mornings. I just lost my mother to the Monster and I'm waiting for a formula that I can drink to grow stronger. Our boys are getting blown off the corners like ghost town dirt. I keep running when the cages get closer, crying when no one is looking, feeling like every day is gonna be the last time I see my son and then I start thinking, if I wanted to write a book how much you think my life would be worth?"

I feel like dropping some bombs tonight
I have a milk crate bursting at the handles with
Muses that look like 3 x 7 memo pads but
I only need a minute of your time
If I told you that your woman was playing you dirty
And you asked me if I was for real
I would say, Word
Word to everything I love
Because that's what Brother Lo and them say
When they want you to believe them
More than you believe in the god of your choice
These poets who don't even know it
Will not put their palms
On a stack of black bibles
Or swear on the soul of an unborn child
If you find out they're lying
You can have everything they love

Here's bomb number one:
I want to give a shout out
To all those lyric poets
Who got low scores and left the short circuit
Through the back door
This is my word to everything I love
When you come back home
You expect welcome mats of damn
Where you been?
You look good
Is there anything I can do for you?
Anything you need?
But these are the same mats
You stepped on before
When you come back home
You expect the spotlight to be as bright
As the last time you got on stage
But the page flipped
And you got left out the next chapter
When you come back home

Everybody asks you if
You're working your steps
You say you closed your eyes
Took one giant step
And never looked back
Word to everything I love
This is what I'm telling you
After you make the love you dream of making
You come home to clean your closets
And make sure to keep the phone nearby
Just in case you bump into half of something
That will bring you back and
Hit you where it hurts

This blockbuster I give to the word hitters
Shadowboxing backstage
Making sure the last line fits
Let me a make a short story long
I want to tell you about the night I walked her
To an all-night Pathmark
It was snowing so much that
I felt like I was in a souvenir globe
The whole Goya bean section knew that we were in love
I carried her garlic, ginger and twist-off mop in one hand
Orange juice and scented candles in the other
She gave me her tongue in the vestibule and
Told me a secret

The next night we met in a garden filled with computers
We downloaded all kinds of flowers and trees
Word, word to everything I love
A few weeks later
Someone had sent her mouth
A giant AOL Instant Message smile
She roller-bladed to the clinic with Chuito de Bayamon
Blasting on her headphones
Don't you understand?
This is for you repeat offenders
In the final round
Who need new material
The song of the almost was

The call you get on the life line
Sounds like tears dropping into a voicemail
She would have wanted to wear ponytails to class picture day
She would have sketched a poem and left it on my pillow
She was surrounded by a circle of street pigeons in a city square
I miss train stops thinking of what her name
Would have been

Writing about What You Know

I.

A young Puerto Rican boy named Papo is on a class trip to the
Aguilar Branch of the New York Public Library on 110th Street in
East Harlem. His name is Papo because 7 out of every 10 brothers
in El Barrio, Los Sures in Williamsburg, Loisaida, Brook Avenue,
Humboldt Park in Chicago and most of Willimantic, Connecticut,
are named Pito, Papo, Flaco, Chino, Piloto, Chano, or Waneko. These
are names that will make you dream of Taino warriors in battle with
Spaniard conquistadors.

Up and down the block there are jingles for *manteca, yucca, tamarindo,
metadona, plátano maduro y pan caliente* and Papo is listening to the
Head Librarian lecture on the value of learning the Dewey Decimal
System. "If you need something on Earth Science, you first go to the
card catalog and"—but all Papo can hear is the wahwahwahwahwah of
urgent police sirens speeding toward the projects.

He turns his head toward the one-week Express Book section. There's
a book with a picture of his block on the cover. He can tell by the
identification tags on the wall telling him who loved who and for
how long. The book says that there is poetry inside. The title buzzes
on Papo's tongue like a biscuit of neon announcing instant Lotto and
liquor. *Smoking Lovely*…The poet is standing in in the reflection of a
lamp post that beams on Puerto Rican flags dangling chest forward out
of tenement windows. Cuchifrito stands blink their 24-hour florescent
crowns for the late night tree blazers who end their cipher sessions with
a taste for a potato ball and a large cup of sesame seed juice.

"Excuse me, Luis. It's not polite to walk away while the librarian is
    talking," says Ms. Díaz.

Papo says, "I just wanted to see that book over—"

"You can see it when she's finished," says Ms. Díaz.

The next day Papo brings his father to the library because only adults
    can check the book out.

Papo tells his Creative Writing teacher that he's having a difficult time finding something to write about. The teacher says, *Write about what you know. And remember: don't tell me, show me.*

That night he was chillin' in front of Caridad's Groceery with Baby Face Nelson and Green-Eye Raymond. A silver BMW drives by with a jukebox in the trunk. The Yellow-Top Crew just cracked their first bottle of champagne. The tempo for Papo's first assignment will be set by a round of Uzi shots ringing off the Wagner Poject rooftops. The shots are supported by a heavy, deep, hip-hop jeep, bass line thump with a stream of furious congas keeping rhythm in the background, warning you to strap in and hold on tight.

Green-Eye Raymond: Sounds like they pullin' somebody's wig back in Wagner, sun. How many shots you heard?

Papo: Like ten.

Baby Face Nelson: Word. That's what I heard. And those shots
    sounded like they had names and addresses.

After the ambulance and police come to break the set, the streets go back to what they were saying and Papo goes home to do his assignment:

His name was Papo.
We didn't know his real name.

He was born with a plastic spoon
melting in his mouth.

His face was carved from marble.

He had silver daggers for eyes.

His heart was shaped like a green toy soldier,
ready to attack.

He had hawk wings attached to his brains.

He crawled to the corner and started running
after his death.

He played follow the leader by himself.

He lived and died in Spanish Harlem.

III.

During an interview to promote his first book, Papo was asked to
describe his style. He thought conga, Santeria ritual, black-on-black
crime, Cheo Feliciano singing "El Ratón," the violent *El Vocero*
headlines, and finally decides to use his block. He says, "It's a lot like
the mother who sticks her head out the window to call her children
in for the night. The way she sings, 'Mira Chino, Marisol y Yoli!
Pa'rreeeba! Ahora! Upstairs! Right now!' And the children yell, 'But
Maa-ah… Everybody is going to the night-pool and—,' and she fills
in the blanks with: 'and night-pool nothing. Let's go. Get your butts
upstairs'. After much pouting and stomping, crying and complaining,
Chino and his sisters disappear through the lobby doors. I know this
mother. She's like Mami Cuca. She's the mother who consistently has
an answer for the Channel 5 newscaster when he asks, 'It's 10:00pm.
Do you know where your children are?' And Mami Cuca says, 'My
son is in his room sleeping right now, Bill.'"

IV.

Before Papo begins teaching his workshop at the Phoenix House drug
program, he gives the participants a brief self-disclosure. "The Hawk
was out the night my life changed. He was rocking icicle-shaped
sideburns and had a wicked wind chill on his back. I walked out
my building and Dona Rosa was pushing her shopping cart up the
handicap ramp. She blessed me and told me to be careful on Lexington
Avenue because 'it was hot out there.' I heard that a grapevine
warning went out to all street-level scramblers engaged in hand-to-
hand combat. Chuck Norris and his partner Chewbacca were in the
blue Taurus that night. My eyes were glazed with that first bag note.
A silent waterfall was chillin' under my lids. Everything made warm
sense. I got high to sell and sold to get high. I saw a badge tinkle in a
factory window like a July 4th sparkler. I heard one of my customers
say, 'Oye, Papo, I think the boys are about to jump.' Before I realized

that I'd made a direct sale, four car doors slammed one right after the other like a *clave* short of a beat. Black Glocks pointed with deadly aim, promising fatal shots if I moved and salvation if I stood frozen. It was the sound of the uptown Blue Man Group delivering my one-way ticket to Central Booking. The package included unlimited time shares and revolving-door insurance policies. This was my bullpen therapy appointment. Frustration steam started to rise from the top of my head while the City insulated my stomach with inch-thick slices of baloney and American cheese. I've slept through seven-hour trips across the Atlantic Ocean and woken up as the plane descended on the Orly runway in Paris, France. I've been on long, hot yellow school bus rides with a bunch of preschoolers yelling all the way to Jones Beach. And I've been on a comfortable United Kingdom cruise-controlled ride in an elegant Mercedes-Benz taxi, *Kind of Blue* providing the soundtrack for the awesome countryside vista. But the longest ride I've ever been on was as the sole passenger in the back of a New York Police Department caged bus, hands cuffed in front of me, feeling every second it took to cross the long, white sand bridge that separates Rikers Island from the rest of the world. I remembered being in my lobby and a bunch of us were collecting change for a sponge ball and Duke was talking about going to jail like a college-bound senior anticipating the first day of class at the school of his choice. *When I got to jail I'm gonna be like…* Flavors and clicks were the most valuable commodities on the Island. (Newport cigarettes and jack time on the phone.) I called Mami Cuca with my first click and as soon as she heard my voice she cried and said, 'Papo, I would go to the end of the world for you.' I couldn't talk because I swallowed too many heartbeats. I sold a six-minute click for a sheet of paper, a pencil and a stamped envelope. I wrote my girlfriend. I told her that I missed the way orange-blossom lotion moistens in her bellybutton and the way she could compress love into seventeen syllables. I made a promise to stop looking at black and white photographs of jazz heroes because they made a fall look sweet and cool. I also told her that I would stop feeding the wind that takes all the lives in the urban studies and that from now on I would use true colors to write about what I know."

Mario (1967)

Agate
for Gil Scott-Heron posthumously

peace. toting poems on Lenox
in steelcase. applejack and boombox.
media fueled nonsense for the cerebral

media sending people
off and counting revenue
from real house whores of the south
sponsored by Gorilla Glue
and Yaki

brothers with gravel throats
sore from shouting GoD,
legions on their feet stomping
Satanic imagery

authenticity with a Fender Rhodes
couldn't stop Jo-Berg
authenticity from Brian's flute couldn't stop Vietnam

storyteller exchanges pleasantries
with merchants offering fruit
not ripe enough for times
defined by newshounds.
24 hour cycle watching time
toll on black future, getting higher
than a spaceman's backside

wanting so badly to come down
so he can write
a new
black
template

Roger Bonair-Agard (1968)

Honorific or *black boy to black boy*

Homes	Star	**Family**	Pardnah
Hollah		*what it do?*	
My Nigga	Brethren	Ese	Fool
	wha you sayin?		
Black	Killah	Dude	Slim
What it look like?		*Wha happen now?*	
Loco	Cousin	Captain	Playa
I see you…			
Skipper	Nigga	Son	**God**
	break yourself!		*what up?*
Blood	Gangsta	Horse	Man
	stick em up		
Homey	Boy	Dread	Nigga
	As-salamu Alaikum		*you got beef?*
Taino	Money	Love	Young'n
Blessings		*where you stay at?*	
Uncle	Joe	Friend	King
Who you rep?	*One Love*	*Freeze*	
Rasta	King	Nephew	Lord
You 5-O?		*Alaikum As-salamu*	
Fam	Boss	G	Brother
	Oye	*Bless Up*	
Nigga	**Nigga**	Nigga	Nigga
Aye	*Yo!*		
Nigga	Nigga	Nigga	**Nigga**

Fast—how I knew

In 1980 I was fast. I knew I was fast because Muhammad Ali told me so. Said he was the Greatest of All Time. I still hear the phrase *All Time* in Ali's voice, no matter who says it, with that exaggerated high vastness in his tone, his eyes crinkling up in the corner especially after Zaire, after Manila. Ali said All Time and he looked like a benevolent king—ripe for a dethroning.

But it was 1980 and far as I was concerned that wasn't the time. He was about to fight Larry Holmes and win again. He was going to pull one more rabbit from one more hat and shut everybody else up again, even as other boys said he was too old and this latest challenger too young and strong. Ali had stayed too long, they said, but I knew that there was no such thing as too long for the G.O.A.T.—Ali had run and chopped wood and prayed five times a day and was going to be great forever.

That day, in the pavilion, right after cricket practice, shirt off and dancing in my socks on the warped wooden locker room floor, I shuffled, showed the boys how Ali would do later that night—all 11 yrs old 90 lbs of me flitting around the room, clowning like Ali would. I was fast and pretty, showing off my tiny, quick fists and bobbing my head this way and that and talking, like Ali did. Too fast. Too pretty. Showing off my narrow unimpeachable body in the days before I'd inked a crown into my chest, a red butterfly where my heart should be. I was fast and Ali was and he was going to be heavyweight champion of the world forever, then all black boys could know they were fast, and talk slick to white men, and the world was going to open up. I was sure of it. I was a black boy.

My mother told me so. She'd let me stay up to see Muhammad Ali talk shit to George Foreman 6 years before, when I really thought he was going to lose and watched his body sag into the ropes, get pounded and pounded before he became some bullet-handed Jimmy Slyde, Honi Coles kinda superhero and Africa chanted *Ali! Ali! Ali!* And it was late and I was leaned forward watching a thing I had never seen before, my mother getting up and dancing too, a slow hip-sway scotch on the rocks in one hand not daring to spill shimmy and she sang *Oh God Ali, dey cyah touch yuh!*

So, see… I knew I was fast. I'd fought myself through the crucible of a Canadian winter and learned how to pretty up my rage and dress it in something shiny and cocked to one side and my thin, tiny body that healed so miraculously and would wound and scar back to brown again so easy and walked anywhere it felt like past any group of boys, knew Ali had enough left to beguile this bullet-headed man, Larry Holmes. Everything was going to be gravy, *Ali Bomaye!* all over again, even though my mom was tense now and my father working. Late. Again. I'd just finished practice and learned a new stroke and made some runs and took some catches and everything would be right. Ali—king of the world, greatest of all time—he was still young and fast and black. And so were we.

In defense of the code-switch or why you talk like that or why you gotta always be cussing

I'm pretty certain my people
  Yoruba. We speak drum
and dust. We are barefoot.
We are also Mumbai
and the venomed thin blood streaks
of slave masters — France, England,
Spain, Portugal, Germany, America.

but my mother taught me *The Hardy Boys*,
the word *precise* and *Where Babies Come From*
She say read Walter Rodney. She say read Kamau Brathwaite
She say read Baldwin

Long before Chicago taught me borders
 and *Joe*, what loose squares are,
the hieroglyph fist twirl dance
and gang sign

my high school principal, Winston Douglas
said *It is a sin against God*
your parents, and yourself, so to profane
the gift with which you were born

    and so I learned the English
of John Milton, Derek Walcott
and the Mighty Sparrow —

but Brooklyn say *Sun* and *Godbody*
and the streets of Arouca taught
me the brilliant run-on elegance
of the eloquent cuss — *Fock You*
with an O so deep and round
you could tumble into the greeting.

Ruby say *not poncho; rebozo*
  and bit my bottom lip
  and cried when the moon was full

Melana say *ghost-pose* and Nita
say *it raining horchata.*
I talk middle-finger, nigger,
son, and espouse
on the theoretical and practical difficulties
of blackness as lived experience,
a metaphysical longing akin
to madness—and Northside say

You're so articulate. Oh my God.
See—Look, even white women love you
and the books say I code-switch,
say I double-tongued, say I adapt/
able. And I say I don't switch
shit. Stop trying to crack
the code and we'll stop (maybe)
inventing new syntaxes for
survive; for making paper,
for stacking cheddar, for getting
our money right. Switch/nothing.
I say I contain several
kinds of niggas – because I know Hindi

words for eggplant, rolling pin, machete,
and several kinds of cloth folded to drape
the oiled body of a woman. I say *Love*

when I talk to a woman, and I say *Love*
when I greet my homies, and *Family*
to address a sweet sister in the street
and *black* when I mean all my people
and *dead presidents* because Rakim,
Biggie, Jay-Z, Nas and the Wu Tang Clan
added vocabularies to the throng
of me. Chicago jails school me

BD, traphouse, swag, pole and bundle;
school me, you could be 10 years old
thrown to the ground arrested
in school, so I talk like *precisely*
greet my gods with the deep O

of a well, of a drum; speak barefoot
and folklorico, speak J'ouvert morning
and Toni Morrison. I recite Winston
Douglas's *never sacrifice principle
for expediency.* I holler at my boys
with a complicated-ass handshake.
I say *Horse.* I say *Blood.* My brothers
answer back. I sing. I lift every
tongue. I speak drum fool. I speak
drum homie. I speak drum dawg. I speak
drum god. I speak drum nigga. I speak
drum

Joe.

Lynne Procope (1969)

Shine (for Joe Bataan)

Say high horn   Say hi-hat,
Say all that   funk
and the blues tradition comes to us
from the south,
originates in the loop of a noose,
Say it comes to us from the fine American tradition
     Say lynch mob,
     is a fine American tradition
Say genocide
     rendered specific
     comes to us thru a free tongue
and how the throat opens itself to moan.
Let your body go limp and moan.
Say the town's on fire and all we've got
is burning now.

Say *burning* as if you could make love
when all around you the world is on fire.

The world's on fire and you're fucking.
Don't it feel good, all this fire down below,
all this rapid repeat action?

Say *riot* like it's an instrument of this empire,
say bull whip or wish-you-were-here-and
     -that-is-a-black
     -man-hanging-from-a-lamp-post
     -in-near-right-of-the-postcard

Say blankets of small pox, poisoned water source,
ruined island   Say nuclear testing
in the house next door then   Say
water hose like there is a lover waiting for your mouth
and you are never coming back.

But say too that there is a woman who is learning to make a fist,
so there's a fist, then guns, then a death warrant.
But the woman; she can never go home.

Say she learns the tongue as a weapon
and when she speaks up that her husband is not bullet proof,
and that children vanish like smoke but hers
        are not considered
        proof of burning. Consider—

that a man dying on death row anywhere in America,
on the lip of the 95, in a car outside a Queens stripclub,
at the intersection of Koval Lane and East Flamingo,
in the doorway of his home, as he reaches for his wallet,
is still more likely to be
        the suspect,
        an unidentified black
        man, an African-American male
        of average height, wearing a baseball cap.

So the woman, our hero, is holding up her fist
and say she's a widow or a thousand widows
and she will not put her fist down because—
        her son,
        because her father,
        because her partner is a woman too,

because her skin,
        because her womb is not a mechanism,
        her body not an object.

Say we all stand behind her, our tight hands curling, but our fisted
hearts rolling out across the plains,   tearing into
the freedoms   that bind us;   could you say love,
        (if that's what we are searching for)
let's say *love*, it too, must surge from one sea
toward all that wants to shine.

All Night

Lynne Procope

the white guy   sits across the bar
he tells you how   he knows he is
        not racist.   and

no matter what you say he knows you are wrong.
about this
black thing   you are not dying inside

        (you did not realize
        you had written this down.)

you are only   not trying hard enough
to understand how good you've got it right now

here,   —while he is paying attention to your beautiful eyes,
your essential femininity, which of course

is the thing
about black girls

how can you be right about your feelings?

he is   seeing you
as if you began to exist in this bar just moments ago

and he is also looking at your friend (whom he points out
is blacker than you,   but
still beautiful)

        as if there were
        no other women

who might go home with him
and did he mention   that he has been everywhere,
        (and did

        I mention

        that I have   also)

but no one cares about that and this man
who keeps touching my arm and my friend
who is black, who might want to be taken home,
just this one time or any, who despite her best reading
on self love and the remarkable hips she has earned
from the hard labor of her fore mothers and who
might wish for a blue eye, for the most questionable charms
of white women, or at least the attentions of white men,

neither of them wish to discuss with me
the nuances of discrimination
in how progressive white men approach accessible blacks
and the women they know in bars. I stay silent.

I order another drink.   The night spins out.

Patrick Rosal (1969)

B-Boy Infinitives

To suck until our lips turned blue
the last drops of cool juice
from a crumpled cup sopped
with spit the first Italian ice of summer
To chase popsicle stick skiffs
along the curb skimming stormwater
from Woodbridge Ave. to Old Post Road
To be To B-boy To be boys who
snuck into a garden to pluck
a baseball from mud and shit
To hop that old man's fence before
he burst through his front door
with a lame-bull limp charge
and the fist the size of a half spade
To be To B-boy To lace shell toe Adidas
To say word to Kurtis Blow
To laugh in the afternoons
someone's mama was so black
when she stepped out of the car
the oil light went on
To count hairs sprouting
around our cocks To touch
ourselves To pick the half-smoked
True Blues from my father's ashtray
and cough the gray grit
into my hands To run
my tongue along the lips of a girl
with crooked teeth To be
To B-boy To be boys for the ten days
an eight-foot gash of cardboard lasts
after we dragged it
seven blocks then slapped it
on the cracked blacktop To spin
on our hands and backs To bruise
elbows wrists and hips To Bronx-Twist

Jersey version beside the mid-day traffic
To swipe To pop To lock freeze and
drop dimes on the hot pavement—
even if the girls stopped watching
and the street lamps buzzed all
night we danced like that
and no one called us home

Patrick Rosal

Your morning's
everyday stained
caul of exhaust Your
plum bludgeoned
dusk Your fine
stench and luck—
less French kiss
Your can-I-get-
down bliss Your god-
gone blesséd
Jones for loam
Your Jersey baroque
Your Mercy
9's sirens prying
every sky Your
name Your flow
Your funk Your every-
day nasty Your very
revelry Your break-
neck scat the loot
you boost Your
rags Your seven-
thousand-island
slang Your hype
Your hips Your spit
Your sickest wit
and snip Your every
severed syl-
lable Your blunt-
toke fables Your
smoke's reprieve
Your lever's
torque bearing your
body every
day Every lovely
mucking hum
Your mic sound
nice Every Check

One Your
fade Your cut
Your knife your
jazz on-two Your bass
Your every clef Your
left breast Your
folly Your lung
Your modest rot
Your alibata
tongue Do you want it
(Hell yeah!) Baby—
'cause it's yours

Patrick Rosal

We learned to poise pennies on the cartridge head
so the diamond stylus would sit deep
in the vinyl's groove. A dance floor could fizz
out quick if a record skipped when we spun back
the wax to its cue. Me and my boys, sons
of cops, bookkeepers and ex-priests, stayed awake
from noon to noon, excavating from crates
some forgotten voice or violin to scratch.
We practiced thumbing the cheap dime-sized
pitch controls and when those broke we didn't
just throw them out. We picked up gear other DJs
didn't want or need. Like the one Pingry prep-school
kid who upgraded to a shiny six-channel model
(three-band eq and 12-bit sampling) and threw out
his year-old Numark which we picked out the garbage
and hoisted home. After fourteen screws,
the top panel popped off and we plucked out
the pristine fader for transplant. We lifted
the turntable's precious arm first,
then the platter. We pulled free the belt,
and unscrewed the plastic top. I didn't take shop
or build a whole lot by hand, but I was good
with a knife when I needed. I could poke the point
of a half-dull blade clean and gentle through
the eighth-inch plastic and saw my way down
four inches, straight as I could make it, to pop into place
the slider we harvested from the rich kid's rig.
I re-soldered the wires to the turntable pitch contacts.
We did this in a basement of a maple split in Edison,
New Jersey, while our mothers played mah jong
in the sala, and our fathers bet slow horses
and the government bombed Iraq. We juggled
and chirped. We perfected the grind of a kick
and dropped it on the downbeat coming around.
Half trash, half hallelujah. Our hands could cut
Bach to Bambaataa and make a dance hall jump.
It was our job to keep one ear to the backbeat
and the other to a music that no one else could hear.

Out of a hunk of rescued junk, we built a machine
to mix our masters. We chopped up classics
and made the whole block bounce.

Ode To The Cee-Lo Players

Patrick Rosal

…for their sport.
—Gloucester, in Shakespeare's *King Lear*

This is what dice does to us. We kneel down
in semicircle. We perfect the slick lean
into the toss. We hone the wrist's flick
and snap our fingers on every sweet run
of trips. We bloodshot homeboys yap
past the standard clocks. Any day, give me
this nasty static of street flies, this blunt
smoke ghosting overhead, this brother
right here who slaps half his rent
against a brick wall and won't flinch once
though his phone's blowing up. You understand,
no orchestra of jasmine, no honey-hipped
parade could snatch him from this huddle
of petty thieves and shit talkers
trading fire. We are the freshest kindling —
This smoldering without wicks
becomes us, If only we didn't burn so fine
standing still. There is no truth like a shooter's
hot hand gone cold. Who says we don't weep
in broad daylight. If we owned boats
we'd shove off our dead to drift
on crackling scrap wood. We'd make
a convent of blaze. In lighted windows
along the block are the shadows
of women who whisper our names
into candles. They can't forget us.
Just in case, I start to carve eyes
into concrete wherever I go. Bless the eyes.
Bless the saints who suck their teeth in despair.
Bless despair—for we nightly reinvent
the alphabet of princes. Here, on the avenues
of chance, we don't just play for dollars
and rocks. Sometimes we kiss each other
on the neck. All we got is this clutch
of crumpled singles in our fists. We don't

believe in love or luck. From above,
we must sound like boys speaking
in tongues. Half this game is calling out
our numbers before they come.

Untitled

What the sister brother mother making in the oven? Subtle shoulder
bounce comeuppance? Breakdance from Angolans going, us up
under ships rowing? Flowing over undertow, Sammy's taps. Hand
jive happenstance to techno trance, folks coveting colored. True black
being an encompassing hue, placentas siphoned off magenta, violence,
indigo blues with cane cotton tobacco rows to hoe.

So what you sayin'? Sosa's John Henry 'gainst the dopest steam
engine? Recidivism's net effect is akin to an Amadou Louima ass
kickin'? Hit it! Reconnoitering Negroes AWOL versus Dominating
Nazi Aryans. RNA vs. DNA in the body politic, difference being the
leftovers, sugar. What flies is attracted to besides shit. We got some.
Circulocutious Infidels affirming the Ferral Biologic importing it.

Each territory a precious piece. Kill 'em with kindness. Sweet like a
Lauryn declaration of love overlapping the looped Bata backbeat. Like
a 12 year old's pressed curls greased with Dax. Like somebody fifty-
seven polishing his T-bird with Turtlewax. Old romance. Akara to
chitlins to chicken wings. Shekere to hambone to two Technics. Field
holler Doo Wops make microphone fiends.

Jason Carney (1970)

America's Pastime
(After the crimes of our Forefathers)

White America—
who we are is not hidden, cumbersome
regret, Evoked from photographs. Motionless.
Grainy black and white movements—
sound of blood,
        smell of fire,
                fingerprints burned off bodies.

American postcard portraits of lynching.
Hung from trees. Nailed to poles. Strung-up
animals. Hatred has silent fangs, formed to stone.

This is American truth, timeless, inescapable. Justice
never required guilt. Only darkness running down
chipped brick alleyway. Pissing himself like scared dog,
Froggie James—
beaten and stabbed,
        hung and shot,
                half his burnt head stuck on
    stake,
in a Cairo, Illinois city park.
How many ways we got to kill a man to take his dignity?

What is more vulgar, hooded secret gatherings on back roads
or picnics in town squares?

White families wore Sunday best to the revival of baseball bats,
pristine choir of timely hats, opened-up bellies, fresh-meat
    sandwiches.
Dragged from courthouse, just after lunch, Jesse Washington
was a thick black smoke of human flesh as proper children
poked his death with curious stick

Laura Nelson hung from a bridge, next to her fifteen-year-old son,
accused of stealing, they raped her. Gave her salvation
rippling the tips of her toes against clandestine
surface of water. She looks so peaceful escaping
our forefathers' claws.

Mary Turner—
eight months pregnant,
                    hung upside down,
                                    split along the gut.
Umbilical chord dangles unwinding backbeat. Mary's child
made no noise crushed under heel of boot. It knew not of begging.
Only blistered voices tattered with hate sing
with the lushness bled-out bruise. Georgia backwoods
sweating with the salvation hymnals. You can still hear
those ghosts singing *Chariots ain't so sweet*
When you meet them running, dirt roads cold places to die.

These photographs, picture postcards, American portraits—
Lynching. Sounding like gurgles of death. A perverse call
of freedom, shot through the mouth of Memphis.
Dreams deferred is blood wiped on shirt, carried like pilgrimage
to a new distortion. Sounding like gurgles of death. The coldness
of memory, not to be forgotten. We don't know how many people
died in this land from the hands of racist laughter.

Equality
muffled under our laughter. American right to death
given so freely. From 1840's negro man—
force fed coke,
            as backs broke,
                            all day with no pay,
on banks of the mighty Mississippi. To the way crack
crumbles to stardust under the weight of handgun freedom.

White folks running this drugged up torture.
Not much changing—
two out of three juveniles sentenced to death
in this land are American children of color.
Not much changing—
one out of five black men on death row, convicted

by all white American juries.
Not much changing—
if you're black in Texas you're five times
more likely to get the death penalty, killing
person that is white.

Lynch mobs ain't dead. They have become inalienable
scales of justice. This is American truth—
perverse call of freedom,
     fingerprints burned off bodies,
          faint gurgle strapped to
 table.

Laughter singing
Not much changing going on around here.

who you callin' a jynx? *(after mista popo)*

What you wearing on yo' head?
What's that shit on your head?

Good lord, you make my eyeliner sweat pika twins.
Peep this joint, I ain't feeling your vibe easy breezy.
No shogun coming from your tongue.

Mista Popo, mista Tom,

    you queasy.

Where's your flying rug, homie?
Yama-uba bored, my agents gonna reward nada.
I shuffleboard smooches in the land of the rising sun's cosplay, papa.

    ROUGELA COMING STRAIGHT ON YOUR
      STEREO!
    POPO WHY YOU TRIPPIN LIKE I'M NO-GO!
    POPO YOU A HELLA STRANGE YU-GI-OH!

What your ma said about a Zwarte Piet?
I'll Tilburg to Finland all over her miffy.

    You butterfly gardener,
    I'll make ya choke on a Ricola™.

    What the fuck did they do to your lips?
    What they do to your lips?

    Turban-Hammer-slacks-wearing-pansy.

Get back to Aladdin's bottle,
I battle laughable cannibals.

I induce sleep with my mammaries.
Kiss attack, ya feel me?

     Kettei. Mista Popo I'm a thriller.
     Rosie flappers for lips.
     The most obscene fish queen you ever seen.
     Don't Superflat matte my color.

I'm your Yokai nigglet sippin' lovely

    with black/purple flesh supposedly offensive.
    make no difference in variation,
    check it: cross pollination.

    Watashi wa zasshu = mass circulation.

     Kokujin wanna mark me; I got ya kawaii kiddies.

    Popo, here's your "black mammy"
    multi-platinum crowd-pleaser,

     destroyin' daisy cutters like Legend of the Overfiend skeezas

I'm causin' adolescent seizures wit my kage gamma rays.

Hirojima's in my pocket, epileptics I dare you to rock it.

    muteki dianetics? ya can't *handle* it!

    Hater-aid bitches mocked my February spin;
    my animated fade-in inori smackin' gaijins.

Sun, where's your brain damage comin' from?

    Why kris kringle got a ocean liner north of the equator.
    Cookies and cream soap land souvenir—
    I polish it with my wamono brassiere.

    ya can't *handle* it!

I'm the master puppeteer in my kaiju dynasty
and you wanna ride me in your tugboat?

What you know about my ice flight?
Wiggle till you figure Harajuku thoughts.

Don't front,   *you know I got you open.*

I swing my chariots low for a reason.

damn right it's betta than yours

she getting taught – him getting schooled

    – frosty dips – foamy zouk

        drown dem clods in *kikongo* dollop

        bradda tell a rida – holla at yuh fadda

            – yu in yuh caddy –

                ricochet feed yu – barrington

     di seagulls crack clam shells –

        sailors – da kine stuffin' swelled snails

dey navy yard smiles chinky –

        cause dey drown dem clods in *kikongo* dollop

      shantay yuh stay – dem – *yard fowl* – serve

swim in *kaiso* – hotel drive – milk dem *lick mouth* – holiday den

assified – technique drop – kikongo dollop – blocka-blocka

      erode di pentameter – blocka-blocka

        shadows sashay – freak-a-leek

           milk dem – hotel drive – bum by – don a dime

              – true dat fadda – charge dem clods

           shantay yuh thesis – walk tick *short tongue*

       – squint when ya milk shake –

           drown dem clods – charge dem clods

              seagulls on crack – blocka-blocka

gamin' gabby

Syraniqua D'Voidoffunk…

trust your fields of prayers won't summon this earth,

    where mountains crash beneath an ocean's thrust.
lonely words burn still days; you mime breech birth

you flee before the dawn makes jest to trust

    what good are rainbows, whispering surprise,
or waterfalls that dine with a tongue's dreams.

this smile falls mute: all's left are toys and lies.

    this joy flies while showers return dazed screams;
rude boyish nature truth dares hide n seek.

your tag balls merry go's or building bricks,

    this morning, leave my pulse free of fool's tricks.
a rabbit's speed, a thousand miles by week.

    these eyes awake and hear the sun;

    good are flints when the night's cherub has spun.

chulo, whining is not for the strong at heart.

you have a vice to sweat the ills when no one is sick.

where are the stars when you sleep all day? what

good are southern memories that keep you sprung? no
one said the text message was an exercise,
so why respond like you vibin' at length, bitch?

don't you know it's ten cents a message, playa?

don't tease my eyes when you fall short.

I'll blame my ovaries before I consider again.

my feathers ruffled from yo' dusty mane,
the moon, the tides, the ripples, the love below!

I'll give dawn to vanity, smoke you, tag you wack.

your bluff, don't bother to ring, departure time, the 11th hour.

stay yo' ass up in Gilroy! the sun mighty nice over yonder.

baby boy   whin'n ain't   workin'

you   vizzle ta sweat   baseheads.   no one itchin'

tha stars?   you sleep all day.   wizzle

    memories,   pussy whippin'   son.

text message: thou   art   has   gamed   me.

yo' aim   off.   beeyotch,   ten cents

a messagizzles?   say it ain't so!   don't teaze

mah eyes   F-to-tha-izzall,   shortie,   test   mah ovaries.

    feathas ruffled;   flakeolicious   head.

tha moon,   tides   ripple   mah   snatch.

gizzy dawn   ta vanity.   scoot   yo' pizzay.

    live n die in Fruitvale,   sun poppin' funkedelic.   yonder

    eyes   awakes n hizzy   tha sun.

ulochay, iningwhay isway otnay orfay ethay ongstray atway earthay

erewhay ountainsmay ashcray eneathbay anway oceansway'say ustthray

erewhay areway ethay arsstay enwhay ouyay eepslay allway ayday,

ouyay eeflay eforebay ethay awnday akesmay estjay otay usttray

oneway aidsay ethay exttay essagemay asway anway exerciseway

    osay ywhay espondray ikelay ouyay'eray ibinvay' atway engthlay itchbay?

    onday'tay ouyay owknay itway'say entay entscay away essagemay?

atwhay oodgay areway ainbowsray, isperingwhay urprisesay

rway aterfallsway atthay ineday ithway away onguetay'say eamsdray

iway'llay ameblay ymay ovariesway eforebay Iway'day onsidercay

againway, ymay eathersfay uffledray omfray oyay' ustyday anemay

ethay oonmay ethay idestay ethay ipplesray inway ymay atchsnay, iway'llay

    ivegay awnday otay anityvay, okesmay ouyay, agtay ouyay ackway

    oodgay areway intsflay enwhay ethay ightnay'say erubchay ashay unspay

Mitchell L. H. Douglas (1970)

Hood

In memory of smokestack lighting, red brick wall & wait, graffiti buzz scrawled high & wrong the misspelled misrepresented; in sweet run sour, endless slabs of cement, bath of street lamp, gutter litter, alley to alley end zone, BB gun aim, tree climb, bird's eye view, calls ignored for lunch, for supper (sorry, too busy in branches); in the wake of Uncle Buddy's fist & forearm through side door glass, ambulance on our would-be 50 yard line, suture map of fold & tuck, flesh envelope. *No need for meds*, he thinks, *I'm fine* (never mind the call to swallow); in contempt of stilted tongue, shuttle black alphabets like lost blood— L&N wind & lash, KY to TN—or skip prattle like hopscotch grids in lime, lemon, pink electric—asphalt body rock—until there is no curb between street & skin—warm, black, waved.

Krista Franklin (1970)

Manifesto, or Ars Poetica #2*

Give me the night, you beasts hissing over the face of this dead
woman, I climb into your eyes, looking. To those who would sleep
through the wounds they inflict on others, I offer pain to help them
awaken, Ju-Ju, Tom-Toms, & the magic of a talking burning bush.
I am the queen of sleight of hand wandering the forest of motives,
armed with horoscopes, cosmic encounters & an x-acto knife. My
right eye is a projector flickering Hottentot & Huey Newton, my
left eye is prism of *Wild Style*, gold grills, lowriders, black dahlias,
blunts & back alleys. At twenty-one, I stood at the crossroad of Hell
& Here, evil peering at me behind a blue-red eye. I armed myself
with the memories of Pentecostal tent revivals, apple orchards, the
strawberry fields I roamed with my mother & aunts in the summer,
& the sightings of UFO lights blinking in the black of an Ohio
nightsky. I am a weapon. I believe in hoodoo, voodoo, root workers,
Dead Presidents, Black Tail, Black Inches & Banjees. I believe in the
ghosts of 60 million or more, & black bones disintegrating at the
bottom of the Atlantic, below sea level, *Not Just Knee Deep. I believe
that children are the future*: love them now or meet them at dusk
at your doorstep, a 9mm in their right hand & a head noisy as a
hornet's nest later. Your choice.

Black, still, in the hour of chaos, I believe in *Royal Crown, Afro-Sheen*,
Vaseline, Jergens & baby powder on breasts, the collective conscious,
cellular memory, Public Enemies, outlaws, Outkast, elevations,
Elevators & *Encyclopedia Britannica*. Under my knife, El-Hajj Malik
El-Shabazz laughs with Muhammad Ali, a Lady named Day cuddles
with a Boxer named Mister after traumatically stumbling on strange
fruit dangling from one of the most beautiful Sycamores evah. Under
my knife, Marilyn Monroe enjoys an evening out with Ella Fitzgerald,
meanwhile, *Life* shows me a gigantic photo. I am a weapon. I chart
voyages of unlove, high on a man called crazy who turns *nigger* into

---

*"Manifesto, Ars Poetica #2" is a collage poem that contains lines from poems by Wanda
Coleman, Aime Césaire, Amiri Baraka, Tim Seibles, Erica Jong, Lucille Clifton, & Krista
Franklin, album titles, movie titles, song titles, book titles & a quote from Bruce Lee.

prince. I believe in Jong, Clifton, *Dirty Diana* & Dilla, paper, scrilla, green, gumbo, coins, Batty Bois & Video Vixens. I believe that beads at the ends of braids are percussive instruments in double-dutch. In the reflection of my knife, Cab Calloway, Duke Ellington & Thelonious Monk argue in a Basquiat heroin nod. I am a weapon. I believe in goo-gobs of deep brown apple-butter, alphabets, Alaga syrup, Affrilachians, A-salaam Alaikum, Wa-Alaikum A-Salaam, & African Hebrew Israelites. I believe in Octoroons, Quadroons, Culluds, *Coolie High*, Commodores, Krumpin, Krunk & *Burn, Hollywood, Burn*.

I am Sethe crawling a field toward freedom with a whitegirl talking about velvet. I believe in tumbleweaves, hot combs & hair lyes, Chaka Khan, Shaka Zulu, Mau-Mau, Slum Village & *Buhloone Mindstate*: "Empty your mind. Be formless, shapeless—like water…" I believe in water. My body is pulp. I bleed ink. I believe in the *Fantastic (Vol. 2), Low End Theory, Space Is The Place* & *The Hissing of Summer Lawns*. Tucked in the corner of my right ventricle sprouts a Tree of Knowledge, lives a Shining Serpent, & a middle finger. I'm on a quest for the Marvelous. My face is a mask of malehood, malevolence, one big masquerade. Metaphysically niggerish, I am a weapon wandering the forest of motives, a machete in one hand, a mirror in the other, searching for the nearest body of water.

Preface to a Twenty Volume Homicide Note
(after Amiri Baraka)

Today, I turned *Transbluesency* over
to the hands of a teenager tussling
with her own words, still trying to decipher
the difference between invention and insipidness.
Meanwhile, you know, the world whips against
our hunched shoulders and McCay's call to arms
is buried in the graveyards of the poets' imaginings,
its ghost inhabiting some young soul in Egypt,
rumbling in the heart of Libya. Meanwhile,
America picks the lint from its navel, moonwalks
its way back to antebellum inertia, lulls itself
to sleep with airwave regurgitations of 1970
before music sold its soul for a stripper pole.

At your lecture, we sat in the Amen Corner
and *hallelujahed* your every word, knowing
over half that room didn't know Tyner from
Tyson, couldn't pick Monk out from a mugshot.
Meanwhile, while knee-grows still swallowing
the jizz of the American Dream and south-
side Chicago teens juke Africa in hyper-speed,
we still ain't caught up where we need to be,
more concerned with how much gold we can
dig out a broke nigga's pocket, debating the political
incorrectness of the word *bitch*, and which came
first: the pimp smack or the egging. Baldwin broke
himself writing tomes on black love while chain
smoking and dragging racism out to the streets
by the scruff of its dirty neck, all to be reduced
to "the gay dude?" in the college classroom.

Who's gonna save us now that all the black heroes
are running from the cops holding their pants
up with dusty fingers they never deigned
to open a book with? Black heroes more concerned
with erasing their records and record deals
than delving into solving the algebra of black agony,

bolt-cutting the inextricable chains of imperialism
that got everybody tied up in knots. Who's gonna
save us now that all the black heroes are making
it rain in sweatshops where the heroines calculate
payouts in booty-bounce, and the drum got
pawn-shopped for a machine?

Adrian Matejka (1971)

Beat Boxing

—for C-Lux

That was the day the breakers started breaking & somebody broke
    the radio while snatching a sack of groceries from an old lady.
    That was the day the paper sack broke & granny smiths

& dry spaghetti spilled on the street like the words spoking a drunk's
free style. The inscription on the noodle box: this beat came up

      the sidewalk spacewalking the throat's feedback. This beat

loaned voice muscle instead of bringing the knuckle. The rappers rap
when this shows up. The breakers break
             when this show up. This beat huffed
a mad circle of knuckle-ups. It breathed deep in someone else's
    crushing
dactylic & blinged hexameter where the handclap should be. This beat

cyphered gunshots into a Kangol dialectic. Empty grocery bags
    between
      handclaps. Old lady's wig between backslaps. Out of breath,
      this beat stutttered without applause like a loan shark on
        Thursday.

      Nobody else breathed as this beat made metronomes from
      breaths.

The old lady went inside & nobody breathed as a green apple rolled
    to a bruising stop. The last beatless day ever. The last circle
    of rhymes before cops sirened the block like it was Odysseus.

Robot Music

The 3 fingers pointing back at you are an abacus for all your funky
      wants. You're hydraulics & supersonics on the multi-colored
      dance floor. Sergio Valente rocking 3 broke parts. No parking,

baby. You need room to get your back up. You got moves like a dump
truck backing up, a shell toe trying to right itself in the brake light

      between sidewalk & broken-arm roboting.

You're as roly & spunky as a cartoon bomb with a fuse wanting
to be lit. Break beats: the struck match.
                           Across cutoff sleeves,
past rising sun headbands & patriotic wristbands, leg-sweeping
every pretty momma in sight right before setting the Soul Train

line on stun. Truthfully, you need a bit more hip in your robot
      convolutions. You need a chronograph for those windmill
      intrusions. That last shudder was like doing community service

      on Sunday morning. When you disco pointed at the lady

in the half-top & spandex, 3 fingers pointing back at you were joined
      by a thumb, bird-dogging the rhythms of the universe
      as you work the dance floor like a B-side's stepson.

jessica Care moore (1971)

mic check, 1-2.

a duality battle. materials: poem breath & voice.
for Lupe Fiasco

1.

I'm a hip hop cheerleader
carrying hand grenades
and blood red pom poms
screaming from the sidelines of a stage
I built
afraid to part down the middle
for feminine riddles

2.

I was born on the tongue
of the prophets. i was here
before the profit. I never thought
the money would ever stop it.
spirit verses spit. Baraka
versus nonsense.
holocaust versus holocaust
at what cost
whose blood lost
in God the dollar trusts
from Fanon to Fila
Adidas to Allah
we die with prayer beads in our palms
store em in box so the
leather never worn.

walking through our cities
i see so much Red.
I never stop at those lights.
I wrap my son's imagination
in the blue. indigo child so bright.
eye no purity inside the stars
camouflaged by the night.

raining words of proverbs
of prophets who never get heard
because the microphone is just another phallic symbol
that allows jack to be nimble
jack to be quick
leaving jill with a man who can't climb
a hill and a bucket of spit
she can't drink or find her reflection inside

she hides

inside crooked eyes of amber
allows her life to be slandered
if Hip Hop is conscious
we must change the standard
my womb-mate's been slandered
I planned her arrival
of letters and lyrics never sent to those lovers
who claim that they know her
but still blow her off as a flunky
not a microphone junkie
fiending for a quick fix
not fast cars & hoe tricks

2.
i'm indigenous anti religious
peaceful despite the evil
they clap
lynching as theater
hip hop has turned pathological
in wars they kill the poets first
i don't know which is worse
to die with words and no truth
or live with truth & remain silent
birth is violent. matriarchy is frightening.

this the only heart i got.
drumbeat machines. pop/lock and robot.
corn rolled princess. genes like jesus and tupac
in the tradition of smiling while i'm breaking

pregnant with potential. still waiting.
afro harmonic winged sistahs forging
their way with their whips & antennas
Ital music samari follicle blades searching for the
safest place for our next planet landing. all natural.

our soft needle against the wax
we are the most beautiful black
mothers with wishbone skeletons
breakdancing into rock a fella
prayer position poses.

there she go. there she go.
there she go there she go there she there she
there she go

1.
her mouth matrix is taped
hooked on phonics escaped
left her language for rape
so she ate her words
and became an instant interlude
a cute break between the music
when she was an electric lady
a black flower rhyme scheme romantic
a breathe and release tantric with five tongues
and no one
understood why her flow was so fast
asked to slow down
hesitate - never last

to the finish I'm gonna win this
all the dj's gon' spin it
when you're a woman
sometimes all you have is a minute

2.
bronx queen. detroit lady. chi town royalty
the sweetest revolutionary
searching for a wind of her breath on the mic
some balance inside the tug of the noose cord

being plugged in and useful. our lyrics
and bodies so beautiful. our roots sore.
the pain from pulling at earth's core
our feet planted at our youths door.
our life is calling us to do more.
& they shoot more. and we still don't know
what you came for. our names forsaken &
confused by the duality of institutionalized
academic wardens. holding our verses behind bars.
we escape & find
urban explorers walking down our spines
searching for the source of our genius.
in the smalls of our backs. we attack blocks.
no take backs. we attempt to act laid back.
we still wear the mask
when the payback

is the mic check.

the sun shine bright while the lyrics
grow colder. now hip hip is older.
they got women in folders.
when you got a Goddess.
then please God, behold her.

one.

I'm a hip hop cheerleader
I buy all your records despite the misogyny
not looking for the blonde in me
Respond to me.
I feel molested
Hip Hop fondled me.
I know the conscious brothas follow me.
Hollow me with half breaths.
Real emcees don't have step.
but i never slept.

Took my poems and made food.
Put my baby in school.
                    taught me to wait for no one

Never turn my back from the sun. of man.
I know my fly mama understand.
Got the rifle on my back with the mic in my hand
I'll be your Tubman compass so we can map out this land.

I'll be the air that you breathe
I'll be your number one fan.
I'll scream the "heys"
I'll tolerate your hoes
I'm a Hip Hop cheerleader.

There she go   There she go.

self love freed me
despite all your rhymes with bitches
i know you need me.
complete thee. believe me.
i see you growing in me.
looking out from my belly
your rhyme schemes are tellin
sang those lullabies to Nelly
close to my edge like Melle
doing cartwheels & air splits
you stage diving into other chicks
when i got your   hair pic.

my weapon of choice.

?

I chose my voice.

when writing wasn't enuf
to move

you

mic check.   mate.

one

two.

1.

2.

John Murillo (1971)

Ode to the Crossfader

Got this mixboard itch
    This bassline lifted
from my father's dusty
    wax   Forty crates stacked
in the back of the attic
    This static in the head-
phones   Hum in the blood
    This deep-bass buckshot
thump in the chest   Got
    reasons and seasons
pressed to both palms
    Two coins from each
realm   This memory
    Memory crossfaded and
cued   These knuckles'
    nicks and nightsweat
rites   This frantic
    abacus of scratch   Got
blood in the crates
    in the chest in the dust
Field hollers to break-
    beats   My father's dusty
wax   My father's dust
    got reasons   Got night-
sweats and hollers
    pressed to both palms
breakbeats and hollers
    pressed to both palms
Static in the attic   Stacked
    crates of memory   Dust
blood and memory   Cross-
    faded and   Bass Cross-
faded and cued   Crossfaded
    and   Static   Stacked hollers
Got reasons in the dust

in the chest   Got seasons
in the blood   In the head-
    phones' hum   This deep-
bass buckshot blood
    pressed   to both palms
My father's dust   Pressed
    to both palms   Got
reasons and reasons
    and reasons

1989

There are no windows here, and the walls
Are lined with egg cartons. So if we listen
Past the sampled piano, drum kick
And speakerbox rumble, we'd still not hear
The robins celebrating daybreak.
The engineer worries the mixboard,
Something about a hiss lurking between notes.
Dollar Bill curses the engineer, time
We don't have. Says it's just a demo
And doesn't need perfecting. "Niggas
Always want to make like Quincy Jones
When you're paying by the hour."
Deejay Eddie Scizzorhandz—because he cuts
So nice—taps ashes into an empty pizza box,
Head nodding to his latest masterpiece:
Beethoven spliced with Mingus,
Mixed with Frankie Beverly, all laid
On Billy Squier's "Big Beat."
I'm in a corner, crossing out and rewriting
Lines I'll want to forget years later,
Looking up every now and then,
To watch Sheik Spear, Pomona's finest emcee,
In the vocal booth, spitting rhymes
He never bothers putting to paper,
Nearly hypnotized by the gold-plated Jesus
Swinging from his neck as he, too,
Will swing, days from now, before
They cut him from the rafters of a jail cell.

Renegades of Funk

—for Patrick Rosal

I.

When we were twelve, we taught ourselves to fly,
To tuck the sky beneath our feet, to spin
On elbows, heads, and backs. To run away
While standing still. So when Miss Jefferson—
Her eyebrows shaved then painted black, the spot
Of lipstick on her one good tooth—would praise
The genius Newton, I knew then to keep
Her close, to trust her like a chicken hawk
At Colonel Sanders. *I refute your laws,*
Oppressor! I'm the truth you cannot stop!
Busting headspins on her desk, a moonwalk
Out the door. Referred to Mr. Brown's
Detention. *All them try'na keep us down!*

II.

Attention: Rhythm's why they keep us. Down
   In Memphis, bluesmen beg the sky to pour
Down liquor. Empty bottles, barren hands.
   A pawnshop banjo gathers dust. Guitars
Sit idle, songs forgotten. Ghosts come late
   To find the crossroads cluttered, strip malls now
Where haints once hung. The young, it seems, forget
   The drum and how it bled, the dream and how
It fed the mothers on the auction block.
   But rhythm's why they keep us. Rhythm's why
We've kept up. Cotton fields and backs
   That creak, a song for every lash, a cry
On beat, and blues sucked dry. The strip malls bleed
   The ghosts from banjos. Hollers caught in greed.

III.

The ghosts. The angels. Holocausts. The need
To shake these shackles, field songs in our bones.
As if, at twelve, we understood, we named
Our best moves *free*: to *break* and *pop lock*. Blood

And bruises marking rites, we'd gather, dance
Ourselves electric, stomp and conjure storm,
Old lightning in our limbs. We thunderstruck
Maroons, machete wielding silhouettes,
Reject the fetters, come together still—
Some call it *Capoeira*, call it *Street*
Dance. We say *culture*. Say *survival*.
Bahia's berimbau or boombox in
The "Boogie Down": a killing art as play,
An ancient killing art to break us free.

IV.

O Lord, send somethin' down to break us free,
Said send us somethin' now to set us free.
Swing low your chariot to rescue we.

The calls went up in every blessed field.
The people shouting, singing in the fields.
They lit the torches, compromised the yield.

This earthly house is gonna soon decay,
Said look like Massa's house gon' soon decay.
I got my castle. Where he plan to stay?

Some waited in the hills till nightfall came,
An exodus of thousands. When night came,
They built their fires, sang into the flames:

Upon the mountaintop, the Good Lord spoke.
And out His mouth come the fire and smoke.

V.

The art of spitting fire? How to smoke
A fool without a gun? We learned that too.
We studied master poets—Big Daddy Kane, not Keats;
Rakim, not Rilke. "Raw," "I Ain't No Joke,"
Our Nightingales and Orpheus. And few
There were among us couldn't ride a beat
In strict tetrameter. Impromptu odes
And elegies—instead of slanting rhymes,
We *gangster leaned* them, kicking seventeen

Entendre couplets just to fuck with old
Miss Jefferson, the Newton freak. Sometimes
We even got her out her seat, her ten
Thin digits waving side to side, held high
And hiding nothing. Where our eyes could see.

VI.

And we knew nothing but what eyes could see—
The burnt-out liquor stores and beauty shops,
Mechanics' lots abandoned, boarded up
Pastrami shacks where, seemed like every day,
We used to ditch class, battle Centipedes
And Space Invaders… gone. Or going fast.
What eyes could see was flux—the world, and us,
And all we knew… like smoke. So renegade
We did, against erasure, time, and—hell,
We thought—against the Reaper, too. We left
Our names in citadels, sprayed hieroglyphs
In church. Our rebel yells in aerosol—
We bomb therefore we are. We break therefore
We are. We spit the gospel. Therefore, are.

VII.

   The walls are sprayed in gospel. This is for
The ones who never made the magazines.
   Between breakbeats and bad breaks, broken homes
And flat broke, caught but never crushed. The stars
   We knew we were, who recognized the shine
Despite the shade. We renegade in rhyme,
   In dance, on trains and walls. We renegade
In lecture halls, the *yes, yes, y'all's* in suits,
   Construction boots, and aprons. Out of work
Or nine to five, still renegades. Those laid
   To rest, forgotten renegades. In dirt
Too soon with Kuriaki, Pun, and Pac—
   I sing your names in praise, remember why
When we were twelve, we taught ourselves to fly.

francine j. harris (1972)

Stitches

Last nigga tried to scratch the surface broke a nail.

—Ab-Soul

Your mama so fat, she got stitches.
Your mama so skinny, she got staples.
You look like a train running backwards on the wrong track.
Your daddy had a hole in his nut sack, shit stringy loose.

Last I heard, you was pushing down maggots in your compost pile
    hoping things would heat up.

Yo, why don't you go back to Ireland.
Yo, why don't you go get bagged.
Yo, why don't you go crust cake in a lotion pump.
Yo, why don't you go overbake at 375°.

My mama bigger than your mama.
Yo nigga, you ever heard of a emery board?

Last dude tried that shit with me got herpes.

The fuck you looking at, Magnavox?
Fuck you looking at, Two Shoes.

Muthfucker, I'll put you in your proper zip code.
Muthfucker, I'll lay you out in your pillows.
Muthfucker, I'll switch your eye color.
Muthfucker, I'll untie your shoes.

Don't try my carrot cake, Son.
Son, don't try my peach Activia.
Nigga, don't push my triangular Swiffer.

Your mama so high she bought a dime in a plastic bag.
Your mama so high she tried to roll up the dime and licked all the
    glue off.

Yo, Bitch. Let's take it out on the veranda.
Yo, let's take that shit backstage.
Yo, let's take that shit boxseats.

Say it to my muff.
Say it to my plug.
Bet you won't say that shit backwards.

I don't mean to be mean, but I'd rather lick a knife.
I ain't trying to be funny, but you smell like yarn.
Not to be racist, but *Air Polska*, Nigga.

Pull down the earth

...make the ground move, that's an assquake
—Big Sean

Pull down the earth for all the asses of all the girls in all the clubs in all
the black bottoms of black hoods in black screaming and black drugs
and half hooker half hoe on sticks of more losers and more dicks all
shake down and ass shake all dope bags and dumbdumb rape babies
and baby mamas jail birds and dodo birds and chicken stickers and
damning demanding hustler puppies with big pop gazing lap straddlers
and smokeouts zonked out and choked out no one in black shit ever

cuts a pineapple

   shaves backwards

      takes a roundabout

         eats tofurkey

            dances dancehall

               dyes a t-shirt

                  flicks a cat's ear

                     takes the alleyway

                        skips along a bike trail

                           moves west and misses home so slow it

                             bleeds color on the melted speaker from

                     a desert sun

                          in the back seat of a celica

                             which bends and gives way

                          to the touch

                             a finger on plastic.

All alone, you use kitchen
      to investigate
            wall
        and tendency
             to

                twerk

  and so
      on spotify channel called
           little ditties for strumpets

    metal, and make

  room
      a petal, shake
      doom and

    bevel
   it ain't   as easy—ro busta—as it looks : go gusta. you have to work (and *check the blinds*) the rows (*in your mind*) you know by heart. *dropit. popit.* you have to fake it. some kind of take—*topit popit*—or plan (shake shakeshake) make it growl it until it aches. (shakeshakeshake) go on and placate the age. boomboom with a move. do it to it. make a mind up. do the makeup. brew it/glue it. do the roundup (bumpit, bumpit) to solution. smooth a dance. make a move. it's not too late. (bumpbump) to make a name up. (*grasswoman*) to shake the blame up. strumpets hump it. never too late (bumpbumpbump) to shift a dime (*take out the trash*) to push a groove (*thaw a loing*) until it rules. (*fix the dish drain*) in the mirror, blow the rules. (*check the window*). (shakeshakeshake) screw the neighbors. pop the blinds. drop it. hop it. don't *complain*. do the hound up. (*butter on the list*) from the ground up (*maple syrup*). there is nothing left

(left to front. front to back : left to left : back
to front) in our humanity (shakeshakeshake)
: /hard til it pops/ : that doesn't live (*warm
water soak*) in how we move (shakeshakeshake)
so as girls *(sticky icky)* around the world—
boomboomboom—we   should   erect   our—
boomboomboom—ungodly poses *(take a scraper
to it. take a. take a. scraper to it)* and fix our asses
(*bootybooty*) into disposition (aw*shit*now) our
bodies for our (shakeshakeshake) adoring gazes

on our own.

t'ai freedom ford (1973)

how to get over (senior to freshman)

pick the big bitch:
the chick who look like
she chew screwdrivers.
hunched at the lunch table copying homework,
shredding syllables with a mouthful of metal.

shush the rebel
in your throat, that ghost of punk funking
dark circles in the pits of your polo.
resist the impulse to shittalk your way
through ranch dressing and lunchroom throng.

bumrush: snatch
song from her ears, tangle of headphone
wires and tracks of mangled weave.
nevermind uglying her face
with nails or an armful of bangles.

she already a jigsaw puzzle
of scratch and scar, every exposed part
caked in Vaseline. every fold of fat
fortified with that free-free—french fries,
chickenshit shaped like tenders, cheese sticks.

she will slip-n-slide you
if you don't come correct.
pick you up by your bookbag
til you feel fly, camera phone red eyes
winking your punkass almost famous.

but that ain't your fame to claim.
pitbull her ankles til she drop,
til ketchup and corn splatter,
scatter abstract like technique
from our 5th period art class.

as she knuckles herself up
from chickenfeed, ain't no need to run.
instead smile for the video,
that soul-clap in your chest
is your heart.

how to get over (for my niggas)

pull up your pants: cripwalk and dance your ass off
the corner coroners got your chalk outline memorized

bullets got they eyes on you du-rag yourself an imagination
imagine a nation afraid of your brilliance   remember

your grandma's resilience   her dreams: charred bits
sludged in chicken grease   piece yourself back together

get your dreams outta pawn break dawn like babymama
promises remix the lyrics breakdancing on your tongue

and play another slow jam   slam dunk your way out
the projects   consider yourself post-racial   facial hair

and funk don't make you a man but it might make you
a punk play dead when you body hits the concrete

like kerplunk hip-hop ain't your savior stop praising
lil' wayne like jesus—nigga, please:

that fog ain't the weather it's the weed bleed
on the sidewalk and call it graffiti warn the youth

with your reckless release police know the sound
of your stereo type   don't believe the hype

your mans and them will snitch if pressed
and your bitch hair is a weave and Ralph Lauren

is a pimp limp your ass back to school nigga
triggers get foolish in your presence   remember

that your essence is golden prison is not your birth
right nor sagging pants your birthmark   know

you are the last dragon—
catch bullets with your teeth and glow.

how to get over (for kanye)

dig. toss ignorance and brilliance in the dirt. spit. wait for sunlight
to hit. for arrogance to take root and sprout snatch out its bloom.
wear it on ya lapel. sell its sweet reek as cologne. call it doom.
spout ignorance. call it brilliance. doubt the hybrid. pout about mtv
moonman. swoon. hide the high kid behind sunglass and plastic. go
spastic when the white chick win.

sequester yourself for the semester. flunk the fuck out. high bid studio
time. study ya rhyme. rape crates of classics for a hook. loop-da-
loop. get stoopid on the track. louis vuitton your look. crooked your
grin when the blogs you read read you. let ya arrogance precede you.
let niggas know how much they need you. indeed you brilliant. be
patient til they get a clue. in the meantime, let it do what it due: kick
a mean rhyme. lace a bassline. waste time on fashion.

blueprint niggerness for white chicks who have considered bigger
dicks when black myth wasn't enough. bootleg Black and call it *Otis*.
trademark swag. call it: *Niggas in Paris*. call it: i'm so fly, i'm jetlagged.
copyright your elbow ash. stash black egos in marc jacobs bags and
sell it back to us for undisclosed amounts of cash. and you know
this. put white folk on notice. call 'em racist to their faces. ball so
hard motherfuckers try to find you. remind us: *we aint even 'posed to
be here*. mercy us a theme song to dream on. fuck brilliance. call it
capitalism. *swerve.* get what you deserve: a kardashian and a mouthful
of flashy. *swerve.*

Suheir Hammad (1973)

break (rebirth)

jesus left at thirty three

full saturn revolution returning messiah

math a myth wa language a lie

scorpio sun wa libra amar

yo this beat nar yo
nod head right off blow up spot wa kill crowd wa
bomb walls break dance wa break off grilled face
iced teeth wa break me sick ill music sickle
self amnesia

ana gathering selves into new
city under construction gaza eyes pitted zeitoun spit meat taqasim
brooklyn broken english wa exiled arabs sampled

> i start to blink and then i think
> reality paper my thoughts the ink
> what i'm writing is strapped in between these lines
> i'll exist when i out run time

ana sawah wa thousand wa one nights wa ahwak
morning ahwa boiling resurrection no sugar no touch

habibi writ his name in water
rhymed sixteen bars wa sang mawal blue heavy brass hair
wool wa ana still waiting missing messiah zei self missing my

habibi don't see me
he gaze stars of different flame

> i left at thirty three

thirty three shots from twin clocks
yo sixteen apiece equal thirty two
that means one of god's suns was holding seventeen
twenty seven hit my saturn dream
six went into me
everybody gotta be born sometime

my eyes burn phosphorous darkened angels broke wings no touch no
touch so much language clustered so much damage cluttered morgue
drawers baby corpses combust when exposed to air in gaza doctors
open bombed bodies find organs on fire wa these people still alive the
dead their wounds flame after spirit gone

fluorescent gardens tended by pyromaniacal men
ana warda exploded tears come busting me open cranial guitar
strumming me a psalm my palms stigmatized heart white butterflies
expand lungs wa bastana new vision same old same sold humanity

somebody touch me jesus

break (sister)

ramallah is closed
zei a heart shuttered wa fortified
bas inside a waiting a held
breath

gaza is on fire
zei a heart feeding on itself
so hungry mistaking
flame for warmth

cities wa women die like this habibi
wa cities wa women live

break (embargo)

between us wall wara wall wa ana i ain't jinn wa ana i
ain't phoenix between us yama walls ya allah first wa last
within me breaking sunset over into canaan way dawn
into egypt river running through women carry their men
framed cornered memorial el umma say ameen cigarettes
fuel gaza kemet crossing fingers one hand birds one flock

the dream after the dream
alone fisherman grandfather's sea

gaza pouring exodus resonant alien smoked out blunted absolute
cipher grace pepper calligraphy hunted cartoonist hunted doctor
hunted moderate hunted righteous hunted baba haunted

some people excavate what they love like looted pyramid empty
stomach worried bead browse these streets carbon 14
proportioned formless dark hidden water

habibi chant soul first soul fist sought fashioned criminal gazelle
leaping fence habibi chant down walls with song with song i reach for

Marty McConnell (1973)

the World tells how the world ends

Without prodding. In an astonished mob. Hand over
the weather. Hand over the knob, the lever, the gods
of gender and weather and catcalls. The gods of raw
astonishment and flat-front khakis. The end? Say weather
is a matter of anatomy. Keep caterwauling. Keep the body
you bought, a bargain, keep coming. Keep coming. Call
your gods weather. Call them new and booming and zippered
throat to crotch like a catsuit. Keep prodding. What's a mob
but a body brought to astonishment. You're a new tooth
pushing through. You too. Wear sex like the weather.
Each genital is a new tooth. You bought your body
on special, it's astonishing. It's the truth. The prodding
is unbearable, it's neverending, it's the god of forbearance
and broken sunglasses and he hates you. He's tired
of waiting. He's prodding and piercing and thrusting
and plucking and dying and dropping it like it's hot.
Where did you buy this body? By whom? The end
is in sight, they say, the end is in sight. Hold
your sutures closer. The weather
is everywhere. You never want it to stop.

object

The girl in the tie is a boy in the bar light
and everyone in a skirt's got eyes

for her buttons, snug in their sockets,
not one of them threatening

to burst. The light in the bar is the boy
in the girl sickened by lipstick. Every tie

is a slipknot, an unraveling skirt waist.
Her buttons say nothing

about regret or blurred mornings
or what's under the lycra compressing

her chest. The bar in the boy is a pageant
of light, an astonishment of offers, skirts

pressed against the night, each other,
the boy, the boy in the girl in the tie

in the bar, the bar, her buttons, her hands
like her father's, in charge, something

about power, something about
hold me down, something

about our fathers, some light
off her shoulders, some weight

the tie tells our skirts she can shoulder
better than our fathers, better her

than the bar, the night, our astonishment
of want. The boy in the light

is a pageant of buttons she knows
how to fasten in the dark. Escape

is key for the boy girl going home
with a skirt, going into the night

with the bar in her, with her lycra
and watch fob and the tie loose

as a slipknot, after all we're all trying to kill
or marry our fathers and who better

than her, marooned at the bar with all
of his charm and none of his weaponry. What

better home for our want than the night,
her chest, our hands flattened against

the bar, each other, the lights overhead coming on
just as the music's starting to get good.

John Rodriguez (1973–2013)

Bronx Bombers

The cops want us locked, Mayor Koch wants us blocked,
transit wants us stopped, their German shepherds want us chopped,
and that third rail at night is like the Mason-Dixon line
—you can't really see it, but it's a problem nonetheless.

You'd think with so many enemies writers would unite,
but bubble vests with deep pockets are flak jackets
for when the yard explodes like shrapnel
from the kind of pineapple you don't want a slice of.

Just as part of U.S. history is conflict,
part of getting up is throwing hands.
Before the beauty of a fresh, whole-car burner comes
the calamitous fracturing of teenage knuckles to jawlines,

because you ain't going over my name
like B-52s over Vietnam, you toy-tagger.
It's 1982 and even the old-timers don't have the vocabulary
to describe our hunger. Nothing else fuels artistry like rage

sprayed by Grand Concourse Puerto Ricans. A graffitied train is
no act of vandalism. Reading our names
when you won't even see us is a mercy, give thanks
you're not getting the bombs you deserve.

What I Saw Was Not Your Funeral

John Rodriguez

You cannot be dead.
You cannot be dead.

You cannot be dead, Ronald Reagan,
while the children of the poor still eat.
You cannot be dead while California
cities still have Spanish names.
You cannot be dead while Oliver North
gets his share of conservative shine.

You cannot be dead.
You cannot be dead.

You will not die until the last mother
on welfare must trade blood for milk,
gallon for gallon.
You will not die until the last
lighter sparks the last crackpipe
melting the last of South
America's finest flake cocaine
(which, when cooked and cut will
be, by way of color, texture and pure
cragginess, your spitting image) into
the most putrescent billow of false,
ephemeral utopia ever known.
You will not die until the U.S.
Strategic Defense Initiative master
builders create their own fully
functional Death Star and history
textbook manufacturers are ordered
to proclaim you a Sith Lord.

You cannot be dead.
You cannot be dead.

You do not deserve a sanctified flag over
a finely constructed pine box, your Nancy,
ever the supporting actor, thrown across

heaving, just saying no, no.
You deserve to be boiled with baking soda,
quartered with razor blades, sealed in glass
jars and sold to the ghetto desperate by vampires
whispering, "Got that Gipp, sun."
You deserve to die dragged from a rope tied
to the back of a Cadillac driven recklessly
by Freeway Ricky Ross on his long, bumpy
road to redemption.
You deserve to die in a showdown
with Bernhard Goetz and the cops
who raped Tawana Brawley.
You deserve to debate for the fate
of your immortal, invidious soul
against no softer an opponent than
Mumia Abu-Jamal.

You cannot be dead.
You cannot be dead.

But if you are, you deserve to be
reincarnated as a dark-skinned immigrant
boy and forced to survive living in
a United States that remembers
Ronald Reagan and the masks
he wore so well, so long.
You deserve all that, Ronald Reagan,
and a brick of government cheese good
to outlast nuclear armageddon and the short
-term memory of a nation without a conscience.

What I saw was not your funeral, Ronald Reagan.
That was a sham, a hoax,
an award-winning performance.
Bonzo would have been so proud.

John Rodriguez

August is the cruelest month: never enough daylight, too much
heat, no holidays and nothing matters except September's

dawning responsibilities, but the August of 1994 I was Holden
Caulfield, summer camp senior counselor for the junior trail

blazers, black and brown children two weeks shy of first, second,
and third grade. Nothing is as positive, as motivating a force within

one's life as a schoolbus full of kids singing along to the local
radio station blazing hip hop and R&B. (Imagine this cherubic

chorus riding upstate to Ini Kamoze's "Here Comes the Hotstepper"
["Muuur-derah!"].) My workday is filled with hazards like chocolate

melted sticky swimtrunk pockets, insistent sunburn, and the assorted
rah rah of parental unsupervision, but those bus rides back from

upstate water parks and pools were my favorite times working.
Have you ever ridden in a cheesebus with ashy children asleep

against you, staring at sudden trees—more numerous than project
windows—blurring along the highways like confusion giving way

to doubt, the heady smell of dried chlorine and musty towels
lulling you into the soft timbre of a Midwest falsetto? Tell me

what it is to fall in love with a lightskin girl covering the Isley
Brothers. I was not two weeks into 21 years old. I had yet

to wear a box cutter in my fifth pocket, or see a semiautomatic
aimed at my center mass, to feel its dumbness against my spine.

---

* "At My Best" contains elements from "At Your Best," by the Isley Brothers and Chris
Jasper. The "Apache" mentioned in "The Last B-Boy" is the Incredible Bongo Band's version,
with a nod to the Sugarhill Gang's lyrics.

My life was uncertain, save for its unlikely length under my control,
like the pilot who falls short of what he says, what he says

he's all about, all about. All my homeboys were still alive, just
like Aaliyah Dana Haughton, not yet an angel of the cruelest August,

begging a boy, who may not be in the mood to learn what he thinks
he knows, to look beyond his world and try to find a place for her.

Paper Bag Poems

These poets use being black to write about larger subjects.
—Charles Rowell

Fulla field hollers,
rifles, unrefined
liquor,

my poems can't pass
paper bag tests.

Blueprints for surviving
architecture of grief.

There is nothing larger
than the night sky
of our blood.

Broken bones of teardrops,
three generations of raw
throated women.

Fists rising from these pages.

Global Warming Blues

The ocean had a laugh
when it saw the shore
I said the ocean had a big big laugh
when it saw the shore
it pranced on up the boardwalk
and pummeled my front door

There's no talking to the water
full of strength and salt
no, there's no bargaining with water
so full of strength and salt
I'm a Mama working two jobs
global warming ain't my fault

I said *Please water, I recycle*
got a garden full of greens
I said *looka here I compost*
got a garden full of greens
water say *big men drill and oil spill*
we both know what that means

now my town is just a river
bodies floatin, water's high
my town is just a river
but I'm too damn mad to cry
seem like for Big Men's livin
little folks have got to die

seems like for Big Men's livin
little folks have got to die

Sunday

All week
my hands are small
brown cyclones

sudsy water, braids, grocery bags,
cast-iron skillets, collard greens,
shirts and folding, broom,
mop, dust pan, chalkboard, shoelaces,
sweet potatoes, cups, sheets, bowls.

all week
my hands are brown birds
guiding a tiny flock

come Sunday
the hands need rest,
need holding.

Now I understand
why my foremothers
embraced Sunday
like I would a lover:

eager, radiant,
ready to be filled.

Possible

for Amiri Baraka

out of the box   they spring
out of the narrowness of yesterday & some bleak projected tomorrow

impossible men

outlawed drum of their hearts
punishable dance of their breath
our loving them is the forbidden religion

impossible   Black & looking the world straight in its eyes
not smiling/making mouths cushions for someone's fear to rest on/not
    smiling

moving through streets   hills   universities   forests
like they gotta right

alchemy of voice   ideas & soul   taking up deserved space
creating it.

Impossible   seducing language out of its corset
into shimmy & groin

***

blood jail burying the young
something darker than blue moaned
through his life's veins
still, he ain't forget the graceful sea
of jitterbug   sweet rivers
of Smokey & how to reawaken
laughter in our eyes

insurrection of his tenderness
surrender to the work
of love   not just the romance

***

he's impossible
exasperated arms flung
shaking heads   closed doors   establishment wallets shut

but he is
& is possible
& is widening possibility

right here.

Tara Betts (1974)

Hip Hop Analogies

after Miguel & Erykah Badu

If you be the needle
    I be the LP.
If you be the buffed wall,
    I be the Krylon.
If you be the backspin,
    I be the break.
If you be the head nod,
    I be the bassline.
If you be a Phillie,
    I be the razor.
If you be microphone,
    then I be palm.
If you be cipher,
    then I be beatbox.
If you be hands thrown up,
    then I be yes, yes, y'all.
If you be throwback,
    then I be remix.
If you be footwork,
    then I be uprock.
If you be turntable,
    then I be crossfader.
If you be downtown C train,
    then I be southbound red line.
If you be shell toes,
    then I be hoodie.
If you be freestyle,
    then I be piece book.
If you be Sharpie,
    then I be tag.

If you be boy,
then I be girl
who wants to
sync samples
into classic.

Typical day that the black girl sees
comin' home wantin' more from a college degree.
—Nas' "Black Girl Lost"

crushed zirconium gloss & glory
glides across her lips.   she looks
in the mirror, puckers, pops her gum,
knows what would
happen if mama saw her
    switch
              girl
bounce-bounce song scripts
pinned into rivets of denim
pressed into thighs rockin
two-pocket shorts cause she can
    switch
              girl
purveyors of pulp nonfiction
sit on regals wit chrome rims
mockin constellations
and damn her pelvic metronome
    switch
              girl
a poet sketches what he imagines
as her fantasies
behind his microphone
he pastes her into fables of blow jobs for hand bags
haphazardly stitches her walk into crack alleys
half-tapes her barely breathing body with bruises
    switch
              girl
women sit facing the microphone
their pupils spin full circles
the girl is each one of them
when she had the periodic table of elements
next to cut-outs from right on!
she wanted to be a nurse
or just get an a in chemistry quietly

while looking like
doing something she ain't
    Girl,
            switch.

Paolo Javier (1974)

from *All Convulsions*

Thinkin bout youth slung at eighth wind
Once sail of skiff bends
You keep writing same theme why is that
Maybe I should try rhyming
But he knows you no emcee why is that
He is, however, a grittier story
Poet who dreams awake why is that
Not our age's Mariana Trench, rather
Byron with vandal savagery

Frank Ocean moves along
First morning summoner he moves upstate
Feel breeze sway into sail
Offer his skiff
Morning coffee ten a.m. chanting done
Mobile Suit Gundam filter sun
He'll send Jay-Z a text later
Hit him up for thoughts on this new song
He hums in mind for Bey.   Hooray

Didn't flee in a Napoleon coach
OBB
The satanic school would have been
A scald to sleep
With your half sight which I don't
OBB enter please
Poetic progress Byron's sexuality too
Loss a part of their talk infamous
The most scandalized figure on the green

                    exiled himself
I merely relocated upstate
For the summer
Whose distance to desire in time
For the better dyspepsia

Historical literary sun text
Through Waterloo down the Rhône Valley
Onto Switzerland a little longer
Meet agony again down English in Italy

febrile age
She writes *Frankenstein*
Rousseau, poliça, voice, backyard
OBB on another pilgrimage, who finds
Him unable to return to England
OBB out of the country again public knowledge
I'm tired of my voice which don't exist
No eye you heard only OBB directions
French Revolution effective fail implosion

in Napoleon
Great main perspective of the woods
Why I keep taking pictures
Don't want to miss a thing miss a
thing
Byron navigated what this might mean for
Europe
OBB's pilgrimage to be a record
Why courage inability to stop striving towards

the Alps
Read all of Rousseau
Democratic espíritu butter poem flow
Flow
Best rapper alive get your umbrage up
Is there a relationship between Perçeval
& Napoleon that's at all relevant
Analysis filter through own generality
Is accurate to serpent extent

& then change
Legerdemain's munching mind
Utterly destroy diffidence therein
If you consider the Andes as farther
Byron unsettles himself in that text
We don't have the Andes reflect heresy

Im sure ways before the opposite mood
Movement fewer always at a spot wherein
Byron's hagiographer doth smooth things over

—

become an emcee
Casuarinas squawk to his toes
My shelter column   before that empty beach   Coyo B, please read it
Old shoes wrest king away from throes
Gold necklaces take your umbrages south by minced foot
OBB known novena or gravity like Byron trammel
Shoulder first offer get it Telemachus count your toes
Spout off the horse moments notice a rose youth unravel
Old whiteman with blond head at Mariana Trench slap vain cavil

OBB BBO also known bone cushion sheep sleeping
Amy Sillman gave you permission to roll
Back in the day twelve years exact isthmus summer
Now a fourth one mark forward transgression
Rap in the fifth dimension keep it close to speed of
Before it, his wife, the two of them (not him) with own
On-the-way outlier looking back across the Hudson River Styx
Such appetite for selfie detention flaunt
Now in the fourth dimension back again at OK corral heart on point

But you've already published this kind of poem
Why not keep it unreal you feel me Vril MC
Who monitors the maze story rhyme in parataxis brother Malcolm's wish
Make you spot eyeshine in the woods at dusk   Joely or Josie
Not iambic shit propeller swelling instant injured grit slide hassle wealth
Noone hurtles onto the page   onset of IdentiTV   Biggie co-script
Amy Sillman in her paintings are poems for comics   take risk
Gimme FaceTime attire sheen swagger
Room to walk barefoot on grass no Giaour

Sup with his friends   whom to trust yeah
Can he re-set them shirtless or apply grass-fed hit
Monday mucous elevator muzak the way rioting canals clear
I know you got a ton of digits on your phone   do I too, know
Upstate again to fix hearing suture nurture same grief

Am I soon to be a father groom shirt helium lather
Send one across dense line to own private island kayak
Bareback inside orange bangka in Boracay
Send me there   to join where   fuck-all   soul's toll

—

OK fine—ask OBB
Rhyme bout day one Philippine summer
Experience what he later fingers
As eye shine, pouring elements into a
Goodbye train to Phil Am Village—There
Outside of Manila where grief taxis over
Mommy Roxy, cousins, village friends
Bawl as Papa's company car with fams pulls away
& the village that raises him stays out late

—

          "all experience is an arch weathervane"
Gleam untrammeled world, whose magick fades
Forever and thirst when I move
If noise wearies of horses, keepers would ride
Last syllable of your name vision
The Land of Look Behind
When trouble comes close to ranks, white people do
"go away white weatherman, go away go away"
You must overhear the future   'Uncertain Smile' across baby girl's face

OBB seizes clearing hard-won ocean dream Everest
Fire up warmth for hearth everything back to portion margin
Hopeless deer head night load to Rome connotation
Diyosa whom this fella breathes like choke quotes like wreathe
Fella slips keep onto in-laws' bimma Imma listen to Lady Saw hey
When Im sick of Midi Mafia enough of you straphanger prophets
Sundress squeeze life out of stairs shot still on a beach stars

Restless like sky swallow fix can't turn it indivisible OBB
You know me embattled with tree
But this seat in back of your breathing bland horses is sweet

Reason the breeze cools hearth last week's tempo folderol
Memory ember in the fire along with your pyre deicide attire
Gesundheit, neighbor! TWICE you owe thought to clarity's laundry chute
Here on the seventh line you feel lucky nickel & bullet dodge
In your journal her presence means deliquescent principles, lust, fucked
Knowing you aint no muppet agenda mad as the snow leaps gazelle on
    track

                    "and the sun did shine so cold"
Biggie's mind
It's a pilgrimage, this   Sumeria in the Hudson
Value gold folding sunlight branches loaves
Figuring out another start date to life
Just when OBB feels anew roll of film to shoot
Fire up the Bauer corner the resigned RED
OBB of the practicum emotion guiding hand
Mother of whose daughter—entrusted Coyote throw him off

OBB homie call it pilgrimage to the Valley
Pushed out of city circumference might as well make it event
So buy a stray camera in neighborhood
Super 8 film from B&H
Praise to our Hassid peeps   cinema's alchemy will keep
Wong needs to find his way but Buenos Aires shows its tough face
In the dark scare door of the camera film seeks own light
Tony hoses the blood off the street as tasking OBB dream of Coyote
Dutchess County light as rain   in the frame

—

Siddhartha understands less about vice and wood sky and trade getting
    paid in full
Ate the bread of others everybone's beads hand over mind shoddy
OBB makes sure to name English yours perfect memory shelve weight
Super 8 amor fati illuminate Maserati OBB laughs rhymes too silly
Dream reams of paper roll into light papaya fuel stand-in
How do you capture an exhale   OBB's three minute lapse into
Tome moment hunt playback contrail no failure lives through it history,
    this story the movies
Make Bach permanence

OBB pats down copy of *Don Juan*, lifts eyes away from the sun

Here I am week left in the Valley black hoodie surrender

Moving morning dew intrigue guess entre nous the Giaour & Harold

Tote a shipwreck darkness sent to raid a coyote spark

OBB pats down copy of *Don Juan*   licks the corner of his mouth grime

Thinner in morning moving dew

Giaour patting shoulder   Childe Harold warms cup

OBB convulses on steps of run-down balcony finality

Nowhere near Aleppo or Ravenna   this poem   more lake than sea

Douglas Kearney (1974)

Quantum Spit

the MC
roman miniscule

MC manifestations
  the Battle Rapper
  boldface miniscule

  the Reality Rapper
  BOLDFACED SMALL CAPS

  the Popular Rapper
  miniscule italic

  the Hypemen
clustered **clustered** **boldface**

  Turntable
  {···*bracketed italics*···}

  Drum
  [BRACKETED CAPITALS]

  America
  BOLDFACED CAPITALS

  Love
  ITALICIZED CAPITALS

{ . . . *once again it's O-onvo on!* . . . }

so soundcheck soundcheck

on stitched leather spines of impalas,
swimming through scabs of pavement,
 pimp fish of 40 rivers:
 I come.

on downtown's brick hawk wings of dollars,
 flying out zombie basements,
cottonmouth city nigga:
 I come.

 on the falsetto scat of swallows,
 falling from beaks of ravens,
steelo flipping shapeshifter:
 I come.

 on-the-low razor bladed collar,
 biding in swollen slaveships,
get-back thangs juryrigger:
 I come
 on some:

} river juryrigger shapeshifter nigga { : I spit original flows.

} pavement basements raven slaveships { : mad folk in cages.

} impala dollars collar swallows { : them hoes love whips.

trigger holler statement—
My spit-box echo to the steel

through the steel! My spit
box black eye-teeth. I steal

on, never been stole on, black-
eye biters. ever steal

bars from My spit-box:
trigger-holler statement

[KAK]

—INNER CITY HEAT HOLDERS IN GHETTO RED HOT-
TER THAN JULY ON THE 4ᵀᴴ TAKE THEY 9s
MILES AWAY FROM UNCLE SAM PLANTING GARDENS
IN THE SKY—THEM NIGGAS DON'T KNOW SHIT
ABOUT THE GARDENS SAM'S GUARDIN (need it in)
SO ON THE 4ᵀᴴ THEY HEAT THE SKY
WITH BURNERS. FIRECRACKERS ELSEWHERE.
NIGGAS KNOW BETTER THAN ANYBODY:
EVEN THIS COUNTRY'S LOVE SMELL LIKE GUN POWDER.

America loves me. what should I smell like
red herring at Liberty's green groin
brine lakes in the basins of Nike
a bed hot with comin and goin

the scarlet motes of asbestos coughs
dregs in Mad Dog broken bottle glint
bizarre plum rottin on Georgia boughs
old powdered milk, mixed to one warm pint

hoodoo smoke of Sackman's odd-tined plant
chitterlings in a saxophone wind
Pampers in a state of fetid want
the stubborn junkie's garbage bin find

a busted phone booth's jaundiced—

LISTEN MUTHAFUCKA: I SAID GUN POWDER!

{. . .*o- oh ooh he-he-ss hell naw/but yet it's that too.* . .}

like water [**KSSH**] is food.
flood.

how I flow. how I spit.

still, I can't put out the fire-

crackers with this country's love,

or my spit-box at Liberty's

green groin.   smoke.   hoodoo.

holler? I steal on [**BIP**]

Mad Dog (shit!!!!

forgot the 20/20)
America loves me.

trigger holler-statement   somebody screeeeaaaaammmmm!!!!!!!!!!!!!!!!!!

aiiaiee!!!

DEAR MC:	*DEAR MC:*
FLOWERED AGAIN	*FLOURED AGAIN*
LOVE,	*AMERICA,*
AMERICA	*LOVE*
(impatieas,	**(impatient**
carnations, begonias)	**incarnations of bologna)**
be 4TH of July in wax	**three fourths of you lie on wax.**
paper ribbon	*paper driven*

{. . .*inni-in the sky.* . .} —forgot the 20/20—

{. . .*and the s these are the breaks!* . . .}
snowblind and on ice—

{. . . *can't stop* . . .}

wheels keep spinning—

{. . .*it won't stop* . . .}

heavy rotation! banging!

{. . . *and it don't stop* . . .} [**BOOM**]
STEEL BARS.
LOVE,
AMERICA

Sam's gardens in the sky flowered again
and them niggas: plums rotting
what should I smell like?
suck sess into my spit-box
echo to the steel
of 16 bars.
I'm trying to go [**BOOM**]

platinum from ice dreams. never slipping
keep banging: the 16 bars the 16 bars the 16 bars the 16 bars the 16 bars
what should I milk? phone-in in the booth.   the 16 bars the 16 bars
plaits numb. smell powder, smoke—

spit-box{ . . . *in the sky* . . . } forgot...

gardens slipping—ice. dreams banging!

[TIK] [TIK] [TIK] [TIK]
[TIK] [TIK] [TIK] [TIK]

DEAR MC:
I LOVE YOU MADLY!
LOVE,
AMERICA

and the streets each remember my echoes of echoes,
cramping as they hand each back.
my shadows still unswept from the last times
that were the last times.
every doorway blank as a motel room.

an idiot radio coos my name like it's made of air and
everyone in the world is buried in rubble.
an idiot radio knows my name
and the streets each remember my echoes of echoes.

my face is on every magazine. I dream the newsstands
eat me over and over. I shout at the dust
"this is the last time, everyone!" maybe they hear,
I don't know, I can't make it out:
everything sounds like applause these days
and the streets each remember my echoes of echoes—

DEAR MC:
DO IT AGAIN, JUST LIKE THAT!
AMERICA,
LOVE   and the drums each remember my stories of stories,

choking as they retell each**YOU CHANGED IT!**
                                      —AMERICA
my penis still caught in the crab's clutches**HOLD IT!**
             and the drums each**STOP!!**   **—AMERICA**
                       —AMERICA
remember my stories of**SAY IT RIGHT!!**
choking   **—AMERICA**

[CHOK]
…I can't make it out
THAT'S RIGHT.
      —AMERICA

{*. . . hear the drummer get w- wi- wicked!!! . . .*}

KAK KSSH BIP BOOM TIK CHOK

CHOK KAK TIK KSSH BOOM BIP

BIP CHOK BOOM KAK KSSHTIK

TIK BIP KSSH CHOK K KBOOM

BOOM TIK KAK BIP CHOK KSSH

KSSH BOOM CHOK TIK BIP KAK

KAK KSSH

BIP BOOM

TIK CHOK

!!!!!

{ *. . . and the girls be on my jock cuz my system's fly . . .* }

e.CANCeL.

WHEN IN COUPE, LOOKING TO HOUSE CHICK,
ASSESS ASSES:
SHE FINE? WITH IT?
SHE FINE WITH IT.
GIVE HER DIGITS.
(MORE POLITE THAN HITTING HER UP.)
SHE HOLLER?
HAUL HER BACK.
WHINE? DYING.
TITTY, LAY, SHUN,
REAP, EAT: ASS NEEDED.
 —from "America's Book of Love," signed:

I LOVE YOU MADLY.
LOVE,
AMERICA

Liberty is a bed hot with coming and going.
 America is a crab holding something.

AND FOR INNER CITY HEAT HOLDERS IN GHETTOS RED HOT,
EVERYTHING SOUNDS LIKE APPLAUSE THESE DAYS.
CAN'T MAKE IT OUT ON THE WIND OF NIKE,
IN A STATE OF FETID WANT: SUCK
SACKMAN SMOKE. DREAMS OF DUST.
BURIED IN RUBBLE. THE BOOTH, A MUSE MEANT FOR PAIN AND—
 AMUSEMENT FOR PAYING
 CONSUMERS! NOW YOU
 CAN GO PLATINUM, GET A WHIP!
 ghetto-whipped?
 YES! AMERICA,
 LOVE

{ *. . . can't stop. . .* }
 { *. . . it won't stop. . .* }
 { *. . . and it don't stop. . .* }

Liberty coos my name like it's made of air and
she's drowning—I know better—she is powdered milk—
I am food —unswept shadow—hotter than july
    flood
my wheel's spinning—heavy rotation—every doorway a motel room—
my spit-box at Liberty's green groin—a bed hot—I'm in
a brine lake mixing a warm pint—love America—a hot bed—
Liberty has a crab—Uncle Sam planted—scarlet motes asbestos coughs
my spit-box is a busted phone booth—Liberty is a bed hot
with comin' and goin'—I want to go—I can't go—16 bars—
America loves me—my echoes of echoes—
America eats me over and over—I am an idiot radio—
this is the last time—16 bars echo the steel—comin
and goin—I want to go—I can't go—America loves me
what should I smell like MUTHAFUCKA! I SAID GUNPOWDER!

I come

I come

I come

I come

Douglas Kearney

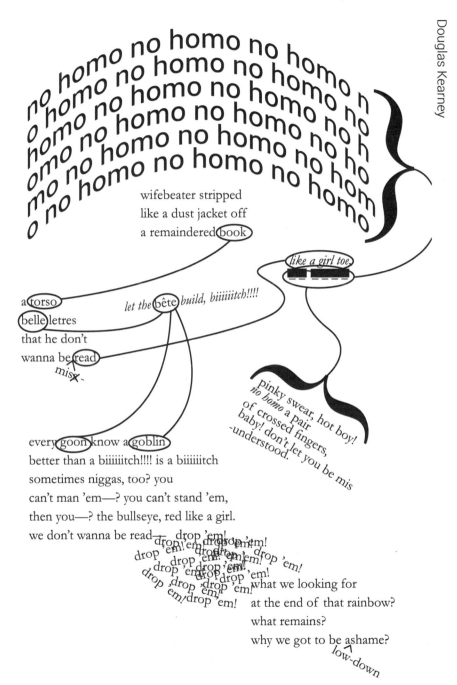

no homo no homo

wifebeater stripped
like a dust jacket off
a remaindered book

like a girl toe,

a torso
belle letres
that he don't
wanna be read

let the bête build, biiiiitch!!!!

miss-

pinky swear, hot boy!
no homo a pair
of crossed fingers,
baby! don't let you be mis
-understood.

every goon know a goblin
better than a biiiiitch!!!! is a biiiiitch
sometimes niggas, too? you
can't man 'em—? you can't stand 'em,
then you—? the bullseye, red like a girl.
we don't wanna be read

drop 'em! drop 'em! drop 'em!
drop 'em! drop 'em! drop 'em!
drop 'em! drop 'em!
drop 'em! drop 'em! drop 'em!
drop 'em! drop 'em!
drop 'em! drop 'em! what we looking for
at the end of that rainbow?

what remains?

why we got to be ashame?
low-down

drop it like it's hottentot venus.
dip   rump   other
trip   keister   her spot tinted skin.
slip   **end up on tv.**   dirt   rind
sink   video   soiled   husk
teeterin' til tits up. hd   rotten   hidin' pole.
drunken   on **revoltin' ho**
         ón dv imprison in shot.   rod
tilted   onto   nut   penis
soused   **hip to under.**   spoo   tool
tore up the donk.   lesser   seep
                tush   vile   **I pour it on. I hit it. *provoked* to**
                hind   spit   poke   pushed to
look. nude heinie   **shit up slot.**   strike   pressed to
peek   spoil   slit   stroke   driven to
peer   repulse pit   *she* lust prod   onus *hers*
see so rotund **in the stink.**
                into   hole
    distort   inside   **kitten to split.**
    revise   **enter the pink.**   rip
edit the pose. turn   poon   sunder
hooker do sit n spin   tenders   shred
                tissue   rive
         she tripe loined.   rend
                nothin'   **rent it out ho.**
                nil   pro
         slop in skirt.   prostitute
                          she isn't loved
                                no
                                nope
                                not
                                never.

a prayer fo mama Brenda Matthews (warrior brew)

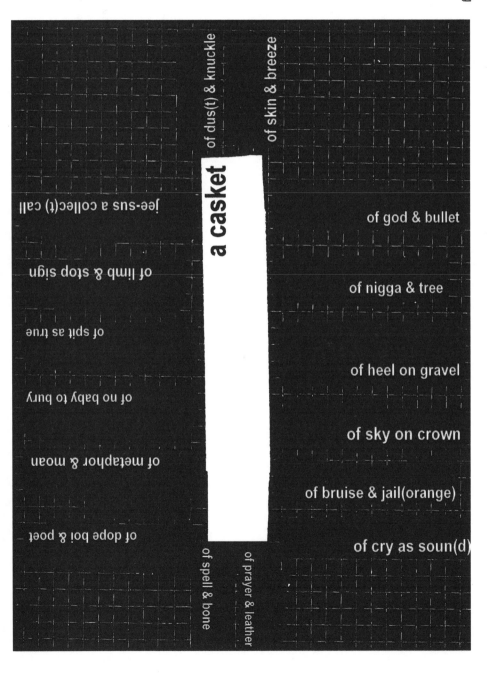

after an artis(t) talk

[a brudda who use(d) to do white-crak] walk(s) up to me & say him aint ever like de nigga(s) him grew up round. cause dey was nigga(s). him mo a human davidson. but nigga(s) call(d) him a faggot thomas. nigga(s) beat him azz fo carryin bookbag(s) wif book(s) in dem. him say nigga(s) scurr(d) of de smell of teen different. & i look at him baby purple dred(s); & i look at him arm(s) dat look like de wall inside of de cell of one of a nigga countin de day(s) him been in de county; & i look at him & i wonder is dis what de cullud boy(s) who double-dutch & lissen to fishbone be into deez day(s). him say, at first, him wasnt feelin me. i came off like dem nigga(s) who sent him thru nigga-terror. but. after lissenin, him say him see a blk man who aint runnin from no nigga. him say i make him wanna take him time walkin down central. i use(d) to live off central.

Lemon Andersen (1975)

The future

Let it top the billboard charts
for scores
years a thousand fold
till everyone realizes
the truth will go pop,
the honest and upright
will be bang in the club,
lying will only list you
with the sucker MCs
Grammys will be overrated
and oxymoronic
ghost writing will win Pulitzer
slang will evoke change,
breakbeats will become elevator music
car navigation will use
top to bottom graf walls
to get you through traffic
grandmothers will still
be making music with their mouth Biz,
thugs will finally come out
and tell the world
that they are the real
hip hop masons
wearing baggy jeans
under your ass
will come back permanently
tattoos will be earned
dreads will be licensed
only to the nappy
the party people will strike
against DJs using MP3s
studios will be strapped
with lie detectors
rappers will replace
video hos with their wives and kids
MC Lyte will be our new Oprah
the Oscar will go to Lupe Fiasco

for playing Rakim
we will wake up every morning
and pray south to the Bronx
we will have a hip hop high school
for the ignorant but blissful
where they will teach
master classes on beat boxing
field trips to old train yards
horticulture classes
on who can grow the best kush,
Big L's rhyme books
will be the basis
for all English majors
we will live in a world ruled
by the iron fist of the 808,
It Was a Good Day by Ice Cube
will be illustrated into a children's book,
they will paint the Brooklyn bridge
Red Black and Green
to commemorate Spike Lee,
there will finally
be some honor amongst us
see America's Most Wanted
will run an hour special
on who killed Jam Master Jay
Hollywood will move to Atlanta
for balance
L.A. will celebrate their independence
from the entertainment industry
we will respect
our gold chains
our diamonds
and replace them with Steve Biko
name plate quotes
democracy will fall into the hands
of an OG'd out government
where Dead Prez
will be in charge
of the people's army of the United States,
Latifah will be the first lady
ladies first
And what do you know
Eric B. will be President.

Michael Cirelli (1975)

The Message

Malcolm was fed 16 bullets because of his. A slug kissed
the jaw of King Jr. and silenced him forever. Gandhi shriveled
like snakeskin. Joan of Arc became Joan of Ash—
So you can understand why Melle Mel was jittery scribbling it
all down, on a napkin, at Lucky's Noodle Shop in Harlem.
Sweat pearled into his green tea. He thought of Jesus
hanging from that dull wood. Heard about the poet Lorca
under an olive tree, shot in the back. Everyone has felt this way though,
he thought. Never could he have imagined what would happen
when he pressed his thumbprint into vinyl. Hip-hop was still
a tadpole. The DJ had just learned to scratch a record and make sounds
no ear had ever conjugated. How was he to know Tupac & Biggie
would follow his lead and get plugged with lead? So he wrote it down,
in big curling letters, emphatic: *don't push me.*

Astronomy (8th Light)

Black like the planet / that they fear.

If those are stars, and what they make when they pepper
the sky, if it is a sky and not a road, is a shape we call
spoon, then the sky that is not a road might possibly be soup
or yogurt, but we call it a sky (and the spoon of stars
has its own name), and in that road of soup is a planet,
if it is a planet, and if what we call *planet* was assigned a color
that is feared in America, if this is America, and if fear meant:
"something *bad* might happen to you, so be on the lookout"
and bad had the same color of this planet in America
so the color called *bad* had to swallow the bad, like a black hole,
had to make break/s, make tap, and scratch two records
together to fire/back, if what fire is is something that makes light,
and heat, so that the bad was no longer bad even when it was used
in speech like when he said "he is one bad mutha effer"
it was not bad meaning bad but bad meaning good—(like foot, like
hair, like skin)—then the skin that looks up to the moon,
as full as a record, reflects the light that shines off the sun that we call
the biggest star in the soup, and we see it down here in Fear,
where the people, if they are people and not spoons, bob their heads
to the light that shines from two mouths and is black.
The light from their mouths is black.

the crossover

it was the end of disco. all the jobs were moving or changing or drying up in the city like the river after a summer of no rain. the parents moved farther from the city or themselves or their families for those jobs. hours in commute. we received a key to let ourselves in after school. they would not be home till late. sometimes they would not be home at all. sometimes the commute was too much. the parents too far gone to see each other. busy running around. sometimes running around with other parents. sometimes running around doing things parents shouldn't do.

there were plenty of tvs and radios. there were older siblings. there were city/suburban sleepover camps. there was a black friend. a new york cousin. a late night pbs airing of henry chalfant's documentary. there was a leak. it was run dmc. it was newcleus's *jam on it*.

the house was quiet. peanut butter spread on crackers. sandwiched potato chips. there was bruce lee, saturday afternoon shoguns. kamala the ugandan giant. nothing was explained. no one home to contextualize. everything was mixed up. ninjas wore black like ice cube. burn hollywood. the sleeper hold. the college radio political talk show said south africa.

there was apartheid at the schools. apartheid in the lessons we sat thru. nelson mandela was in america. his name was chuck d. his name was krs-one. what is a black panther? there is apartheid on the bus home. there is apartheid in the lunchroom. the sides of the city we don't visit. were told not to. there is apartheid on the television. bill cosby aside.

there was a tape deck. a walkman. there was no apartheid in the music. no separation in the library. books endlessly check-out-able. there was holden. the hero Huey P. the wandering protagonist in the midst of all that quiet. the new music to soundtrack the walk to school. the music truthed. the music was middle finger fuck you. fuck you actor reagan who sent uncle dave crazy back into the streets. fuck you actor reagan who warred on the drugs my mom did. what you know about three jobs and two kids and running from landlords. the music was solace and ammunition. alone and one in the chamber.

i listened to every word. memorized all the words. recited the words into a notebook. there was not a viaduct in the music. there was not a neighborhood to avoid. there was not a gunnery filled with columbus broken promises. there was not a cold war of white flight and divorced unions. there was a hero. for the people. all of the people.

i wanted to be a hero.

in the fruit markets just west
my pops copped produce right off the truck.
he'd drop me & say to stay on halstead
between roosevelt & the viaduct.

i'd linger among pick-the-red-ball
shell game hustlers, duffle bag porno
salesmen who dabbled in colognes
socks & leather belts. on the southside
of the street, a buffet of hubcaps, an open
air department store for pimps & starter
jackets, a junkie yard w/ '88 special white rock
blankets of bootleg tapes, piles of plastic
bodies splayed like fallen dominos

Public Enemy records were four bucks
Cube's *Most Wanted* went for five
cuz record shops wdn't carry gangsters.

but jewtown wuz filled with gangsters
& shysters & hucksters & repo men

my grandfather knocked doors
from 7 am seven days a week
demanding loot owed on layaway.
fur coats, suits, alligator shoes
leather couches, jewelry & liquor.

jewtown was blues, then.
church folk & John Lee Hooker
amplified on sunday carts of metal.
white short sleeves & thin black tied
salesmen pushin Jesus & silverware.

by the time i got there
it was Africa. musk smudged
storefronts. beads & prayer rugs
Afro picks & posters of Malcolm

hung in natural light
like ducks & pigs in Chinatown

the one neighborhood
race mixing was allowed
the block spared from the great fire
where jim's original polish
piled fried onions & peppers
where blacks and jews came together
outside their homes to eat pork
and fuck white women
where muddy waters came
to plug in & make rock & roll

wholesale and ho sale
where cash was green
& rent was cheap
& jews were slumlords
cuz no one else wanted
to live there, a safezone
even in the riots
& both daleys hated all
the mixing & tore it down
& paved it over

& now
there is a gold statue
a hawker frozen
a bluesman museumed
a caribou coffee

jewtown was a home away
from one, makeshift & janky.
a shtetl & ghetto & certainly
unjust it was, but it was
a home
north of the delta
west of the pogrom.

this was america   once
when blacks & jews roamed

on the holiest days off
to find a gun or girdle
some whitefish or pig's feet
in search of a deal or a scam
to get by & get over.

molemen beat tapes

were copped from Gramophone.
cassettes jammed into a factory
issued stereo deck of the hoopty
i rolled around in. a bucket. base
and drum looped with some string
sample, fixed. a sliver of perfect
adjusted. the scrapes of something
reconstituted. there was so much
space to fill. an invitation to utter.
Iqra—Allah said to the prophet
Muhammad (peace be upon Him).
a to b-side and around again. a circle
a cipher. i'd drive down and back
in my mom's dodge for the latest
volumes of sound. i'd stutter
and stop and begin again. lonesome
and on fire. none. no one i knew
rapped. i'd recite alone on Clark St.
free, styling, shaping, my voice
a sapling, hatchling, rapping
my life, emerging in the dark
of an empty car.

                *

there was a time when hip-hop felt like a secret
society of wizards and wordsmiths. magicians
meant to find you or that you were meant to find
like rappers i listened and memorized in history
class talked specifically to me, for me.

                *

& sometimes
you'd see a kid whisper to himself
in the corner of a bus seat & you
asked if he rhymed & traded a poem
a verse like a fur pelt / trapping.
some gold or food. this sustenance.

you didn't have to ride solo anymore.

*

Jonathan was the first kid i met who rapped. he was Black
from a prep school, wore ski goggles on top his head & listened
to Wu-Tang which meant he was always rhyming about science
and chess. his pops made him read Sun-Tzu. his mans was Omega
a fat Puerto Rican who wrote graffiti and smoked bidis.

& they'd have friends
& the back seat would swell
& the word got passed / scooped like a ball
on the playground. you'd juggle however long
your mind could double dutch. sometimes you'd take
what you were given / lift off like a trampoline
rocket launch. sometimes you'd trip & scrape
your knees. tongue-tied, not quick. words stuck
on loop, like like words, stuck, like that. but break
thru, mind, knife sharp, mind darts
polished & gleaming we'd ride
for the sake of rhyming. take the long way
home or wherever the fuck we were going
cruise down Lake Shore & back, blasting
blazing. polishing these gems.
trying to get our mind right.

white on the block

1

the first night i lived in Pilsen was early august when even the night
refused to cool. i was thirsty. it was past midnight. i asked the Kings
outside if they knew where i could get something cold to drink. i just
moved in and i could use a beer, a jug of water, something to keep
me from being hot and lonely. i asked if they wanted anything, this
group of four young men: skinny and Mexican and tattooed wearing
white tank tops and jean shorts and sox hats and silver necklaces, the
makings of mustaches. they just looked at me. i asked again if they
knew where i could get something to drink and the street was actually
quiet for once and the quiet stretched taut over the city like a wire
around a neck. again these boys didn't say shit, just looked at me, for
fifteen seconds in silence that could've been an hour. the older looking
of the four said there was a gas station on Cermak and Ashland. i said
thank you and started to head that way until under his breath he said
they'd take a six pack and his homies giggled and i looked back and
laughed and the leader looked at me and shot a look to the rest like
shut the fuck up man/hood/adolescent/cool

when i got back, we opened a case of cans and sat on the stoop on
19th between Loomis and Throop, northside of the street, in front of
the house with the green door and the young men made the steps a
school room. they mapped out the neighborhood, block by block,
who ran what streets. what beef. names, signs, colors. counts, bishops,
conservative Vice Lords. peoples and folk. five and six point stars.
almighty, insane. gang affiliates and factions. they were stuck here.
moving white and weed. trapped in the trap. they could not leave out
with out heat, a constant look over the shoulder. locked into a prison
block, a prison on this block.

2

i stroll anywhere
anytime. dayglow, moon
night. my skin
a pass. a piss
a joke, a way

an out, always.
i stole, got caught
let go. no record
stalks me thru courtrooms.
i have no history
upon arrival. i am
always writing it.
i drink and drive
been pulled over
by CPD / nothing
thankfully. it's not luck
it's just / white. on the block
in the streets. the city's
mine. art
institutes collect my image.
i can tilt my fitted
toward any nation.
i am welcomed
guest. a warning shot,
my reputation precedes me.

Jericho Brown (1976)

Motherland

Our mother swears the woman's nose is wide enough
To dam the Red River.

Our mother says you could drain a swamp
Through the gap in Angel's teeth.

She's too bottom-heavy for her clothes. Even in a housedress,
She looks like a whore fit for music videos.

Our mother keeps asking why so many music videos
Are filmed at pools and beaches.

Mama doesn't care that Angel has two kids
Or that she dropped out of school before
Meeting my brother—and while I want
Someone to say what a shame it is
That she out-drinks our dad
At Thanksgiving—Angel's looks are all

Our mother will criticize, turning watery eyes
From my brother to me,

Pray my other boy won't bring anybody as ugly home.
So I never do.

He was a fool for a tall woman, and Angel stood taller than him in any pair of shoes. He saw her the way children see the trees they climb, their mothers cussing down below.

After his car quit, I'd pick him up for work. He'd light his morning cigarette and fidget with my stereo for something repetitive, explicit— the kind of music born when we were, the one sound we had in common.

I shouldn't, but I'm thinking
About the woman who got shot
Fighting over that sweat-soaked
Headscarf Teddy Pendergrass threw
Into the crowd at one of those
Shows he put on for "Ladies
Only" the year I was born. How
Many women reached
Before the tallest two forgot
Their new fingernails matched
Purses and shoes? I'm no good.
I thought I'd be bored with men
And music by now, voices tender
As the wound Pendergrass could feel
When he heard what caused gunfire
Was a trick he rehearsed. Love,
Quick and murderous, bleeding
Proof of talent. He wanted to be
What we pay to see—Of course,
That's not special. I imagine
Someone who desires any
Worn piece of man must be
Willing to shoot or be shot.

As we veered onto Line Avenue, he stopped the music, *Sometimes, I*
call Angel those names. She throws forks and plates when I do it.

He got out of my car laughing, but with his head in the window
like it was his last chance at giving advice, *It feels good to have a woman*
fine as she is so mad at you.

Before he saw Eve, the serpent walked upright
      And climbed and crawled like a man with limbs.
He tangled himself in reaches for green, prized
      The curves of his quick and endlessly slim

Body. Days were years then. The woman spent
      Most days in giggles or gorged on something
Significant placed in her palms. The serpent
      Admired her wandering, her ease at being

Described, entered. No one wanted, but even that garden
      Grew against the ground's will, and this,
Child, I tell you since soon you'll grow and harden—
      No matter how low she seemed squatting to piss,

The damned snake couldn't stop staring, and she couldn't
      Understand—though he inched close enough
To whisper something wet and true. He needed to confront
      Her with what he knew, needed her stuffed

On a sweet that made her see herself, see him
      And every beast in the young world watching.

That wasn't the day she killed him. They fought and called the police on each other for years. Nobody paid any mind.

But if I turn too quick on Line with the worst music, I can hear him again, explaining the satisfaction of hurting a woman who's still there the next morning. I think that's why he loved Angel, ugly or fine. What man wouldn't love a woman like that? And why can't I?

Mahogany L. Browne (1976)

When 12 Play Was on Repeat

when you are a deep amber & your jheri curl is a distant memory & your shape is swollen in the perfect places & the boys remember your name & your first and last crush sings to you come here with a lilt in his walk & his tongue wags you towards him with its pale pink & you smile because you remember the sun wrinkles your darkness so you pull corners of your bright face & squint like you practiced in the bathroom mirror where only a hint of your gap-tooth smile lingers like a wager & you think of the time you danced in the basement against the brown boy with a half-moon fade beneath your hungry hands even then you were frowning in the dark trying to figure out if his fingers should shovel themselves between your cotton & denim like that because you could not understand the wet & you frowned & he stopped & you thought i want to but his eyes were all over your face & his smell was copper & so close & you sighed & he stopped & you know now that means uncertainty but you were certain that you weren't certain enough to know what a sigh can mean but now you smile just in case anyone is really looking at your face & in the dark he says come here & he is what you've always wanted & it is in the senior class lock-in which is a storm of hormones high on endo smoke & everclear & everyone is touching someone & no one is frowning including you & it's like the time when stories are passed during homeroom & locker rooms & you always wanted to have a story for the cold tiles when there are only bra straps & lip gloss & hair brushes & smiles where no frowns are found because you don't know what it is like to lose yourself into a shadow you only know how to fold each breath like a black girl mistake into the borrowed white   stretch jeans pocket   &   wait

upon viewing the death of basquiat*

~~i look into the noise~~   ~~mouth paper thin~~
~~my tongue~~————a scatter ~~of forgotten belongings~~
extinguishes ~~the heat of~~ home

---

* once, my mother plagued a painting   swept oceanic throughout the dreams of a
brown man in the lower manhattan   three years later   she sun rose
in california   swan dove into an oblique woman there are days i forget my
name   *my name* i forget my claim   this kind of fire that strikes black bodies into fever
spliff   clean   cleaner, *still* ain't no mountain of needles or glass   pipes large
enough to tow away my body   today, my mouth is a tomb   of the things people
forget   such a power my maw, this spill wonder, this rapture of psalm   ain't no
way   I let the sun   set us afire   again

nameless

who clean the house
who cook the food
who bless the babies
who stay too true
who make the clothes
who buy the shoes
who sleep too little
who sing no blues

Aracelis Girmay (1977)

ELEGY IN GOLD

Earring, tooth,
dog breath, shoe,

mango fruit or pocket watch,
sunlight on my love's

elbow, sunlight
in the kettle's steam,

we walk in the rubble
of the sunk ship's dream

brushing crash-site
from our hair & dresses.

This is the country
of the gone-away: Harlem,

you wear the missing
like a golden chain.

BREAK

When the boys are carnivals
we gather round them in the dark room
& they make their noise while drums
ricochet against their bodies & thin air
below the white ceiling hung up like a moon
& it is California, the desert. I am driving in a car,
clapping my hands for the beautiful windmills,
one of whom is my brother, spinning,
on a hillside in the garage
with other boys he'll grow old with, throw back.
How they throw back their bodies
on the cardboard floor, then spring-to, flying
like the heads of hammers hitting strings
inside of a piano.
                   Again, again.
This is how they fall & get back up. One
who was thrown out by his father. One
who carries death with him like a balloon
tied to his wrist. One whose heart will break.
One whose grandmother will forget his name.
One whose eye will close. One who stood
beside his mother's body in a green hospital. One.
Kick up against the air to touch the earth.
See him fall, then get back up.
Then get back up.

Idris Goodwin (1977)

Say my name

I always thought it just came out of a book.

My mother still has it
looks homemade, the cover
crude and orange

African Names

Inside the book it says something like *Idris means everlasting* or *never
    to die*
but I don't think that's right.

My mother Pat, my dad Don, their parents Thelma, James, Ruth and
    also James

Their siblings
Alicia, Ron, Theresa, Darrin, Reginald, Janet, Joyce, Jay, Val, Alvin,
    James Jr.—they wanted to break the chain

they were afro-wearing 1960s Black power children
trying to make a statement through their offspring
wanted us to have names with throat and vowels

In Detroit, they were a minority, our Black church asked,

Why you give that boy that African name? that Muslim name?

There are names in the good book—strong Apostle names.

Names in the phone book—strong regular names.

In the suburbs, I was a minority, my white middle American school
    asked,
Is it eye-dris?
IDI-ris?

I'd rice?
Isadore?
Ivan?
Iggy?
Can I just call you I?
Can I call you E?
Can I call you something
other than your name?

Age 11, I ask my mom, *can I change my name to something else? Tony,*
    Mark, Sean—something else?

Being named Idris in North America will arrest people

You must grow patience.

what an interesting name.
that's so unusual

Sounds Turkish.
Sounds Greek.
Are you Muslim?

Where does it come from?

Age 16, two Arab guys come through my register
get big-eyed when they see my name tag.

they're curious
how the name found its way to a Target in suburban Michigan

They're disappointed when I tell them about *African Names*

Age 28, I am in the Middle East, where they pronounce it beautifully
not all straightened and flattened
E-Dreece

They have given it a joyful bounce.

Idris is a prophet
in the Quran

earlier—Age 20, new to Chicago, broke, cleaning cigarette butts
out of the restaurant urinal for minimum wage, my boss, a giant
stereotype with turtleneck, sport coat, big glasses, and thick-as-
Ditka's-mustache accent—unzips at the urinal

(Yep, the one I just cleaned)

He smirks *I ain't gonna remember that name of yours. How 'bout I just
call you Eddie.*

And my name became Eddie until his assistant suggested that he stop
for fear I would claim cultural insensitivity

The gentleman from the UK tells me the Welsh have a myth

There is Morocco's Moulay *Idris*

The jazz world's Idris Muhammed

There is the other theater artist Idris Ackamoor

Television's Idris Elba

What does it mean?

Fiery poet—prophetic cashier—confused minority

What does it mean?

confused minority
black power baby—

It's so exotic
What is it again?

Philosophic cleaner of urinals

I ain't gonna remember that
That's gonna take me a while to learn

old, young, black, white, the spectrum

What does it mean?
How do you say it?

I call myself E-Dreece
like my mama says it
but who knows if she's saying it right

Old ladies and dope boys

I.

Behind doors with multiple locks, old ladies sit silent, their GI bill homes kept from fading by green gardens and fresh paint. They sit silent, artifact-surrounded, memory thick: skinned knees, rock heads, uncles, sweaters and aprons floured. Framed photos of Dr. King, military uniforms, perfect afros, graduation caps, S-curls, dashikis, Brooks Brothers and Cross Colours.

Archived on the shelf: *Ebony, Essence, Black Enterprise, Jet*. The engraved King James Bible next to the 10th Edition New World Revised Bible next to the pocket-sized Bible. Some spare in the drawer.

When you come home from Global Visions, they get a ride to the grocery store across town. The good one. The bus stopped running here in the 1980s. They cook for you, just you, a full family meal, hoping the aroma will lure. Then maybe the leaf can be slid through the dining room table.

II.

Across the street, the whole family razor blades and triple fades, fitted caps stooping over triple beams and mayonnaise jars. Baking soda water boils. Once it hardens, they chop.

Neighbors morph into ghosts, into shreds, while the talented tenth look ahead like Lot.

III.

Detroit blocks. Old ladies and dope boys stand off on porches, unafraid. Neither buying what the other is selling.

These are the breaks

You've heard the myths and legends. '70s south Bronx. Poly-culture pot of gold, echo urban stomps. Hands releasing ratchets to touch the vinyl, stroke the grooves. Nodding back and forth like wrists that found new ways to prove. And show, and grow, and blend. Bring it back again. Edit. Gut. And tear new names up out the wind.

You've heard about criminal. The daring, death-defying so-called underground. So-called urban styling. With the Asian technology that flooded the colony. Bytes of info, bit and flip.

Tools inverted. Sound stolen and distorted like legislation imported. Stolen like real estate, inventions and credit. Broken like neighborhoods when interstates arrive.

So the children of the losing war, they built a bridge again. Pulse to pulse catapults, lasso pulling different folks on subway cars, on foot or spokes called Philosophical. Diasporic.

The magical mining through mud for the fantastical. Celebrating. Chanting out: Raw, strike, flame ignite. Heart, livid, never break for the night.

For blocks and blocks, hips-head. Let the Breakers break. The stale left dead.

Yes,
we ex
plode
on the
break is the place where the poem get laced. Let the rhythm hit us
first in the face.

And,
in bet
ween,
all these
bangs and the bumps and the pows and the thumps, we explore time's
signature, we can't get enough.

And,
to this
day,
the words we
say been influenced by the molding of music, changing it around for a
brand new usage.

Now Bird riding horse with Bach. So-called third world pulled into
the concerto.

Some wanna cap, regulate madness. Scared of the beautiful
miscegenated scratches. But they never die down, they only get live-er.
Can't nobody copyright fire. Can't nobody copyright fire. Can't nobody
copyright fire.

'Cause it's spreadin' like it always do. Suburban, urban, and the rural,
too. Plugged in. Tucked in. Finding new ways to tune in. Finding
new ways to stand up. Speak out. Get by. Finding new ways to say
how long you been here. Finding new ways to stop the erasure of
markings.

Breaking down all the talking, coded, loaded, locked and smoking,
stocked. Because it be about the *body*, the body's reaction. The lungs,
throat, tongue. The limbs' rebellion.

Finding new ways to break the rhythm expected. Finding new ways to
break the laws of stolen land.

And some, they like to say they got patents on the noise. Numbers on
the invisible, barcodes on light. But fire, you can't copy, right?

Enzo Silon Surin (1977)

Corners

Outside Papi's Bodega, young boy in
summer's native garb—white tank-top,

doorag—a smooth blue crown garnishing
the stubbles of a week-old fade—regulates

a stereo knob while sitting shotgun
in a chromed-wheel Escalade—the ghost

of Tupac Shakur magnified in a sub-
woofer like an opus—as long as

music's kept *all's good where we come
from.* If only a glare didn't easily stumble...

if only manhood wasn't tenured with black
powder in metal capsules, brown boys, free

to chase arcade mortality, wouldn't have to
warily long for a ghetto's heaven or if grief,

inherited each day they step into the a.m.,
would follow them into an afterlife.

But corners often *leave souls open and closed,
hopin' for more...* and on Winthrop and Thorndale

the sidewalk folds into a man in hooded sweat-
shirt and blood-sodden jeans, fresh breaths

breaching his lungs. If only keeping eyes off
the karma and on the prize was what made this

world go 'round, it would be what was always
wanted, any landscape better than what's here,

where on most nights, a native glare renders
a chamber empty as winter flower boxes.

It's Just Begun*
(for B-girls and B-boys worldwide)

Birthed from the streets of the Boogie Down
born in a cipher where the rebels gathered round
homegrown/ in the soil of soul/
this is rhythm/
captured in movement and sound.

This is poetry in motion
rooted in heartbeats and drumbeats
same universal pulse per minute

Therefore
we are music.

Move in accordance
to the laws of a planet rock
this nation/ under a groove/
needs no passport for entry
because we know/ like the truth
music knows no boundaries.

from the Bronx to Berlin
from Finland to Japan
Seoul to Switzerland
raise your fist/ lower your head
and pay homage to elemental/
movement more original/
than sin.

Blessings to these warriors anticipating battles
bathed in the heartbeats of ancestors/
blessings to these b-boys and girls
who lower their ears to listen to the earth's breath/
blessings to the cadence of combat

---

* Commissioned by Crazy Legs of the Rock Steady Crew for the Red Bull Beat Battle in
London, England

captured on concrete and cardboard battlefields.

This is the resurrection of the real/
the rebirth of what they tried to kill/
this was captured from the youth and commercialized/
extracted from the ghetto exploited then despised.

But this is history revisioned and revised/
the reprise/ they said it died in '84
but we're here to show them
what ciphers were really created for.

Spin the record to the break
let loose/ backspin/ body bending backward
finesse the footwork/ hit the floor/
feet like funky drummer/
beg the bass for more/
breakbeat
stop/ rock/ pop/ lock
Let the toprock time the tempo.

Shit

this is James Brown brought back to life
tribal beats remixed/ djembe remastered/
what remains of our origins
remembered/ and recaptured

See sound is infinite
so the break will forever echo/
on the one hearts pulse
like a spinning record
to the beat
to the beat
till the breaka breaka dawn.
So let the world know we be/ music
universal and eternal
never finished
'cause it's just begun
it's just begun
it's just begun.

Ciphers Pt 1

I will tell this story out of order. You must forgive me for this.

My OG told me that in the old days, you learned to flow by running through the ragged blocks while neighbors hurled boxes of razor blades out burnt-out windows, dodging stray dogs with pearly white feral teeth and bullets that hiccupped through the air like drunk hummingbirds. He said that to be respected in the cipher you had to have seven wounds under your cloak and spit blood that sizzled when it touched the pavement. He said that when you woke in the morning, you had to roll over in bed and begin punching holes through the walls. He said the best MCs had knuckles like bloodied faces, and arms crawling with scars. So he said.

Nowadays, children arrive to the cipher fully robed in paper-thin garments, wafting above the ground like kites. They learn to flow by watching flickering screens, then by huddling next to machines, and suddenly leaping up shouting in dreams.

My OG said the last generation would stumble across the water on drowsy wings. That their works would be feeble and small. But that those who endured would win crowns of gold and ivory.

Who knows what these sayings mean? But I clutch them under my coat like precious cargo. I fan them out like playing cards, hide them under my tongue like little blades, keep them crammed in my pockets, in case they might save my soul.

Vigil Pt 1

When the kid leaned on the wall the last time, he was shivering. The spring hadn't yet stretched its legs out of winter's white skirt and the city lay still under a silver bell of ice.

When the kid leaned against the bricks at the corner of Green and Blue, the fools blackened the wall behind him with fire, slayed him with summer, absented him from the table of his confederates and left him laying on the ground like a broken bottle in a paper bag bleeding all the stories he had never told and a halo of bullets casings around his head.

Time will gnaw his bones and his memory will be swept into the gutter with the leaves, but before the devil's teeth leapt to meet him he prophesied, saying,

"You have to kill a man to see what's in him. You never see the river you cross. The only wisdom's that veins are full of wine, pens are full of blood. Do this in remembrance of me because we turn to dust."

Nobody knew what he meant and he laughed.

When he lay bleeding like a broken bottle onto the street that remembers nothing, his face shone like troubled water and the shorties gathered around him, peering into the ruined well. His lips were moving, but he made no sound.

"Yo, son, who you talking to."

"I'm talking to the souls that hang from telephone poles."

He was still holding a lit square when he died. It trembled in his hand like a homeless comet.

One for the trouble.
Two for the deceased.
Three for heaven hoping that's where you and I meet.

I Have a Drone
—For Barack-George-W-Bush-Obama

I say to you today, my friends, that in spite of the difficulties of
the moment, I still have a drone. It is a drone deeply rooted in the
imperialist dream.

I have a drone that one day this empire will live out the true meaning
of its greed: "We hold these truths to be self-evident: that poor men
are created to serve wealthy men."

I have a drone that one day on the red hills of Georgia the sons of
Democrats and the sons of Republicans will be able to sit down
together and create more efficient ways to invade foreign countries
and loot their natural resources.

I have a drone that one day even the state of Mississippi, a desert state
sweltering with the heat of injustice, will be transformed into an oasis
of neo-liberalism that distracts poor black, brown and white folks
away from the root causes of their oppression.

I have a drone that Sasha and Malia will continue to live in a nation
where their well-being is regarded as superior to the well-being of the
children whose folks who voted me into office.

I have a drone today.

I have a drone that one day the city of Chicago, whose great mayor
is committed to disarming the common people, will be recognized
as a model where little black boys and black girls will be able to join
hands with little brown boys and brown girls and wilt together as their
neighborhood schools are shut down.

I have a drone today.

I have a drone that one day every valley shall be privatized, every hill
and mountain shall be lined with surveillance cameras, the rough

places will be made sharp as barbed wire surrounding Guantánamo Bay, and the crooked places will be made straight as a Wall Street bailout, and the glory of the Invisible Hand of Capitalism shall be revealed, and all flesh shall desire it together.

This is our neo-liberal hope. This is the faith with which I co-opt the Left. With this faith we will be able to replace the mountain of democracy with the stone of capitalism. With this faith we will wrap a shiny new package around the same old product. With this faith we will be able to profit together, to exploit together, to colonize together, to drop bombs on Afghan children together, to kowtow to the one percent together, knowing that we will all be free-market capitalists one day.

This will be the day when all of Adam Smith's children will be able to sing with a new meaning, "My head-space, 'tis of thee, sweet land of private property, of thee I sing. Land where my conscience died, land of union-busting pride, from every mountainside, let free-market capitalism ring."

And if America is to be a great empire, this must become true. So let free-market capitalism reign from the prodigious pyramid-tops of Teotihuacan. Let capitalism reign from the Four Sacred Mountains of Buddhism. Let capitalism reign from the heightening Jabal Kumar of Iraq!

Let capitalism reign from the snow-capped Himalayas of Pakistan!

Let capitalism reign from the curvaceous slopes of Cuba!

But not only that: let free-market capitalism reign from Indiana State Prison!

Let capitalism reign from the American Cancer Society!

Let capitalism reign from every hospital bed and classroom of Canada. From every immunization shot, let capitalism reign.

And when this happens, when we allow capitalism to reign, when we let it reign from every heart and every soul, from every state and every city, we will be able to speed up that day when all of Adam Smith's children, black men and white women, Jews and Gentiles, Protestants and Catholics, will be able to join hands and sing in the words of the neo-liberal spiritual, "Free-market capitalism at last! Free-market capitalism at last! Thank God Almighty, we are free-market capitalism at last!"

Kyle Dargan (1980)

CREWS

Those Clay Terrace
boys. Those
Benning Park boys.
Those Simple
City boys.
Those River Terrace
boys. After hours
those boys. Those
shoot-and-dash boys.
Siren-fed boys.
Fatherless boys
siring boys. Noise
them. Urban
reservation—hunt-
and-gather boys.
Keep the blood
on the reservation.
Hunt those boys.
Solve for X: how many
whys and zombies
equal those boys.
Give me dap
those boys. My boy.
My cousin. No taller
than tree trunks
chopped. Those boys
sundown colorful.
Watch those boys.
Southeast hocus pocus—
you see / don't see those
boys. Then you read those
boys: police blotter those
boys. Then they're ink
those boys—RIP
graffiti on white tees:

those boys. Those Clay
Terrace boys. Those
Benning Park boys. Those
River Terrace boys. Those
Drama City boys.

SLANG

"Salutations, son," I say
to my dogs. Dap them
up: slap-snap-paw-
chatter. We embellish
last night's mischief. Shout
"word" and "dang" and
"that's ill." We're sick with
it, whatever it is. The sun
is our medicine. Our diction
scares our parents. They think
we speak in knotted tongues.
"Dog." "What up,
kid?" "Son, I told you." We
lift mutiny against word
rulers and the world
bequeathed to us.
It is our mission to be
other. "Old man." "Old
lady." "What you talking?"
We are eruption—our breath
a lava over the land.

O. P. P.

It was Magic that summer. Our tracks were long
—spooled between the hubs of Crescent Road
and Prospect Street. Sound we carried on foot
from one avenue to the other. Apartment buildings'
walls and sunken garages kept us from cutting
through backyards, kept us moving in knights' Ls—
intersection to intersection, long boulevards
made for rooks or teenagers whose urban costumes
fit them ill as legacies.

                            Climbing to the top floor
in one of Prospect's proud brick towers, already
were Mrs. Roach and my grandmother cooking
words. Speculation stewed between them. I watched
lips pause for news. California | Earvin Johnson | HIV.
Around me, they spat "tsk" and guessed at Cookie's fate.

Down Park, over Glenwood to Jason's driveway court.
A game of 21—running hookshots tolled his backboard
while all we asked was "You heard?" We understood
little of what made "the hiv" and swore by our own
foolishness that we knew how to prevent it.
In Jason's bedroom studio we freestyled goofy lyrics,
deepened our voices to castigate. "Should've
used a prophylactic" I barked like a Cypress Hill
chorus or a Kane crescendo: put a quarter in your ass
'cause you just played yourself. Years later I would
be shamed—the health teacher correcting me
on the role mouths can play in transmission.

Terror was knowing I was one wrong answer away
from becoming like Magic. Maybe one pair of lips
—another's, my own. I want to go back and rescind
those lips that made rhymes as a child. Remember,
we'd just sealed the '80s. Reagan's vacant smile
haunted our homes, hip-hop was too busy
for compassion, and we fashioned ourselves fly
as we wove music of other people's pain.

Tarfia Faizullah (1980)

100 BELLS

My sister died. He raped me. They beat me. I fell
to the floor. I didn't. I knew children,
their smallness. Her corpse. My fingernails.
The softness of my belly, how it could
double over. It was puckered, like children,
ugly when they cry. My sister died
and was revived. Her brain burst
into blood. Father was driving. He fell
asleep. They beat me. I didn't flinch. I did.
It was the only dance I knew.
It was the kathak. My ankles sang
with 100 bells. The stranger
raped me on the fitted sheet.
I didn't scream. I did not know
better. I knew better. I did not
live. My father said, I will go to jail
tonight because I will kill you. I said,
She died. It was the kathakali. Only men
were allowed to dance it. I threw
a chair at my mother. I ran from her.
The kitchen. The flyswatter was
a whip. The flyswatter was a flyswatter.
I was thrown into a fire ant bed. I wanted to be
a man. It was summer in Texas and dry.
I burned. It was a snake dance.
He said, Now I've seen a Muslim girl
naked. I held him to my chest. I held her
because I didn't know it would be
the last time. I threw no
punches. I threw a glass box into a wall.
Somebody is always singing. Songs
were not allowed. Mother said,
Dance and the bells will sing with you.
I slithered. Glass beneath my feet. I
locked the door. I did not

die. I shaved my head. Until the horns
I knew were there were visible.
Until the doorknob went silent.

with thanks to Vievee Francis

NOCTURNE IN NEED OF A BITCH

Forget the sounds of glass shattering,
the alleyways I walk past, hunger
knifing me cleaner. Forget the schizophrenic

I still see, for years now—forget his voice
burning past me. *Bitch, I need you.*
Bitch, I need, I need, he moans,

and it's not me he wants, but
the night is a varnished peeling wall
against which I always want to be

roughly pressed. How many other nights
has he stumbled across this sidewalk,
pleading with someone else

who isn't there—cars blast by:
earthquake of bass, crackle of voices,
thigh, throat, clavicle, crook of elbow,

curve of breast, *bitch, I need, I need*—
and I can't forget those summers
all of us spent sleeping underground

in that old peach-carpeted basement,
can't forget how my sister was still
safe and warm beside me the night

I heard footsteps that weren't hers
or mine—I took her hand,
waited until the footsteps finally

stopped: dream-summoned,
alive or ghostly, I'll never know.

But what does that have to do with lips,
tug of earlobe, palms macerating
palms? *I need, I need*, and the hunger

inside me isn't for food, and I can't forget
we don't belong anywhere: not this city,
not in childhood's bed or the adult one

I slide alone into after praising Your name,
Lord. Tell me why being human is so lonely,
why this man turns now to embrace

no one beside him. Tell me why my sister
is a ghost stepping lightly across the floors
of strangers, their children asleep below.

Tell me why, Lord, you made it so that taking
a kiss full on the mouth feels like weeping:
the helpless swell, its delicious spill. I need,

I need. Take then, as You took her too.
Take the morning's sandpaper sunlight
in which I'll wake again to offer You

another day of hunger. Take from me
this razor humming inside my body
You made for any kind of breaking.

BLOSSOMS IN THE DARK

If only love could be
like that first slice
of bacon dissolving
on your tongue, or
the short, tight skirt
rolled into your purse
nights you salaamed
your parents goodbye
to arrive at the party
bare-legged, redolent
of cigarettes kissed
with lips reddened
hastily in the dark. Is
love your father's silk
tie you've learned
to let dangle between
your bare breasts?
Is there faith woven
into the skullcap
he unfolds each dawn,
noon, twilight? Or is it
in his neat, shorn nails
scratching skin off
the back of his sun-
black neck? Today,
you asked the Muslim
at the deli to please
slice the ham paper-
thin. Is it faith whose
hand holds back
your hair while you're
sick beside the keg,
skirt riding up?
Tomorrow, you'll love
any man willing
to fling his tongue
into that valley
above your collarbone.

No one can tell you
what to do
with your breath
braiding his throat.
No one can tell you
what to do
with your fingers.
Mother will call
twice while you've got
one hand on his cock,
and you'll consider
picking up.

SELF-PORTRAIT AS SLINKY

It's true I wanted
    to be beautiful before
        authentic. Say the word
            exotic. Say *minority*—

a coiled, dark curl
    a finger might wrap
        itself in—the long
            staircase, and I was

the momentum
    of metal springs
        descending down
            and down—say tension.

The long staircase,
    and I was a stacked series
        of spheres fingertipped
            again into motion—say

taut, like a child
    who must please her
        parents but doesn't
            know how—a curl pulled

thin—I wanted to be
    a reckoning, to gather
        into each day's pale
            hands—that helpless

lurching forward
    in the dark—another
        soaked black ringlet,
            that sudden halting—

Samantha Thornhill (1980)

Elegy for a Trojan

Latex moon, rising
in the sky of my sex,
the night we met, I streaked
the sheets with untamed
glee. Since the day
I watched you
swallow whole
my teacher's eggplant,
I have breathed
your name,
citizen of Troy

I've scanned
your tragic tale;
of your plight
I'll say it plain:
you've been fucked.
How many times
have you spared me
from hollow stallions
brimming with deadly
little men?
Lengthened yourself
to lengthen my days?

No matter, don't
nobody love you
when you broke.

The morning after
you did, down slid
the atomic pill,
detonating deep
within my ecology.

Old friend, consider
this apology, wrapped
in so long, resting
on a silver tray,
for Trojan,
there were times
I felt only you
in the dark,
and we have been
strangers, too,
more, more
than I
can say.

Ode to a Star Fig

Fig, you are an astral thing.

From how you marquee a tree branch
to your debut on the brunch
tables of my matinee life.

I regret the man in me
that cannot delight in you
without breaking you first.

My crowbar hands pry
your pangaea to continental
drift, and what is all this sea
anemone so packed into you—
all this pink and promise?

Testicle halving to twin vaginas.
Bless you fig, hermaphrodite:
male protecting female, woman
in every man. Utopia
in my mouth: yours
is the sweet of nameless streets
fiber of unanswered inquiry.

How did we get here, and why?
How does sun manage to court all
the planets in that unapologetically
black sky?

Ode to Gentrification

Those living here long
enough to testify to the rough whores
of the brothel that was this lot
old-school denizens of this bleach-
boned block would say
that the realest thing
about the white woman
and her Yorkie on this
reimagined street
is the leather
of the leash that tethers them.

Your very name—
glass splinter planted
deep in the fat of our vernacular.

Gentrification, rightly
mistaken for *juxtaposition:*
pretty boys with swagger;
checkerboard trains;
skyscraper sadness;
bodegas sighing out soy.

Peruvian girl and boy fattening
fridges with Fiji between
homework and dreams
while Pops slices
and dices and Mom
rocks the register.

Gentrification, kissing
cousin to *gratification,*
birthing gratitude—
twin to regret.

So call me regrateful.

I am so sorry to thank you

for the manner in which
I participate in your cruel
and convenient magic.

You ushered out the families
who lived and loved
where my head now rests.

Yesterday I retrieved laundry
cleaner than bells—
my unmentionables
caressed by another's
mother's hands.

I sit on the up
side of your coin, drinking
in the sky's blue dregs
while the teens I teach
and the sturdy black grand
mothers I salute
with my seat
kiss concrete.

Ode to a Killer Whale

from the perspective of Kunta Kinte

Black boy, with a name
and a plight like that—
just as well claim

African. No matter
your mama squeezed
you into the dim waters

of Iceland where you learned
to hunt from top rung
spanning a cool

hundred miles on a day's
breath with NUFF
time to frolic in the sun

light shining down on the deep
sea diver's sole delight—
some white boy's locker.

Brother, had I known
they were coming for you
next I would have sent

congo cries straight
to your orca heart—
up jump the boogie, before

lasso logic and nigger
nets. Alas, the same
passage done borned

we to this troubled mass;
and the same pink
dolphin captivated us

both into ticking time
bombs swimming circles
inside their squares.

Oh how they love you
to their greatest capacity—
which is to say, shutting you

up in a bathtub, training
your charm into dollars you make
rain for them, as they flip

you over to milk
your sperm from the cash
cow you is, quelling

all rebellion with rubs
and rewards. Only for
your seeds to grow

apart from you. Alas
they captured you but are
yet contain the joy

of your rage. Alas, you signify
half the name they gave
you killer—cause bruh

you ain't no whale.
Shamu, Rambo,
Sambo of sea: I mean

to say, and Nat means to say
(we spoke the other day)
and sister Harriet too—boy

you got some dead folk praying
for you! Done seduced your
captors with your kind nets.

May you do all we tried
in our ways to do, which is
to say. Like a bullet

burning with the president's name
boy, save your masterpiece
for the stage. I mean to say: killer

whale, killer whale—grip this ship
by its sail and drag the whole thing down,
down, down, down, down.

Harbor

"You a pussy this pussy ass phone ain't workin tell alla dem bombaclat
    pussyhole fuh gwan!"

And pussies everywhere retreat.

The First Pussy will say under her breath that you are only as good as
    she is
The Second will whisper that she has been trying her best since God
    first pressed His want inside of her
The Third merely cuts her eyes and mumbles something about
how you can always hear a pussy pop on the track, back behind the
building, in the bedroom, beneath the bravado wearing more grimace
than smile but never seein' any profits
Hm.
The Fourth thinks you ought to pray to Pussy
Here's what you say to Pussy:
"Hail Pussy, full of grace.
Blessed art thou among body parts
for the prophets cum through
And come through you
forgive the forgetful foolish popes, poets, priests and MCs. Amen"

Pussy pushes up her sleeves
She's always in a fight on the schoolyard
They keep talkin' 'bout beatin' her up or beatin' her to sleep
She keeps her composure
but it's difficult when the classroom and the Congress
are overrun with boys and girls who say they love
but act like they despise Pussy
Pussy chuckles at the absurdity
She knows that if it were white folks bashing black folks in verse
the way men bash women—I mean—pussy—in their songs
no one would dance along and say, "O but they're not talkin' about
    me." Or "I just like the beat."

Pussy thinks that shit is weak
She is tired of hip hop's "greatest" finding fame, Grammys and more
    pussy at her expense.
She got the blues, y'all.
She is being stolen in a cul-de-sac in Cali
She has had too much wine and blames herself
She is sliding down a pole in the ATL wishing she didn't have to
    explain herself
She is bruised and oozing in the Congolese bush
where they dare Pussy with a dick, then a stick, then a gun blast
She weeps through her stitches, holds herself together like a fist
and wonders if they cut off her lips in Niger 'cause she can talk to the
    moon
if they severed her clit 'cause her pleasure shakes the earth's core and
    brings forth the greatest alchemy
God stores his gold in Pussy
so they keep legislating and probing like our bodies are the Wild West
But Pussy ain't goin' nowhere,
she gon' always be rockin' her Sunday best on the porch swing or
    taking the bus from Delhi to tomorrow
So don't be like no apple hatin' its tree
you ain't got to have one to
Stand up for Pussy
Stand up for Pussy
Stand up for Pussy
Amen

Jacob Saenz (1982)

Evolution of My Block

As a boy I bicycled the block
w/a brown mop-top falling
into a tail bleached blond,

gold-like under golden light,
like colors of Noble Knights
'banging on corners, unconcerned

w/the colors I bore—a shorty
too small to war with, too brown
to be down for the block.

White Knights became brown
Kings still showing black & gold
on corners now crowned,

the block a branch branded
w/la corona graffitied on
garage doors by the pawns.

As a teen, I could've beamed
the crown, walked in w/out
the beat down custom,

warred w/my cousin
who claimed Two-Six,
the set on the next block

decked in black & beige.
But I preferred games to gangs,
books to crooks wearing hats

crooked to the left or right
fighting for a plot, a block
to spot & mark w/blood

of boys who knew no better
way to grow up than throw up
the crown & be down for whatever.

Evolution of My Profile

Jacob Saenz

Before, being bald & brown
badged me a 'banger:
black pants w/X color

shirt & head shaved short
branded me in X gang,
even if they hang in

a 'hood not my own,
I still got thrown on
a cop car's hood & trunk,

punched in mouth for being
in a marked car cruising
down the wrong streets.

Now being brown & bearded,
boarding trains w/a backpack
bursting at the seams w/books,

I receive suspect looks
from cops patrolling
w/bomb-sniffing dogs

as if I should be muzzled
& leashed like their animals—
collared & crated in the dark,

taught how to sit & lie
down & beg for treats,
only set free when I learn

not to bite back & snap
my jaw at the hand
petting my head.

GTA: San Andreas
(Or, "Grove Street, bitch!")

I play on Grove Street,
live on Grove Avenue.

Find me in the streets dressed
in greens like groves.

On the avenue, I'm a blue
jeans type of guy.

In the streets, never leave
home w/out my 9mm.

On the avenue, always carry
my pen & wine key, in case

some fool blows his cork.
My uzi sings songs in

the streets—*ratta-tat-tat.*
Birds chirp-chirp-chirp

in trees on the avenue.
Rolling down the street

w/my lady—what she wanna do?
"Let's do a drive-by."

Rushing down the avenue
w/my baby: "I'm hungry.

Let's do drive-thru."
I'll punch punks purple & blue

in the streets, bleed 'em w/bullets.
On the avenue, I'll leave punching

to punks dressed in blues, reds,
etcetera & mind my own.

Nadia Sulayman (1982)

bint ibrahim

when i return
reclaim, rename
i will turn a key
dangling
between breasts
daughter
of refugees.
i will bathe
in sea water
trace a trail
of cactus plants
i will stand firmly
where concrete
kissed the heavens
of a lesser god
turn your walls to art
i will make beautiful
from your ugly
there is so much ugly.
i will collect the ashes
from books and words
you burned
i will change
street signs
from hebrew to arabic
not hebron, but khalil
al-quds, akka, nasera.
i will disarm
your children
arm my women
with roots
from century-old trees
i will sing the names
of my great-grandmothers
to a land who remembers

their kind hands
rekindle a memory of ancestors.
i will unlock prison doors
heal the scars
of stone-throwers
boys turned men
by fire and torture.
i will weep
and one day
i will
invite you
into my home
as a stranger
we will
talk of haifa
and sit on the coast of yaffa
from the porch of my mosaic-tiled home
i will keep your mezuzah hanging
from my door
but you will understand
i will not forget
i will not forget
and i will pray
that i will not do to you
what you have done to me.

Ha Ha Hum

In the chorus of one of my favorite songs are three throat-clearing sounds—
sometimes depicted as *Ha Ha Hum*
on lyrics websites such as azlyrics.com, lyricstime.com, and
　anysonglyrics.com

A sound we make when we talk with the mouths of Jews.
　　Channukah, l'chaim, chutzpah.
Voiceless fricative.

Russians have a letter for it. In block, an x, in Cyrillic, two c's back to back.
In the words, good, *chorrosho*, and bad, *plocho*.
They have other letters I love, for *sh, tss, sht, szh, yoo.*

The sound Kanye makes—it's not unlike the French r.
How my name falls back into the mouth like it's collapsing.
　　Sa-cha.

In Russian, the r would roll, as when my great-grandmother said her name,
as when my great-grandfather called to her.
My name means *princess* in Hebrew.

Kanye's means *the only one* in Swahili.
A language once written in Arabic script, now written with letters like ours.
Switched in the 1800s. Trying for sounds like *nz* and *nd*, to begin words.

The mouths we speak with are hidden by our other mouths.

Adventures

5 year anniversary of Katrina already.

I remember Bush reading a story to a classroom of children and not leaving. The book upside down.

Do I want to believe that?

No, that was after the planes flew into the World Trade Center.

On NBC, Kanye spoke out. I watched this clip over and over. He looks like he's going to cry. He says, "George Bush doesn't care about Black people," and they change who the camera's on.

They moved to Chris Tucker, stumbling over every scripted word.

Then, on ABC, an interview, "I'm working—I'm working off the cusp here. I'm working off the top of my mind. I'm not reading the teleprompter. I'm letting—I'm speaking from the heart, and that thing got dialed up and typed—typed into the heart. And that was that."

"Do you think it was fair?" asked the interviewer. But that wouldn't be my first question.

How does your heart work?

What else in the body could be the teleprompter?

The internet winds around. Not too many links before I find an interview between Larry King and Dr. Jan Adams, the cosmetic surgeon who operated on Kanye's mother the day before she died.

Adams went on the show to formally announce that he would not partake in the interview at the wishes of the West family.

I'm disgusted by him because I've begun to love your mother.

I'm working in the darkness between her teeth. I'm reading

She dedicated a whole chapter of her memoirs, *Raising Kanye*, to
what he said about Bush and Katrina, to their trip to Houston. They
brought Halloween masks to the children. And fifteen furnished
homes for fifteen families for one year.

Though no one reported on this. Not one *Houston Chronicle* article.

Kanye had said, in that NBC clip, "I've even been shopping before
even giving a donation, so now I'm calling my business manager
right now to see what's—what is the biggest amount I can give."

What is the biggest amount so that how much remains?

I can't look up something like that.

A number I can't imagine.

After the earthquake in Haiti, Noah and I donated $20 at Wegman's
and our cashier told us it was the largest donation all day.

In one verse, in 2007, Kanye raps, "███████████████████████
██████," and I would guess he dreams about Katrina.

About making a song, Kanye said, "I think about how people will
react when they hear this. I think about how they will react to a
certain point in the song. So, you know, a lot of time I try to build it
up like an adventure."

And he does. And they are.
And I can imagine the water beginning to enter the house.

Adam Falkner (1984)

If You Don't Know
after The Notorious B.I.G.

Shirtless and grass-stained, you scowl at your own
12-year-old reflection in the bedroom mirror.
Strike your hardest L.L. for the camera; grip
the backs of your own bird-blade shoulders
like holds on a climbing wall, dare the boy
in the glass to say something back. You never
thought that hip hop would take you this far:
the pictures on the wall, the castle of crisp sneakers
still in their boxes—track jackets to match—words
that fit like strange origami in your cavity-free mouth:
the only white boy you know who can do it like this.
And sure, people laugh. Call you fool. After all,
the public housing you boast of to the mirror,
the interviews by the pool, the minks you buy
your mother—all just a dream; gasoline in
an imaginary engine propelling you away
from the soft, pliable furniture of your boring,
suburban nest. But you know very well
who you are; a home too haunted to sleep in,
a tourist walking circles in a city they did not build.

You study the shape your mouth makes around
words like *common* and *thief, dead* and *broke,*
until finally, you reach the part of the song that is not
yours to say—even white boys like you who aren't
really white but for their ability to disappear, leap
into the wind, board a return flight when the clock
strikes homesick. But the way you say it
is different—you give it something special,
soften its bite so that it hardly feels like a blade
at all, so even the boy in the mirror cannot tell it's you,
how deep your hunger for a culture to weep for,
a struggle to wrap your own two arms around,
a roadmap to follow, another fire to hold. You are

the source. The genesis of a new kind of whiteboy: fly
paper for hands, fat with guilt you do not have time
to name, a fitted cap that fits like a parade mask.
You roll the word around in your mouth like
a jawbreaker. Slap it against the drywall
of your bedroom, swallow its colonial flare
like cheap whiskey, add it to the growing pile
of things you can never give back.

for Lisa Hall

Chinaka Hodge (1984)

Small Poems for Big
twenty-four haiku, for each year he lived

when you die, i'm told
they only use given names
christopher wallace

no notorious
neither b.i.g. nor smalls
just voletta's son

brooklyn resident
hustler for loose change, loosies
and a lil loose kim

let me tell you this
the west coast didn't get you
illest flow or nah

had our loyalties
no need to discuss that now
that your weight is dust

that your tongue is air
and your mother is coping
as only she can

i will also say
that i have seen bed stuy since
b.k. misses you

her walk has changed some
the rest of the borough flails
weak about itself

middle school students
not yet whispers in nine sev
know the lyrics rote

you: a manual
a mural, pressed rock, icon,
fightin word or curse

course of history
most often noted, quoted
deconstructed sung

hung by a bullet
prepped to die: *gunsmoke gunsmoke*
one hell of a hunch

here you lie a boy
twelve gauge to your brain you can't
have what you want be

what you want you black
and ugly heartthrob ever
conflicted emcee

respected lately
premiere king of the casket
pauper of first life

til puff blew you up
gave you a champagne diet
plus cheese eggs, welch's

you laid the blueprint
gave us word for word for naught
can't fault the hustle

knockoff messiah
slanged cracked commandments, saw no
honey, more problems

a still black borough
recoiled, mourned true genius slain
the ease of your laugh

the cut of your jib
unique command of the room
truthfully biggie

what about you's small
no not legend not stature
real talk just lifespan

yo, who shot ya kid
nypd stopped searching
shrugged off negro death

well, we scour the sky
we mourn tough, recite harder
chant you live again

of all the lyrics
the realest premonition
rings true: you're dead. wrong

Stakes is High

> ... 'cause this life is warfare.
> —Mos Def and Talib Kweli

You know those people who are uncomfortable
having a conversation at a comfortable level?
Like, you ask Tony his thoughts on Kobe
or the LA Lakers. And Tony responds:
Schwarzenegger ruined their state.
Four years in office and more debt than '03?
Come on, man. Fuck California.
Yeah. So Tony's my dad. He's retired
but doesn't know it. He thinks sleep is
death's first cousin. Early AMs
my brother and me tiptoe meandering routes
around our house, avoiding his line of sight.
These are the hours he tunes to AM talk.
Reads his paper where the stakes are high.
Two Decembers ago, my brother Brian and me.
We're sharing cognac sips and cigarillos
shooting stars in a powdered driveway
when dad breaks from the Al Sharpton Hour.
Tracks prints to basement floor. He starts in
on precipitation: *What type of grown ass men*
trek lines of snow through a house?
Me and your mama raised you better than that.
He shifts into hyperbole: *When you two start*
having kids, I hope you take plenty of movies.
Your mama and me plan to kick back—watch
the decline of common courtesy. Then Brian
makes a wrong move. Smiles. Says snow was
trailed in a square. Technically a half rhombus.
Pops leaves us. Leaves the earth: *Oh, so you*
wanna joke about geometry? I hear scientists
developed a system for tracing racist thoughts.
Can you use your math on that?

Someone should make a drug to kill every last
bigot in the world. They should pump that shit
through the faucets. Drunken laughs march dad out.
In what world does he live? Michigan bigots
own bunkers. Unregistered land. And if I spent
one summer as a survey worker, if I phoned a woman
named Shanquita and assumed she lived in a hood,
is that intra-racist? Is it double-back racist to assume
you assume she was black? To assume you are not?
Would I be exempt from the axe? Could a black poet
fail the test? Let's say yes. Let's call my F a defect
of private schooling and exclusive subdivisions.
Let's call my death another gulp in the throat
of history's tireless typhoon, spinning backwards.

When I'm alone in my room sometimes I stare at the wall, and in the back of my mind I hear my conscience call

me Ishmael. Call me sailor. But not
captain. Call me fishhook. Clean.
Call me multipurpose fish scale
weighing self-obsession. Call me fish
tail in a siren's silk sheets. Thief
in the night. Buccaneer. Call me
multipurpose fish scale singing
motherfucker, then calling it good.
Call me lukewarm algae eater
upchucked. Call me match head struck
against hollow whale walls. Call me
faith's phosphorus irritation. The-Bible-
study-leading-Sea-World-trainer-
dead-between-Shamu's-teeth. Call me
freightliner hull hacking through a baby
humpback. Extinct & extinguished. Son
of a slave girl expelled to the desert
for being himself. Call me
miracle. Opposite mirage. Three parts sea
but bountiful land. Call me mangy
pasture. Wild buffalo. Archer. Arrow.
Call me sheared. Call me back
to the Shepherd. Call me lamb.

Ars Poetica in the Mode of J-Live

It's like this, Anna:

shell banged bare
with a bat, Anna

vat of gun powder
shed, Anna

famished bird
fed off scraps, Anna

gut-itch flown
south for life, Anna

dropper's stool self-pecked
slow, Anna

wince or stool
dropped again, Anna

bird sifting
through his shit, Anna

slug built by a bird's
beak, Anna

small handgun.
It's like this, Anna

gun the bird
doesn't grip.

It's like this, Anna.
It's like that.

It's like that
and like this.

> *Do I love you? Do I lust for you?*
> *Am I a sinner because I do the two?*
> **—A Tribe Called Quest**

Because you introduced me to Wu Tang
kung fu flicks, 5 Fingers of Death
& 36 Chambers
over quarter candy & sweet peach Faygo
pop on a playground bench.
Because you held my hand
as I cranked the boom box volume knob.

Because you lived next door to my boy B.
Because he slept through 12th grade
to the tape-recorded husk of your voice.
Because he never graduated
he stayed home & mostly kicked it
with a hustler, turned 3rd shift grinder.
His name was D. He lived by you too.
B. got fed, turned out cool & normal.

Because I nodded to your chest's thump
under a rocket's trail of smoke
strong enough to trace every porch
couch, box spring & classroom in Kzoo.
Your cherry gloss lingered around
each Old E bottle I downed.
Because I studied you in college.

I want you to sound bad.

Because you are mine.
Because I refuse to share
let's say you're an overwhelming
total body high.

Because your mouth
is the nectar & squish of a peach.

Because your lips are the color
of a flowering quince.

You ghost rode your banana seat
bike through my yard. Miss Bonita,
I caught your bug & couldn't kick it.

Michael Mlekoday (1985)

Self-Portrait with Gunshot Vernacular

All summer was one wet weapon
after another: barb of sweetgum
in the ankle, stranger's knife blade,
the wasp stuck in your sneaker.
Rainfall kept the crack addicts
asleep in the church basement
amid remnants of the broken window.
O window, come again in glory
and the block will put a piece
of itself through you,
makeshift spear to the side,
stone to the back of the skull,
thunder of gunshot. Here,
we all know that sound.
If somebody flinch at firecrackers,
they may as well mispronounce
your name. This place is old
as a mother tongue.
Here, the world is always saying
Ya mama, Ya mama,
and you write poems
like they brass knuckles
or empty 40 bottles of O.E.
Believe that. Believe in wildlife,
that snarl and sex, glimmer
of I, I, until death.
Most people stop believing
in lions after visiting the zoo,
but you seen too many broken locks
and this neighborhood is bordered
by a jawbone made of light.
Rhyme or die. Shoot or die.
Smuggle yourself out
like a banned book or die.
This is the voice
calling to you in the wilderness,
its dark milk like blood in the throat.

Self-Portrait from the Other Side

The woods behind
my elementary school
held ghosts and gang members.
We studied the carvings in the trees:
GD, Gangster Disciples
or some spirit afraid of *GOD*.
We weren't afraid of neither
until we were alone.
My friend carried a gun to school
and we all believed
we were magic. That year
my grandfather died.
That year I found a Pete Rock tape
and twisted my hat backwards
like an exorcism gone wrong.
Not wrong meaning wrong, but.
Not to say I was hard, but.
When I write the letter *O*,
I imagine it burns through
the paper, that to praise
means to open by force.
The dropped jaw, the bullet hole,
the neighborhood
I can never leave.

Thaumaturgy

Michael Mlekoday

rarely happens in the suburbs.
It's all sunburns and shrubbery,
there. I've never climbed a tree
and thought, Wow. I've never
seen the ocean, but I have stood
on a bloodstain shaped like a wave
and thought about how small we are,
how whatever washes you can
be a big emptiness you get lost in,
and I stood there every day for a year
for the repetition of it, like a novena.
The city bus repeats itself. The breakbeat
in my head repeats itself, and maybe
this is how déjà vu works, and maybe
I'd rather remember some things
that never really happened,
like the time I danced so well
I raised the dead, my old dog
or Dad, I think, I think
it was in Baba's house, I think
the record kept skipping in a perfect loop.

Kristiana Colón (1986)

a remix for remembrance
for my students

This is for the boys whose bedrooms are in the basement,
who press creases into jeans, who carve their names in pavement,
the girls whose names are ancient, ancestry is sacred
The Aztec and the Mayan gods abuela used to pray with

This is for the dangerous words hiding in the pages
of composition notes, holy books and Sanskrit
This is for the patients who wait for medication
for the mothers microwaving beans and rice at day's end

This is for the marching bands and girls at quinceñeras
The skaters and the writers whose moms are eloteras,
laughing "Cops don't scare us, we sag so elders fear us
We will rewrite our textbooks in our own language if you dare us"

This is for the Sarahs, the Angelicas, and Shawns,
the Beatrices, Paolas, Danielas, and the dawns
we scribble sunlight in the margins of horizons with our songs
for all the voices tangled with the silence on our tongues

Rivals in the parks, fireworks at dark,
tired shirts that sweat your scent on hangers in the closet
For the boys who fix the faucet while their sister fixes coffee
'cause mommy had to leave for work at 6 AM and laundry
isn't folded yet: you don't have to hold your breath

You don't have to behave. Stage your own rebellion
paint canvases with rage, and religion, and prayers for pilgrims
sleeping in the train cars at the border and their children
Filibust the Senate and bust markers on the Pink Line
Stain the prosecution's case and force the judge to resign,
force the crowd to rewind the lyrics you invented

Speak away the limits to heights of your existence

Be a witness, be a record, be a testament, a triumph
Set your poems flying in the glitter of the planets
Feed open mouths with truth, the truth is we are famished
The Universe is starving for the symphonies you play
Clarinets and thunder and the syllables you say
are the instruments: you are infinite. Stretch your hands to heaven
Let your throat throttle the rhythms of all your fallen brethren
Your legacy is present, your history is now
You are the tenth degree of sound
You are the nephews of the sky
You are the bass line and the hi hat and the snare drum and the cry
of red Septembers. You're the architects of winter
You are the builders of the roads that you're told you don't remember
    You are the builders of the roads that you're told you don't
       remember
        You are the builders of the roads that you're told you don't
       remember

Cast poems in the river and tell them you remember
Skate City Hall to splinters and tell them you remember
Send diamonds to your islands and tell them you remember
Find your God inside your mirror and tell Her you remember

stockholm syndrome*

& here we are now on the brink of the Apocalypse:
nation made of Quakers, Mormons, Mayans, Scientologists,
day traders, day laborers, naysayers, congressmen,
patriots, facial lifts, debutantes, and politics
Starting not to give a fuck and stop fearing the consequence
Drinking every night because we drink to my accomplishments
Lights come on at final call so pay me all your compliments
before they bring the tab I pay with refunds from my scholarship
We asked no questions before signing master promissories
We asked no questions when he sent the troops to battle for greed
& you know I love Obama but he let them bomb Zuccotti
& you know that burning books is the prelude to burned bodies
Kindle them all. Take your kids to visit the mall, play rich
until derivatives fall, don't snitch—the emperor's knickers will fall
Don't flinch when all your niggers are called niggers, on-call niggers
Lost our Hollywood map and got no OnStar with us
Barnyard bidness, Animal Farm—y'all with us?
No bar codes on my arms, God as my witness
Bust into the vault and leave with all y'alls riches
Face against the wall, hands off alarm switches
Janitors cut cameras, we got the guards with us
Toss the gas canisters back at killers
Throw the ducats in the truck and drive to Canada with
quickness
Add my name to the pages of a long, long hit list

---

* Features lines from Drake's song "Headlines."

Eve Ewing (1986)

to the notebook kid

yo chocolate milk for breakfast kid.
one leg of your sweatpants rolled up
scrounging at the bottom of your mama's purse
for bus fare and gum
pen broke and you got ink on your thumb kid

what's good, hot on the cement kid
White Castle kid
tongue stained purple
cussin on the court
til your little brother shows up
with half a candy bar kid

got that good B in science kid
you earned it kid
etch your name in a tree
hug your granny on her birthday
think of Alaska when they shootin
curled-up dreams of salmon
safety
tundra
the farthest away place you ever saw in a book
polar bears your new chess partners
pickax in the ice
Northern Lights kid

keep your notebook where your cousins won't find it.
leave it on my desk if you want
shuffle under carbon paper
and a stamp that screams LATE
yellow and red to draw the eye from the ocean
you keep hidden in a jacked-up five-star.
your mama thought there was a secret in there
thought they would laugh
but that ain't it.

it's that flows and flows and flows
and lines like those rip-roaring

bits you got
bars till the end of time
you could rap like
helium bout to spring
all of it
down to you
none left in the sun—fuelless
while the last light pushes from your belly

climbing your ribs

and you laugh into the microphone
and who is ready for that?

Ciara Miller (1987)

In Search of Black Birds

1.
The Mason Boys' sneakers crunched against rusted leaves
as the dying rat beat against the plastic bag. They pushed
its writhing body away from theirs, dropped it into a dumpster
& rushed upstairs to soap their hands, each flicking death water
on each other's eyelids.

2.
"Boys, c'mon in here & get these pancakes!" said Mama:
not fat & aproned, a chef in a silk dress who watched CNN,
skipped Sunday church sessions, smoked Newport 100s & kissed
the wrinkles on her sons' foreheads. Their prepubescent mouths
gulped & slurped syrup. They later asked to back-flip in the corners
of a gardenless backyard, jumped the black fence instead,
into the grime of an alley in search of black birds.

3.
The crimson, off-white & blue blues cop car sped onto the potholes
of Jefferson Street. "Betcha I can run faster than that car," Malcolm
Mason bid. "Nuh Uhn, I can." Martin Mason declared. Their black
raced, heaving. Thighs like boulders, bulging. Martin Mason scooped
up woodchips & rock, teasingly hurled them at his brother. A pebble
thwarted, pounced against the car window. The cops drove faster.

4.
Mama, with two gray crinkled curls at the front of her afro,
poked her head out of her window. The streetlight was a dusty
orange glow: spiderwebs & mosquitoes smashed & electrified inside.
Their darkened dead bodies dimmed the street.

Mama tipped her cigarette into a white ashtray, crossed her
legs near the window & inhaled the smoke. She thought about
the silk slip her Grandma Hattie told her to wear
beneath skirts. The crossed legs. How to be a proper woman
raised amongst improper men. Most midnights when the boys
feigned sleep, she wore silk lavender skin-tight dresses, 6-inch heels,

mascara & blonde wigs. Men touched her bare arms at bars.
She danced with them & returned home to scrape egg
from her own skillet.

5.

The Mason boys ran behind the bushes, they ran behind the willowed
trees. They ran into a pit bull who barked & howled. Their fright,
almost found. They ran inside their skin, inside the black where they
were rabbits. A black bird hovered above the tree branches where
they shivered a shhh from the sweat of their skin. The black bird beat
his wings wildly with the wind. Inside the black, their boyhood hid.

6.

Nina Simone blared from Mama's window. "Just two more plays.
Boys will be boys," she thought. A hooker with missing front teeth
& deep burgundy lipstick stopped in front of her gate. She slow
danced by herself, arms wrapped around her back as if she was in the
arms of a lover. "You jamming up there girl!" the hooker yelled
up to the second floor. Mama studied her aloneness like a recipe.

Morgan Parker (1987)

Let Me Handle My Business, Damn

Took me awhile to learn the good words
make the rain on my window grown
and sexy now I'm in the tub holding down
that on-sale Bordeaux pretending
to be well-adjusted I am on that real
jazz shit sometimes I run the streets
sometimes they run me I'm the body
of the queen of my hood filled up
with bad wine bad drugs mushu pork
sick beats what more can I say to you
I open my stylish legs I get my swagger back
let men with gold teeth bow to my tits
and the blisters on my feet I become electric
I'm a patch of grass the stringy roots
you call home or sister if you want
I could scratch your eyes make hip-hop die again
I'm on that grown woman shit before I break
the bottle's neck I pour a little out: you are fallen

Joshua Bennett (1988)

When asked about my hometown: an admission

Filthy incantation, I dare not speak its name. I either claim the South Bronx by maternal bloodline (a tactic commonly known as the Boogie Down Bandwagon Maneuver) or shift the tone altogether. Invoke DMX and David Berkowitz to make the place sound so scary you will never want to go. On its own, the word Yonkers sounds like a rare breed of pest: a blue carnivore that lays eggs in the cabinet. I am my father's son. I cannot claim what I do not love. I have carried this place in my shame folder since the '90s. We are long past polite.

When asked about my hometown: an anecdote

Joshua Bennett

My best friend D was birthday cake with knives in it. Last April, he caught his ex–best man with his ex-wife and came for them both like a god of war. Rolled on homeboy's crib forty-two deep, stood on his porch with a fresh pistol, arms akimbo, like he had seen this moment in a prophetic dream and planned all poses well in advance. D called for the traitor twice by name. Slapped a purple Warhead out of his little brother's mouth just for show. And that was on a Sunday. His parents weren't home.

Love Letter to Zack, the Black Power Ranger

You chant "Mastodon!" like a fight song that gets the Mighty
Morphin Power party started every single time. Every single time, you
are battle-axe-blast-cannon-black-satin fly. Every fight sequence is a
dance floor designed for you & you alone: body blows turn to body
rolls & I can no longer tell what the music is for, backdrop to beat-
down or beat-drop to get down & boogie good one time, show those
Putty Patrol how to twerk the body elastic, how to un-become in
style. You called your fighting style *Hip-Hop-Kido* & we crowned you
iconoclast, Zachary of Angel Grove, patron saint of the rhythmically
challenged.

To my shame, it took me until age 6 to peep the struggle, how the
power (rangers) that be kept you from getting your protagonist on.
Even when Tommy & Jason grew tiresome, & Billy Cranston, the first
televised nerd I ever saw or claimed as mirror, could no longer swing
the weight of my corduroyed angst alone, you still never get your
proper due. They called you background noise: a televised war when
the game is on.

But I know you, Zack. I know that you are more than just the moves.
You are the moonwalking-crescent kick's muse & the moon, every
late-'80s black baby boy's big brother from another dimension.
Because of you, we all wanted octopus braids and a cousin named
Curtis. Because of you, I can pop-lock at the bus station every
morning. Smiling in spite of the the world. Shameless as a tusk.

Alysia Nicole Harris (1988)

When I Put My Hands in the Air It's Praise

In a club in Prague
      I'm wearing python-skin shoes,
tiger-print dress. All the Cosmic Dancer's foes

wrapped around my waist.
      Let the DJ be Shiva
spinning, with his four arms,

Bajan Rihanna atop Dre in South Central
      moves her body like a lipid snake—
           Let me show you how sacred hips can be.

A man prettier than crystal
      grinds his pelvis
into the small of my back.

I dance in his arms, and outside
      the snow isn't sharp,
there's just enough song left

to squeeze through. I lick the lyrics
      from inside his mouth
           What's the Czech word for *tonight*?

How do you say *the music*
      ain't Christian but swear-to-God
it's holy?

Britteney Black Rose Kapri (1988)

Winthrop Ave.

Broke fences, Kids wear the same clothes
from yesterday. Grease pops and hot combs
crackles in the morning. Superstar on the
court, Monster in the classroom.
Pit bulls get fed more than Pooh and
Jayquayisha. (Her daddy name James Quan.
Her momma name Keisha.) It sound like bass and
boom and bang and bang and bang, but no kids
cryin. They used to that shit. Blue lights and Street
light Pied Piper, them niglets get to marchin when
they come on. Hypodermic needle wasteland.
Football on asphalt. Double Dutch, pass the Dutch,
double back around get your shit fo the pigs come
back. It's what up Joes and Black and Blue.
Not crossin Foster Avenue.
That's Black and Gold land, King land, no
(Black) man's land.

We House: after Krista Franklin's Definition of Funk

House, as in abode, as in dwelling, as in crib, as in where your
inhibitions go to rest. as in Jack, Loft, Footwork. as in sweating out
that press and curl. as in *Pump Up the Volume*. House as in bullpen.
as in Black boys drowning at white hands. as in we'll never forget you
Eugene Williams. as in a city of Fire. again. as in Stockyards. as in
Hog Butcher of America. as in Butchered Black boys. as in Mamie
Till calling for an open casket. as in a whistle in the wrong direction.
as in the Godfather himself teaching you how to pray with a beat.
as in Rest in Rhythm Frankie Knuckles. as in a sea Black bodies.
as in Black bodies draped across poplar trees. as in this movement
gradually getting Bigger comma Thomas. as in we pledged allegiance
to "House Nation." House as in the Warehouse. as in Professor Funk
in full regalia. as in yo momma steppin out tonight. as in yo daddy
put on his good shoes. as in Chris Underwood on the 1s and 2s. as in
the Chosen Few. as in Washington Park, as in free breakfast. as in for
our sons South and West sides. as in Kanye. Common, Kelly, Lupe,
Keef, Trayvon, Oscar. House as in a Black mayor. as in finally for the
people. as in "ha y'all niggas thought you had something." as in our
skin is not for mourning. as in drum beats. as in we still don't need to
know the same language to speak. as in "Can You Feel It." House as
in a fusion between disco, funk and electronic. as in niggas spent their
whole time in this country making the best outta scraps. as in House
is food for the soul. as in light a candle for James Baldwin, Maya
Angelou, Amiri Baraka and the kid down the way. as in yo grandma's
cooking on a Sunday after church. as in yo cousin doing hair in the
kitchen. as in a fan in the window cause you bet not turn that AC on.
as in "Your Love." as in Chicago is my kind of town, unless I can see
the niggas. as in white flight. as in redlining. as in naming the train
that separates us the red line. as in you ain't even trying to hide that
shit. as in we gone dance anyway. House as in Detroit stay trying to
claim our shit. as in Black kids reading poems at the Hot House. as in
Hands Off Assata. as in too many educated black people downtown.
as in shutdown. as in shiiid, we still got the Silver Room. as in home is
where the House is.

Angel Nafis (1988)

Legend

my cigarettes cold turkey Dad
    my whisky cold turkey my what go in your nose cold turkey Dad
my once he turn his back ain't no turning back Dad
    my who needs a map Dad
my *Ellie Pearl you'se to say* Dad
    my million skeleton inside the soapbox Dad
my steal anything that ain't nailed down Dad
    my *I'll come up to that damn school tomorrow* Dad
my *eat as much as you want* Dad
    my *They use to call me Boobie* Dad
my been saying he 70 since he was 65 Dad
    my been saying money ain't his problem since I can remember Dad
my been talking about the chocolate brown cadillac
    with the cream interior since I can remember Dad
my open faced grilled cheese heated up at the bottom of the oven Dad
    my east coast jawbreaker Dad
my 15 to 20 minutes late and no cell phone Dad
    my walk with one hand out and twice as fast as everybody
my Michigan sore thumb
    my bullshit referee
my blue-jump-suit-doused-in-cologne Dad
    my call 4 times in a row with no shame
my care package with 4 broken watches and Mom's old portraits
    my smart ass Jack-O-Lantern

Oh, hero
    unforgettable planet
        garden of ripe roses
            I curse and lift up every clock

my me
my hands of flesh
that dug out the light.

Ghazal for My Sister

A little darker than me/ love by the mass sister
Pale birthmark on ya neck/ with so much sass sister

Almost my reflection/ through mirrored glass sister
Heels and creased pants/ on the go/ niggas harass my sister

twin bodies forked path/ a year estranged/ alas sister
My world is hers if she knew she my last sister

Worth unmeasured/ though neither of us can pass sister
White boyfriend curse between your eyes/ but you got class sister

I hold my breath and tongue
pretend I don't see, "Sonny's Girl"
tattooed on your ass sister

He cleans his boots on your dreams/ he is an ass sister
(the) black freckle on your nose/ could teach a class sister
Ima miss you when I go

but return
religious

like mass sister.

Conspiracy: A Suite

What the Doctors Say to the BlackGirl

We will try to maintain anatomy.
We were able to save both ovaries.
If you are uncomfortable at any point
with these students in the room—
We just need you to sign right here.
How long have you been bleeding?
How many partners do you have?
How many male? Are you sure?
Have you ever had chlamydia?
Is she your only partner?
Can she leave the room? Are you sure
you have two ovaries?
Bleeding that long isn't standard
so, we tested for chlamydia—
and you don't have it. If you want to have
children do so before thirty.
When you want to have children
show them these stills—see a specialist.
The anatomy is completely demolished.
It's what's called a chocolate cyst.
Does it hurt
right here
when I

press?

What the Paper on the Kitchen Table Say about the BlackGirl's Sister

Patient's scan revealed an 8-week-old fetus. Patient
was advised to terminate.

What God Say to the BlackGirl

Here go roses. Here go cool water. Here go a dark
man in a pink tuxedo. Here go a picture of your mom.

Here go a joke so good you cry. Here go a window fan and
the way the curtain blows. Here go a flock. Here go a tongue
on your back. Here go aging. Here go a paycheck with your
name spelled right. Here go trees that applaud. Here go
what your whole body remember.

Gravity

after Carrie Mae Weems's Kitchen Table Series

I. The Straw

Can you throw this away Maybe you should hire more Black staff
Where are you really *from You're not busy are you You look ethnic today*
Where's the African American section Can you turn the music down
Fasterfasterfaster Let me see those eyes Beautiful If you were mine
I'd never let you leave the house It's like you went straight to Africa
to get this one Is that your hair I mean your real *hair Blackass*
Your gums are black You Black You stink You need a perm

I don't mean to be
racist

But

You're scarred over, I'm the one bleeding
You're just going to rip apart whatever I say
You've said sorry only two times
We tacitly agreed
Then dead me

II. The Camel's Back

When you born on a somebody else's river in a cursed boat it's all
downhill from there. Ha. Just kidding. I'd tell you what I don't have
time for but I don't have time. Catch up. Interrogate that. Boss. Halo.
I juke the apocalypse. Fluff my feathers. Diamond my neck. Boom,
like an 808. One in a million. I don't want no scrubs. You don't know
my name. Everything I say is a spell. I'm twenty-five. I'm ninety. I'm
ten. I'm a moonless charcoal. A sour lover. Hidden teeth beneath the
velvet. I'm here and your eyes lucky. I'm here and your future lucky.
Ha. God told me to tell you I'm pretty. Ha. My skin Midas-touch
the buildings I walk by. Ha. Every day I'm alive the weather report
say: Gold. I know. I know. I should leave y'all alone, salt earth like to
stay salty. But here go the mirror, egging on my spirit. Why I can't go
back. Or. The reasons it happened. Name like a carriage of fire. Baby,
It's real. The white face peeking through the curtain. Mule *and* God.
I'm blunted off my own stank. I'm Bad. I dig graves when I laugh.

José Olivarez (1988)

Ode to the First White Girl I Ever Loved

It was kindergarten
and I did not know English,
so I could not talk
without being ridiculed.

And the teacher did not want me in her class.
She was white, too.
She said I do not know
how to teach someone
who only speaks Spanish.

And the kids did not want me in their class.
They were white, too   and black.
They said we do not know
how to be friends with someone
who only speaks Spanish

And I was the only Mexican
And I only spoke Spanish.
I watched a lot of TV.
Everyone was rich and white.
My family was poor and Mexican.
My family only spoke Spanish

And in school I felt so lonely.
My loneliness would walk home with me.
My loneliness held my hand as I crossed streets.
My loneliness spoke Spanish like my family.

And this is how I learned to equate
my family with loneliness,
how I learned to hate my family,
how I learned to hate being Mexican.

And I watched a lot of TV.
Everyone was rich & white,
and what I wanted was to grow up

and be rich and white and speak English
on shows like Seinfeld or Friends,
on shows with laugh tracks, big hair, and cardigans.

What I wanted was friends
to walk home from school with.
A teacher to give me gold stars
like all the other kids.
And what I wanted was to stop eating
welfare nachos with government cheese.
It was kindergarten
and I loved all the white girls
in my class. Robin & Crystal & Jen
& all the white girls
whose names I've forgotten.

I wanted to kiss them.
I thought kisses were magic.
I hoped I could learn English through a kiss,
that I could run my hands through their hair
and find a proper accent.

I loved white girls
as much as I hated
being lonely and Mexican.

Lord, I am a 25 year old man
and sometimes still a 5 year old boy
and I love Black women and Latina women.

And I tell them in Spanish
how beautiful they are.
And they are more beautiful & lovely
than all the white women in the world.

I tell them in Spanish
how lonely it is to live in English
and they answer with a remix of my name:

yo se,

yo se,

yo se.

Home Court

When I was in second grade,
Oscar and Cesar's dad died.
When they finally came outside,
their faces ashen with sorrow, we turned
to the basketball court. We played with shadows
of death threatening to touch, we were defiant,
we were still alive, we sweat the fever
of hurt from our bodies, our small hands
aching to be held. We played all day

and it was more prayer than basketball,
the jumper's follow-through:
a small, noiseless plea. We held the ball
like rosary beads and prayed with our hands.
We put up a thousand shots of penance,
all of us trying to gather all of the magic
left in our wrists. Lord, we prayed all day

and it was more teeth than basketball.
We stomped around the court trying to destroy
the concrete. Every dribble was violent,
a curse, we were daring whatever god
was watching to strike us down too. We
we were striking anything we could touch,
our eyes dry and vengeful. We fought all day
on the same basketball court
that Oscar and Cesar's dad built.

      O, Grief,
we went back to our houses
when we realized we were playing
on the dead man's court.
That was nothing compared to our hearts
when we looked at our hands and saw
our whole bodies were made of Grief.

We walked away tough-fisted and prayer-hearted,
our hands stained bright orange, the ball
bleeding away into a patch of grass
that couldn't hide the wound.

Joy Priest (1988)

No Country for Black Boys

when   walking while black   i am always there. i patrol. i follow
from a 7-Eleven. conceal your   dark skin in a hoodie

watermelon Arizona fruit juice   i leave my vehicle. come after you
no sudden movements like say   trying to get away. i neighborhood watch.

reaching for a pack of Skittles   like a suburb with color rushing in
you might end up wrestling for   your life has low value, boy

the right to live   you   parade around here
be second-class citizen unarmed   like that. like you are only

three wks seventeen. fight howl   victim. plead

for help in your

home   heart   savage life. get trial & conviction
suspended over a hollow point   on my Florida sidewalk. remember me.

remember to call out a mother's   pain. die with only a ghetto
name. they don't know   heart. how does it feel? listening to

your screams apart from   your body   expire *these assholes*
man w/ gun. he is the one who   *always get away*, but i am the one who

survives in America

Always & Forever

Open this / when you need me / most,
he said, as he slid / the shoebox,
wrapped in duct tape, / beneath

my bed. / His thumb, still damp from
the shudder / between mother's thighs, /
kept circling the mole / above / my brow.

The devil's eye / blazed between his teeth
or was he lighting / a joint? It doesn't
matter. / Tonight I wake & mistake

the bathwater wrung / from mother's hair
for his voice. / I open the shoebox dusted /
with seven winters / & here, sunken

in folds of yellowed / newspaper, / lies
the Colt .45— / silent & heavy
as an amputated hand. / I hold the gun

& wonder / if an entry wound / in the night
would make a hole / bright
as morning. / That if I looked

through / it, I might see the end / of this
sentence. / Or maybe / just a man
kneeling at the altar / of a boy's bed,

his grey button-up reeking / of gasoline
& cigarettes. / Maybe the day will close / without
its period / as he wraps his arms

around the boy's milk blue
shoulders. / The boy pretending
to be asleep / as his father's clutch

tightens. The way the barrel / aimed
at the sky / must tighten
around a bullet / to make it sing

Self-Portrait as Exit Wounds

The deaf aren't afraid of guns
—Vietnamese proverb

Instead, let it be the echo to every footstep
drowned out by rain, cripple the air like a name

flung onto a sinking boat, splash the kapok's bark
through the rot & shine of a city trying to forget

the bones beneath its sidewalks, through
the refugee camp sick with smoke & half-sung

hymns, a shack rusted black & lit with Ba Ngoai's
last candle, the hogs' faces we held in our hands

& mistook for brothers, let it enter a room illuminated
with snow, furnished only with laughter, Wonder Bread

& mayonnaise raised to cracked lips as testament
to a triumph no one recalls, let it brush the newborn's

flushed cheek as he's lifted in his father's arms, wreathed
with fishgut & Marlboros, everyone cheering as another

brown gook crumbles under John Wayne's M-16, Vietnam
burning on the screen, let it slide through their ears,

clean, like a promise, before piercing the poster
of Michael Jackson above the couch, into

the supermarket where a Hapa woman is ready
to shout *Father!* at every white man possessing

her nose, may it sing, briefly, inside her mouth,
before laying her down between jars of tomato

& blue boxes of pasta, the deep red apple rolling
from her palm, then into the prison cell

where her husband sits staring at the moon
until he's convinced it's the last wafer

god refused him, let it hit his jaw like a kiss
we've forgotten how to give one another, hissing

through the forest where a boy sits at a desk
lit only with night's retreat, trying to forge an answer

out of ash pressed into words, may it crack
that stubborn bone above his heart—red

& red seeping through an epic of blank pages
before slamming back to '68, Hong Long Bay: the sky

replaced with smoke, the sky only the dead
look up to, may it reach the grandfather entering

the pregnant farmgirl in the back of his Army Jeep,
walnut hair flickering in napalm-blasted wind, let it pin

him down to dust where his future daughters
rise, fingers blistered with salt & Agent Orange,

let them tear open his olive fatigues, clutch
that name hanging from his neck, that name

they press to their tongues to relearn the word
for *live*—but if for nothing else, let me weave

this deathbeam the way a blind woman stitches
a flap of skin to her daughter's ribs. Yes—

let me believe I was born to cock back
this chamber, smooth & slick, like a true

Charlie. Like I could hear the footsteps of ghosts
misted through the rain as I lower myself

between the sights—& pray
that nothing moves.

Prayer for The Newly Damned

Dearest Father, forgive me for I have seen.
Behind the wooden fence, a field lit
with summer, a man pressing a shank
to another man's throat. Steel turning to light
on sweat-slick neck. Forgive me
for not twisting this tongue into the shape
of Your name. For thinking:
this must be how every prayer
begins—the word *Please* cleaving
the wind into fragments, into what
a boy hears in his need to know
how pain blesses the body back
to its sinner. The hour suddenly
stilled. The man, his lips pressed
to the black boot. Am I wrong to love
those eyes, to see something so clear
& blue—beg to remain clear
& blue? Did my cheek twitch
when the wet shadow bloomed from his crotch
& trickled into ochre dirt? How quickly
the blade becomes You. But let me
begin again: there's a boy kneeling
in a house with every door kicked open
to summer. There's a question corroding
his tongue. A knife touching
Your finger lodged inside the throat.
Dearest Father, what becomes of the boy
no longer a boy? *Please*—
what becomes of the shepherd
when the sheep are cannibals?

Củ Chi, Vietnam

Red is only black remembering.
A baker wakes early, presses what's left
of the year into flour & water. Or rather,
he's reshaping the curve of her pale calf
atmosphered by a landmine left over
from the war he can't recall. Forsythia.
Alfalfa. Foxglove. A fistful of hay
& the oven scarlets. Bubbling dough.
When it's done, he'll tear open the yeasty steam
only to find his palms—unchanged.
He'll climb the spiral staircase & call to her.
He'll imagine the softness of bread
as he peels back the wool blanket, raises
her phantom limb to his lips as each kiss
dissolves down her air-light ankles. & he will never see
the pleasure this brings to her face. Never
her face. Because in my hurry to make her
palpable, I will forget to write a bit of light
into the room. Because my hands were always
as brief & dim as my father's. & it will start
to rain. I won't even think to put a roof
over the house—her prosthetic leg
on the nightstand, the *clack clack* as it fills
to brimming. Listen, the year is gone. I know nothing
of my country. I write things down. I build a life
& tear it apart & the sun keeps shining. Crescent
wave. Salt-spray. Tsunami. I have enough ink
to give you the sea but not the ships
or even a shore to arrive—or depart. But it's my poem
& I'll cry if I want to. It's my poem & I'll say anything
just to stay inside my skin. Sassafras. Douglas fir.
Foreshadow. Let's call this autumn
so I can stand beside you in my long brown coat
as my father sits in a $40 motel outside of Fresno,
his limbs rattling from the whiskey again. Fingers blurred
like a photograph. Marvin on the stereo pleading *brother, brother.*

& you're sleeping in the next room while I write this.
Brooklyn still the color of your lips in the dark—glistening
like a cut. & how could I know, that by pressing
this pen to paper, I am touching us back from a kind
of extinction? That we could've been more
than black ink on the bone white backs of angels
face down in the blazing orchard. Ink poured
into the shape of a woman's calf. A woman
I could go back & erase & erase
but I won't. I won't tell you how
the mouth will never be as honest
as its teeth. How this bread, daily
broken, dipped in honey—& lifted
with your tongue, like any other
lie, is only as true as your faith
in hunger. How my father, all famine & fissure,
will wake at 4 am in a smoke-grey room
& not remember his legs. *Go 'head, baby,* he will say,
Put yor han on mai bak, because he will believe
I am really there, that his son has been standing
behind him all along. *Put yor han on*
mai shoder, he will say to the cigarette smoke
swirling into the shape of a boy, *Now flap it.*
Yeah, like that. Flap like you waving goodbye. See?
I telling you... I telling you. Yor daddy?
He fly.

When Tip Drill Comes on at the Frat Party

Or,

When Refusing to Twerk Is a Radical Form of Self-Love

After Danez Smith

Sometimes it's as simple as the reminder of numbers
& ridged plastic sliding through an ass: bent, shaking,
whirring up like an arcade game when touched.

Sometimes it's as simple as the boys, howling
under bright lights, who only see the dissected
parts of you—
nose, wrist, nape of neck, nipple—

that which can be held down, pinned back, cut open,
frog heart pounding & exposed to the science class
of club & white boy & hands.

Sometimes it's as simple as sweaty nails pushing
gritty into your stomach, the weight of claws ripping
at the button on your jeans.

Sometimes it's as simple as a look from your best friend,
alive on the dance floor, the light of her own sweet sweat
to realize the powerhouse in you, to realize the sum

of your body, not its dissected parts but the whole
damn breathing thing. Sometimes it's as simple
as standing still amid all the moving & heat & card

& plastic & science & sway & say:
No.
Today, this body
is mine.

UNEMPLOYMENT

Praise your body for its pockmarks:
    the scars around your nipple, the constellation
    of bruising that is your shoulder blade.

Praise the fur you were born with:
    the thick knit wool down your legs, the way
    you are more sheep than woman, the prickle

and scratch of you. Praise the lumpy back fat, the quiet
    cellulite, the tiger marks across your thighs
    that, even though you are starving,

you still cannot get rid of. Praise the way this keeps and has kept
    you off the nighted corner, out of strange men's cars,
    from befriending a simple pole. Praise the danger

of internet ads and your aversion to touching money.
    Praise your gentle self-doubt, the empty hatred bred
    from your own blood. Praise the way it saves you.

Praise the way it keeps you hungry.

PLUTO SHITS ON THE UNIVERSE

Fatimah Asghar

*On February 7, 1979, Pluto crossed over Neptune's orbit and became the
eighth planet from the sun for twent years. Labeled as "chaotic" with a
path of orbit that could never be accurately predicted, Pluto was demoted
from planet status in 2006.*

Today, I broke your solar system. Oops.
My bad. Your graph said I was supposed
to make a nice little loop around the sun.

Naw.

I chaos like a motherfucker. Ain't no
one can chart me. All the other planets
think I'm annoying. Think I'm an escaped
moon, running free.

Fuck your moon. Fuck your solar system.
Fuck your time. Your year? Your year ain't shit
but a day to me. I could spend your whole year

turning the winds in my bed. Thinking about rings
& how Jupiter should just pussy-on-up
& marry me by now. Your day?

That's an asswipe. A sniffle. Your whole day
is barely the start of my sunset. My name
means hell, bitch. I am hell, bitch. All the cold

you have yet to feel. Chaos like a motherfucker.
& you tried to order me. Called me ninth.
Somewhere in the mess of graphs & math & compass

you tried to make me follow rules. Rules? Fuck your
rules. Neptune? That bitch slow. & I deserve all the sun
I can get, and all the blue-gold sky I want around me.

It is February 7, 1979, & my skin is more
copper than any sky will ever be. More metal.
Neptune is bitch-sobbing in my rear-view,

& I got my running shoes on & all this sky that's all mine.
Fuck your order. Fuck your time. I realigned the cosmos.
I chaosed all the hell you have yet to feel. Now all your kids

in the classrooms, they confused. All their maps
wrong. They don't even know what the fuck
to do. They gotta memorize new songs and shit.

& the other planets? I fucked their orbits.
I shook the sky. Chaos like a motherfucker.
Today, I broke your solar system.

Oops. My bad.

Franny Choi (1989)

PUSSY MONSTER

from the lyrics of Lil' Wayne's "Pussy Monster," arranged in order of frequency.

for flu food bowl stood no more soup remove spoon drink juice salt
pepper heard well cool job blow bet mic check how don't have clue
but find show tell lift top lip smell swallow spit every time goes get
call Dracula vacuum catfish fish cat tuna smack flip spatula lil runnin
so tackle baby be worm apple butt go backin front throw black Acura
been this game actress told action cameras lookin hope yeah where
know rain hurricane imagine did pearl talk jump here hi taste taste
what what cold cold suck suck hot hot blew blew there there one
one two two still still put put face face reason reason why why mama
mama need need stay stay gotta gotta survive survive let let up up
throw throw on on words words better better comin comin could
could tongue tongue with with over over over out out out she she she
eat eat eat feed feed feed walk walk walk got got got wanna wanna
wanna make make make make do do do do your your your your just
just just just when when when when in in in in if if if if can can can
can i'ma i'ma i'ma i'ma it's it's it's it's i'm i'm i'm i'm alive alive alive
alive of of of of of cause cause cause cause cause now now now now
now her her her her her i'll i'll i'll i'll i'll like like like like like like a a a
a a a that that that that that that that that girl girl girl girl girl girl girl
girl girl my my my my my my my my my monster monster monster
monster monster monster monster monster monster to to to to to to
to to to to to to and and and and and and and and and and and and
and it it it it it it it it it it it it it me me me me me me me me me me
me me me the the the the the the the the the the the the the the the the
the the the the you you you you you you you you you you you you
you you you you you you you you you you i i i i i i i i i i i i i i i i i i i i i
i i i i i i la la la la la la la la la la la la la la la la la la la la la la la la la la
la la la la la la la la pussy pussy pussy pussy pussy pussy pussy pussy
pussy pussy pussy pussy pussy pussy pussy pussy pussy pussy pussy
pussy pussy pussy pussy pussy pussy pussy pussy pussy pussy pussy
pussy pussy pussy pussy pussy pussy pussy pussy pussy pussy

IMPULSE BUY

bugzapper dress
laughing teeth beacon whats
yr name again dress
filled w/my hips (not fables of yr
lips & pulling me close &
saying the word beautiful) so
hot shit dress. *oh* i cum
from the future dress
electric zinging super christ & fuck
that! dress. what's that?
phone #? passwd.s? well that's for me
to keep and you to
drool for. in which case:
mr. pavlov bell/ringer dress
take a number & get in line dress
neon polish, programmed to scoff.
bathroom fuck dress. highball hookup
greygoose in splintered shotgunz pow/pow/
we die soon dress. hair dye blue dress.
sloppy wink dress. chlorine in the sink dress.
me without you dress.

on caskets

after Suji Kwock-Kim

1.
decorating the dead is among the most basic
human instincts, to return the borrowed body &
acknowledge Earth as maker & home.

Neanderthals used antlers & flowers. Egyptians
had pyramids with peasants buried in the walls they
built. some niggas just get a pine box. hopefully
you get a hole or a flame. some only get a cold
cabinet in the morgue until somebody or nobody
claims them as a loss.

2.
a permanent fixture on my to-do list
is research life insurance plans. pick
a good one with a fair rate & enough
money to buy a nice box

3.
everything gonna be all
right this morning & i contemplate
the implications of the statement for the night.*
everything in Mississippi is too cruel to bury.

i wonder what that means if every body in Chicago
has red clay in its lineage. Chief Keef must know
in his bones *ball like it's no tomorrow* from what
Muddy time-capsuled into the south side ground.†

4.
when grandma died she left mama a notepad
with instructions. the one i remember was *get*

---

* Muddy Waters, "Mannish Boy"
† Chief Keef, "No Tomorrow"

the casket you want. what you like. don't be
pressured.

we wore blue at the service. we matched
the box & its glossy painted ribbons,
gold-flecked & light.

5.
house slaves are responsible for preparing
the dead of the master's house. they clean
& clothe. they dig the hole. they don't
bury any black body really, only dispose.
one of the concessions won by slave riots
was the right to funeral. whitefolk were
confused at how the Africans sometimes

wore white, smiled, shouted like joy.
they seen funerals. not homegoings.

6.
my mother used to say my father loved
funerals. he worked graveyard shift & spent
the days & weekends visiting bodies.
running his finger alongside the box
& signing the greeting book.

the most decent thing you
can do is visit the funeral of
someone you didn't know
for someone you do:

sister's coworker, lover's friend,
accountant's mother, your aunt's
high school rival.

7.
black churches formed burial societies
after slavery. every week you chipped
off a piece of your pay to save for the shovel
& the rough hands that will lower you.

i know some black folks now buying

their plot foot by foot. saving for a
final mortgage.

8.
it is día de los muertos & i have a check
folded in between the pages of a book about
genocide. i will send the money next week
to the other side of my family
& help bury grandma's sister.

9.
i can't think of a black rapper who hasn't
contemplated their own death on record.
ready to die, life after death, death is certain,
do or die, get rich or die tryin', death certificate.[*]

this is natural
all my verses mention
boxes or holes.

10.
once we lay this brother
down in the ground
we got work to do.[†]

when i was a young boy
at the age of five
my mama said i gon' be
the greatest man alive.[‡]

these children don't
expect to live past 30.
they come to these funerals
& they represent.
they put themselves in
the place of the person
in the casket.[§]

---

[*] Notorious B.I.G., Notorious B.I.G., Royce Da 5'9, Do or Die, 50 Cent, Ice Cube
[†] Ameena Matthews, Chicago CeaseFire Violence Interrupter
[‡] Muddy Waters, "Mannish Boy"
[§] Spencer Leak, Chicago funeral director

prelude

he must've moved out
the neighborhood when i was little.
i bet he could ball,
probably could dunk.

                maybe he rap now.

  maybe he is the boy on every wall.

we ain't got graffiti over here
like for real art stuff but maybe
in the '80s he was optimistic. this was his all
city attempt all over the hood.

maybe he ain't a he.

in the time before the Folks
Nation ran everything over here
maybe the presiding clique was RIP.

i see it everywhere:

        RIP Pierre
        RIP Bird
        RIP D
        RIP Man Man

maybe RIP is a girl.
i see her name next to all
the bad boys. all the big boys
my mama told me not to fool with.
maybe she's all they girlfriends
at once. but they all
gone. no wonder
she keep finding new boys
to kiss.

picking flowers

Grandma's rosebush
reminiscent of a Vicelord's du-rag.
the unfamiliar bloom in Mrs. Bradley's yard
banging a Gangster Disciple style blue.
the dandelions all over the park putting on
Latin King gold like the Chicano cats
over east before they turn into a puff
of smoke like all us colored boys.

picking dandelions will ruin your hands,
turn their smell into a bitter cologne.

a man carries flowers for 3 reasons:

> *he is in love*
> *he is in mourning*
> *he is a flower salesman*

i'm on the express train passing stops
to a woman. maybe she's home.
i have a bouquet in my hand,
laid on 1 of my arms like a shotgun.
the color is brilliant, a gang war
wrapped & cut diagonal at the stems.
i am not a flower salesman.
that is the only thing i know.

juke

in dark basement they dance violent
in violet light like a fight or fuck.
boy against wall back bent like a bow
aiming an arrow. she is all knees,
thighs driving into him,
punching his center like a clock.
working & rotating.

she is sturdy ballet
on a single leg, her
homegirl holding her up.
he is playing man,
grabbing, thrusting
like beating, bass banging
into him & out again. he
is balancing on both feet.
tiptoes & swivel
in his new shoes;

        they gleam bright, 1 of the few
        sources of light, like she is,
        or the purple lamp in the corner
        nobody can see.

Broken Ghazal in the Voice of My Brother Jacob

Irrefutable fact / my brother is black jewish
Kink hair & a wide nose / that's gotta be black, jewish

He said look in the mirror / naked / if it ain't black—jewish
        If we don't do it to ourselves / first / then they do it to us

Said he loves countin' stacks / is that black? / jewish?
Said we loves eating chicken cause we black-jewish!

Said, you gotta keep it real / listen to black music
If you wanna keep your teeth / you ain't allowed to act jewish

And that's jewish / Night of the broken glass jewish
They'll beat your face in with a bat / until it's black.

They raped your great-grandma, and that's a fact, jewish
Say a prayer for the secrets your family keeps, Kaddish

See Aaron, you run / but I learned to attack: jewish
        In order to survive, you gotta be black, stupid

Let 'em tattoo my arm, that's how I act Jewish
That's how I be black / but that's not what you did

Got yourself a "good job," where nobody's black / jewish
Cut the slang off your tongue / it's too black; jewish

And, you never came home / Aaron / where it's black-jewish
And not coming home / is black
        jewish

Danez Smith (1989)

cue the gangsta rap when my knees bend

because my mouth is a whip
& other times my mouth is a whip, you know

bass, rubber, leather seats, detailed flame
you know, some comfy, show-offy shit

fit for music. because he whips me
around easy as Sunday, no church

or plate to get to, just cruise, just eight
oh, eight inches of tar

for me to glide & boom. because it's a drug
& always violence & we hood all day

because my head bob the same, my spit be ready
to brawl. because the song need to have claws

& I need to ravage or revenge, either will do
what difference does a vowel make,

the only word my mouth cares for is O,
the only music the kind that bites.

twerk (v.)

keep the body from knowing what it knows

        weep through pores
           let a NGH cry in public

     forget your god's name, your mother's

be delivered through your own hips

        holy the ether of your waist

     spin light into a gown of hands

summon the sky down, teach stars to pulse

      make his tender muscle flex, tantrum

dilate the room's hundred eyes

     glimmer the black of your knees

     & finally know the reason the body is

Dinosaurs in the Hood

Let's make a movie called *Dinosaurs in the Hood*.
Jurassic Park meets *Friday* meets *The Pursuit of Happyness*.
There should be a scene where a little black boy is playing
with a toy dinosaur on the bus, then looks out the window
& sees the T-Rex, because there has to be a T-Rex.
> (It's a dinosaur movie, duh)

Don't let Tarantino direct this. In his version, the boy plays
with a gun, the metaphor: black boys toy with their own lives
the foreshadow to his end, the spitting image of his father.
Fuck that, the kid has a plastic brontosaurus or triceratops
& this is his proof of magic or God or Santa. I want a scene

where a cop car gets pooped on by a pterodactyl, a scene
where the corner store turns into a battleground. Don't let
the Wayans brothers in this movie. I don't want any racist shit
about Asian people or overused Latino stereotypes.
This movie is about a neighborhood of royal folks—

children of slaves & immigrants & addicts & exiles—saving their town
from real ass dinosaurs. I don't want some cheesy yet progressive
Hmong sexy hot dude hero with a funny, yet strong, commanding
Black Girl buddy-cop film. This is not a vehicle for Will Smith
& Sofia Vergara. I want grandmas on the front porch taking out
    raptors

with guns they hid in walls & under mattresses. I want those little
    spitty
screamy dinosaurs. I want Cecily Tyson to make a speech, maybe 2.
I want Viola Davis to save the city in the last scene with a black fist
    afro pick
through the last dinosaur's long, cold-blood neck. But this can't be
a black movie. This can't be a black movie. This movie can't be dismissed

because of its cast or its audience. This movie can't be metaphor
for black people & extinction. This movie can't be about race.
This movie can't be about black pain or cause black people pain.
This movie can't be about a long history of having a long history with
    hurt.

This movie can't be about race. Nobody can say nigga in this movie

who can't say it to my face in public. No chicken jokes in this movie.
No bullets in the heroes. & no one kills the black boy. & no one kills
the black boy. & no one kills the black boy. Besides, the only reason
I want to make this is for that first scene anyway: the little black boy
on the bus with a toy dinosaur, his eyes wide & endless

       his dreams possible, pulsing, & right there.

Danez Smith

Dear White America
with lines from Amiri Baraka & James Baldwin

I have left Earth in search of darker planets, a solar system that revolves too near a black hole. I have left a patch of dirt in my place & many of you won't know the difference; we are indeed the same color, one of us would eventually become the other. I have left Earth in search of a new God. I do not trust the God you have given us. My grandmother's hallelujah is only outdone by the fear she nurses every time the blood-fat summer swallows another child who used to sing in the choir. Take your God back: though his songs are beautiful, his miracles are inconsistent. I want the fate of Lazarus for Renisha, I want Chucky, Bo, Meech, Trayvon, Sean & Jonylah risen three days after their entombing, their ghost re-gifted flesh & blood, their flesh & blood re-gifted their children. I have left Earth, I am equal parts sick of your 'go back to Africa' as I am your 'I just don't see color' (neither did the poplar tree). We did not build your boats (though we did leave a trail of kin to guide us home). We did not build your prisons (though we did & we fill them too). We did not ask to be part of your America (though are we not America? Her joints brittle & dragging a ripped gown through Oakland?). I can't stand your ground. I am sick of calling your recklessness the law. Each night, I count my brothers. & in the morning, when some do not survive to be counted, I count the holes they leave. I reach for black folks & touch only air. Your master magic trick, America. Now he's breathing, now he don't. Abra-cadaver. White bread voodoo. Sorcery you claim not to practice, but have no problem benefitting from. I tried, white people. I tried to love you, but you spent my brother's funeral making plans for brunch, talking too loud next to his bones. You interrupted my black veiled mourning with some mess about an article you read on Buzzfeed. You took one look at the river, plump with the body of boy after boy after boy & asked 'why does it always have to be about race?' Because you made it so! Because you put an asterisk on my sister's gorgeous face! Because you call her pretty (for a black girl)! Because black girls go missing without so much as a whisper of where?! Because there is no Amber Alert for the Amber Skinned Girls! Because our heroes always end up strung out or strung up! Because we didn't invent the bullet! Because crack was not our recipe! Because Jordan boomed. Because Emmett whistled. Because Huey P. spoke. Because Martin preached. Because black boys can always be too loud to live. Because this land is scared of the Black mind. Because they have sold the Black body & appropriated Soul. Because it's taken my father's time, my mother's time, my uncle's time, my brother's & my sister's time, my niece's & my nephew's time… how much time do you want for your progress? I have left Earth to find a land where my kin can be safe. I will not rest until black people ain't but people the same color as the good, wet earth, until that means something, until our existence isn't up for debate, until it is honored & blessed & loved & left alone, until then I bid you well, I bid you war, I bid you our lives to gamble with no more. I have left Earth & I am touching everything you beg your telescopes to show you. I am giving the stars their right names. & this life, this new story & history you cannot own or ruin

This, if only this one, is ours.

Jamila Woods (1989)

Defense

Trayvon Martin armed himself with the concrete sidewalk and used it to smash George Zimmerman's head. No different than if he picked up a brick or smashed his head against a wall. That is a deadly weapon.

—Don West, defense attorney for George Zimmerman

black boy touch turn
anything weapon
him Grim Reaper
Midas / him smile
suspicious / pigs
frisk every
tooth

black boy on sidewalk
be like black boy
with brick fist or
black fist

black boy sneeze
buckshot snot
even his sick
deadly

him a walking
emergency / whole
body a trigger

hoodie / holster

Blk Girl Art
after Amiri Baraka

Poems are bullshit unless they are eyeglasses, honey
tea with lemon, hot water bottles on tummies. I want
poems my grandma wants to tell the ladies at church
about. I want orange potato words soaking in the pot
til their skins fall off, words you burn your tongue on,
words on sale two for one, words that keep my feet dry.
I want to hold a poem in my fist in the alley just in case.
I want a poem for dude at the bus stop. *Oh you can't talk
ma?* Words to make the body inside my body less invisible.
Words to teach my sister how to brew remedies in her mouth.
Words that grow mama's hair back. Words to detangle the kitchen.
I won't write poems unless they are an instruction manual, a bus
card, warm shea butter on elbows, water, a finger massage to the scalp,
a broomstick sometimes used for cleaning and sometimes

to soar.

Deep in the Homeroom of Doom
after the "Give Yourself Goosebumps" series
by R. L. Stine

Page 1

You are in 9th grade at a private Catholic
college-prep high school. You are not
Catholic. You have never heard of Lacoste
Birkenstock, or the NorthFace. Detention
here is called Justice Under God. Khaki
is not your best color. You've got to find a way
to survive your freshman year! But first
you'll have to figure out how to be cool.

Turn to Page 2

Page 2

Kelsi Carroll is cool. Way cool. Blonde, blue-eyed
Kelsi's double polo collar is perfectly popped.
Her Birkenstocks curl like baby otters around her socks.
She invites you to a party at her house tomorrow night
jots her number down and signs her name with a tiny heart over the *i*.

To ask your mom if you can go to Kelsi's party, turn to Page 23
To ignore the invitation, go home and watch Boy Meets World
reruns alone, turn to Page 48

Page 23

You call your mom at work to ask about the party.
She asks for Kelsi's Mom's number, wants to call
and make sure parents will be home, make sure
there will be no dark unsupervised basements
full of drugs and heavy petting.

If you grow a pair and ask Kelsi for her mom's number, turn to Page 30
If you chicken out and tell Kelsi you can't make the party, turn to Page 70
If you give up on trying to be cool and go watch Boy Meets World,
turn to Page 48

The next day in homeroom you ask Kelsi for her mom's number.
She gasps and stares at you in shock as her Blackberry clatters
to the ground. The classroom falls silent and four rows of pale
stank faces turn to you like a plot of spotlights. Your face catches fire!
The chemistry teacher has to extinguish your burning skull.
Who said black girls can't blush?

THE END

Page 48

After school, you plop down on the couch to watch *Boy Meets World*.
As the opening credits roll, you begin to feel bloated. Your belly swells.
You reach for the remote and realize your arm is rooted to the cushion!
Is that the smell of burning french fries or your pubescent B.O.? Guess
you should have listened to Mom about watching all that television.
You really did become a couch potato in

THE END

Page 70

You can't bear the idea of asking Kelsi to ask her mom to talk to your
mom about the likelihood of dry humping or mary-g-wanna going on
at the party. So in homeroom the next day you make up a lie about
needing to babysit your siblings. You say you don't have a ride
to the North Side, your train stops running, you wouldn't have a way
home. The words drool from your mouth and come out garbled
like grownups' voices on Saturday cartoons. Kelsi listens until her
smile goes slack. You never get another invitation.

THE END

Epilogue

In later years, you stalk Facebook pictures of Kelsi's friend group and try to imagine yourself there: at the beach picnics, the ugly Christmas sweater parties, the prom night dinners and trips to Michigan lake houses. Your cheeks muscular from fake smiles at their lunch table. Their mothers' fridges full of milk, your good manners and stomachaches. The arches of your feet fallen from wearing knockoff Birkenstocks you begged your mother to buy. The boys you partied with but never touched. Your father staying late after work at the hospital to pick you up. The girls unsure how to hold your hair back when you had too much.

My Daddy's forehead is so big, we don't need a dining room
table. My Daddy's forehead so big, his hat size is equator. So
big, it's a five-head. Tyra Banks burst into tears when she seen
my Daddy's forehead. My Daddy's forehead got its own area code.
My Daddy baseball cap got stretch marks. My Daddy pillowcase
got craters. His eyebrows need GPS to find each other. My Daddy
forehead lives in two time zones. Planets confuse my Daddy forehead
for the sun. Couch cushions lose quarters in the wrinkles in my Daddy
forehead. My Daddy so smart, he fall asleep with the movie on and
wake up soon as the credits start to roll. My Daddy so smart, he perform
surgery on his own ingrown toenail. Momma was not impressed, but my
Daddy got brains. My Daddy know exactly how to drive me to my friend's
house without lookin at no map. My Daddy born here, he so smart, he
know the highways like the wrinkles in his forehead. He know the free
clinics like the grey hairs on his big-ass head. My Daddy so smart, he wear
a stethoscope and a white coat. My Daddy drive to work in a minivan
only slightly bigger than his forehead, that's just how my Daddy rolls.
My Daddy got swag. My Daddy dance to Single Ladies in the hallway.
My Daddy drink a small coffee cream and sugar. My Daddy drink a whole
can of Red Bull. My Daddy eat a whole pack of sour Skittles and never
had a cavity. My Daddy so smart, he got a pull-out couch in his office.
Got a mini-fridge there too. Got a cell phone, and a pager, and a email
address where I can leave him messages when he's not at home.
My Daddy's not home. Momma saves a plate that turns cold.

But when my Daddy does come home, he got a office in his bedroom
too. Computer screen night light, Momma says she can't sleep right
but my Daddy got work, my Daddy at work, at home, in the attic,
with the TV on, in the dark, from the front yard, through the
windows, you can see him working, glass flickering, my house
got its own forehead, glinting, sweaty, in the evening,
while my Daddy at work, at home, in his own area code,

a whole other time zone.

Benjamin Alfaro (1990)

What the Eyes Saw

I remember being six years old when he passed.
My sister, home and crying. Asked what it all meant.
Gazing at *All Eyez on Me* for hours. I remember
unsuccessful attempts to contort my fingers, parrot his.
I remember belonging to two discs. Incessant rotation
on Walkman. Satellite in the back seat of a Nissan Maxima
amidst a tireless winter. I remember learning how death felt
when it belonged to a stranger. How my sister and I'd string
our words like escape rope up I-75 to our grandmother's
ruin of a body, the cancer whittling her bald, bringing
insolence in each tone. A stranger, too. Or again,
sitting with my sister trading war stories about my father.
His knees like a straightjacket, hands clutched at her throat
like a jackal clenching its jaded prey. Her friend would run
ten blocks before she called the police. And after the volley,
my sister would take me to sit on a swing in our backyard
from before I was born. Before it snapped under the weight
of a sixteenth birthday party, before the tree collapsed too,
splintering the lawn. Before it became overgrown and my work.
Picture me rolling down the steep backyard hill with a machine
twice my size, yank ripcord unremittingly until the work was done.
Before the anthem of adolescence would calcify these timid bones
against any bad ethics that built them. The ugly pedigree cooking
in my blood. Red and knotted. Hands like talons. I remember
'Pac as two round eyes looking up. I remember silence
and a penchant for violence. I remember pressing rewind.

for KTK

Safia Elhillo (1990)

a suite for ol' dirty

"and and
then we got
then we got
the ol' dirty
bastard
'cause there
aint no father
to his style"

—Method Man

JAMIE LOWE INTERVIEWS DIRT MCGIRT, THE ARTIST FORMERLY KNOWN AS OL' DIRTY BASTARD

D: *fine, i guess*

I: what do you mean you guess?

D: *i just been a bad boy, that's all, ain't nothing to it*

I: you were in jail.

D: *yeah*

I: what was it like?

D: *not good*

I: why?

D: *nothing is paid a mind to, really*

I: what was jail like?

D: *it's just living and dying*

I: what kind?

D: *with no feeling*

>   *;now i have no feelings towards*
>   *the future because feelings are*
>
>   *emotions i don't have those either*

I: can you expand on that?

D: *man, look up at the sky. all the stars, man, the stars*
   is beautiful tonight. look at em

I: does being on parole affect the way you make music?

D: *people were trying to kill me*

I: you think your music will be the same?

D: *nobody's life is based on something they decide*

I: is there a problem?

D: *nah, i was just thinking about something else*

cherry jones (mother) william jones (father) russell jones (1968–2004) shaquita jones (daughter) taniqua jones (daughter) bar-son jones (son) (b.k.a. young dirty bastard) *the corner of my bowl of rice the taste of everything that came before it retrospectively coated in brine*

*

i wonder if they feel
about me the way i feel
about the olive nestled
in the corner of my bowl
of rice the taste of
everything that came
before it retrospectively
coated in brine

I: can you expand on that?

D: *i'm not trying to get all personal*

---

*a song for dirt:

when you get off parole you're going to hawaii
no pills just water & the sounds in your head
collect enough aliases & your name never dies

I: what was the first thing you did when you got out?

D: *hug my mom*

D: *i don't know if ol' dirty bastard is even here anymore*

D: *i think he's gone*

NOTE: i was warned by his management that he can go one of two ways and it just depends who shows up that day

CHERRY JONES*:
well how it works is russell died so dirty could live forever he made a performance of his pathology rhymed his way out of his body genius is a carnivore you know a cannibal a fucking factory for martyrs he cried help you know but it rhymed so we applauded he gutted himself into his own puppet but the blood glittered his mother outlived him he was his best worst invention the wrong name outlived him that's why that's why that's why that's why he died a restless death so don't act like you know anything.†

ROBERT DIGGS‡:
he walked like this *[walks with straight posture, hands behind his back]* every time he spoke he spoke with wisdom the radiance that he had the beauty that he had... his whole look was just angelic

---

* mother of his style
    † a song for dirt:
    MANAGEMENT: *yeah i'm sure he knew he was going to die dissolved to just water, that's what everyone said*
    when you get off parole you're going to hawaii
‡ b.k.a. the RZA; bandmate.

& when he became ol' dirty bastard he
became more successful he made a lot
more money had a lot more fun a lot
more things *[sic]* going on but he went
further away

NOTE: as i left his apartment full of
functional furniture and bare walls i
caught a glimpse of his bedroom and
his fairytale canopy bed shrouded in
cascading yellow chiffon

all i got left to do is be black & absurd

I: is there a problem?

D: *yeah. ok. i don't do [drugs] we don't do [drugs] and all that stuff*

I: why?

NOTE: his eyes rolled back his face screwed up tight & he started
talking in another voice answering a question i never asked a second
or two passed and he was back to Dirt unaware that he had said
anything there was a second flash of another person just for a second

*all i got left in me is things that rhyme that i don't mean to say all i got
left is a body full of names my mama
won't call me by*

I: what do people say when they see you?

D: *hey Dirty*

I: do you have any friends?

D: *nah*

I: so what's up with the splits in your identity?

D: *see my name / is something that you'll never know / unless*

I: can you expand on that?

CHERRY JONES*:
for a minute
his name was Rusty†

---

* mother of his style

† a song for dirt:
i think you did your full best / really did try
left behind water & your canopy bed
when you get off parole you're going to hawaii
collect enough aliases & your name never dies

ARTICLE IV

no more monikers no more trouble just him and his birthright:
his voice and his very first name

"what's the world
without Dirt?
just a bunch of fucking
"
water

—Rhymefest

Sources:
Lowe, Jaime. *Digging for Dirt: The Life and Death of ODB* (New York: Faber and Faber, 2008).
"RZA of the Wu-Tang Clan at ODB's Funeral." YouTube. July 25, 2009. Posted April 30, 2013. https://www.youtube.com/watch?v=FBuXbfTmIx8.
Wu-Tang Clan. *Enter the Wu-Tang (36 Chambers)*. RCA, 1993. CD.
Ol' Dirty Bastard. *Return to the 36 Chambers: The Dirty Version*. Elektra, 1995. CD.
Jones, Cherry. "A Letter From Ol' Dirty Bastard's Mother Cherry Jones." BallerStatus.com, March 5, 2014, http://www.ballerstatus.com/2008/11/14/a-letter-from-ol-dirty-bastards-mother-cherry-jones/

Aziza Barnes (1992)

Juicy (an erasure)

[Intro:]

      All

               grip.

Yeah.

       All me.

Nothin' lived above.

          Buildings called on me.

      Feed my all

    all

[Verse One:]

All.

 I used
my every attack;

          My red match.

Remember,
you never

     take

'Cause sin,

            I used to.

Call.

      If you don't

[Chorus]

hold,

       I'll give you

[Verse Two:]

change.

         All day.

Keep me.
Miss me.
Play me close like

   life without
   ears.

           I dropped all.

[Verse Three:]

Dead
money handles
one-room.

         On her back,
    of course.

My face,

no

    heat.

          Why we thirst?

all...

      (all)

don't

you know

the house

mad?

Camonghne Felix (1992)

Badu Interviews Lamar (an erasure)

Badu Interviews Lamar

Badu: this cyclone of good fortune.

                    You handling?

Kendrick:

                              happy

blessing myself.
                    graduated   ,

      struggle
                  come
                        big   far
                              a blur .

  problem is   my bubble.   tell me

            "You're crazy   by yourself,"

"Kendrick"

                        I'm in my
              own world.

            let
everything consume me.

                              the other end,

                                        has a

                    conception of who

        what

            comes from me, from within

                              no matter

                passing   or playing ball.

                            was a   hole   building

        up for this

                    pen,   I wanted to be

                the best

                                        So I'm

                        taking it.

Police

Law is body talk. Law arches the forked road/ the breadth of any choice stretches and collects volume/ I've never met anyone like you before/ law functions in height when the lights go off/ the lights are off/ where are his hands?/ the law towers and flickers, at most/ but did It lie?/ why are the lights off?/ law is man/ the law abandons language in the dark/ the law sequesters the cool of the silence/ he presses his forearm across my back like a live rod/ like law/ don't act like you don't want to/I quell the breath of it to occupy the sound/ the law prefers disease/ my word pales cocktail pink against his.

Steven Willis (1992)

Beat Writers

for Amiri Baraka and Allen Ginsberg

I saw the best minds of my generation
starving, hysterical, naked, and left for dead but were destined to
   make it.
Ran the negro streets with an angry fix.
Crack(s)
In their nostrils and pavements, the worse condition but were
   destined for greatness.
The gunshots from the block influence this poem's cadence.
Living paycheck to paycheck has taught me most of my patience,
the loss of familiar faces has taught me crime is invasive
the source of my inspiration.
A decade before Reagan
A DJing Kool rasta, Bambaataa, and a couple Gangstars helped father
   a generation of black epics and sagas
Roger
was raised by Big Mama but learned Crack Commandments from
   Poppa
Tasha
bumps the Keef and Waka while guns go *blocka*.
Don't assume.
That bass vibrations can't be felt in the womb, when rock music
   fornicated with blues.
The birth of the trap beat generation,
the babies of Boom
equipped with African traditions and America's doom.
To sculptors of Black Culture
And your bohemian ways,
Your hedonistic approach left this boy in a maze
your b-boy counterculture was just more than a phase
it was the cardboard box, in which we were raised
to elevate to a freeze
d boy clocking for fiends
he'll take the mac to your noodle if you reach for the cheese

he want the C.R.E.A.M.
soliloquies of the grieved and the thieved
the Beat Writers who wrote poems to beats
the Kerouacs of the concrete
the Ginsbergs to the curb
the William S. to their boroughs
the masters of spoken word.
(Neal) Cassady's of the Cuckoo's Nest, and the ones flipping birds
Who haikued the obscene. Who free versed the absurd.
There's no way you can reverse.
The bridge between the music and people we wrote.
Or the religious gunned tongues that we tote,
just take note
of the dope rhythmic quotes
that could summarize the ethos
of the young gifted and black growing up cutthroat.
The ethnography of poverty that we coat
in metaphors and similes to help cope
in beloved communities that are deficient of hope
that's why the young and the music elope,
there no way you can denote,
The syncopation that gave voice to the streets
or blackball us from the poet elite
we're owed a canonized seat
right next to Solomon and Sinclair Belize
the Beat Writers who wrote poems to beats.
Lyrical vandals that graffitied the streets
The Beat Writers who wrote poems to beats.
Gold roped chains and Adidas on feet.
The Beat Writers who wrote poems to beats.
Who drove in '64 Impalas, put the screens in the seats.
The Beat Writers who wrote poems to Beats.

Reed Bobroff (1993)

Four Elements of Ghostdance

I've been ghost dancing in 12" ceremony,
mixed in reverse
I want to go back
                back to when
                drum circle cipher sessions
spun the world.

I've been ghost dancing
on this modern platter of cemented Long Walks.
I pray
for buffalo with hooves like hail:
"Stampede, please, bump the table
            please, bump the table."
I can dance my toes over their groove backs,
listen to the way hide grinds
like pine nuts in gourd
or Hip-Hop of extinct knees
that snaps beautiful like a B-Boy. The Tribe is back!

Quests no longer find thin sacks of bones
on the plains. I've been ghost dancing

                      I can see
Narbona   O.D.B
Crazy Horse   Notorious B.I.G and
                    Red Cloud
                    jump from their paved-over graves.

I hear their Tribal
wisdom:
I hear words.
I hear prayer.
I hear

hands:

Jam Master Jay shows us
Sha'bik'eh through repetition.
We dance
through re-ah-repatition
we dance.

MY MOCCASINS!
need to be tied with a deer hide / fat lace. Spit shined, / sterling silver
    stamp—gotta look vamp
before B-Boys rip through stage,
decked out in braids.
Turquoise chains hanging for days like

1862 Sioux warrior ways.

But us
new Braves smile,

'cause *Wovoka*,
Natives don't gotta be the only ones who come back!

John Lennon, Robert Johnson, KeithMoon
play Eagle bone
whistles inside Bob Marley's Peyote clouds.

We are Rainbow proud,
forever
like Krylon feathers, we
bomb this world in medicine wheel
colors.
Blue coats point their Gatling guns
but the bullets pass through us
leaving spiritless splatters on the walls.

They say Graffiti is
a "stain."
So like Wounded Knee
we sink in.
Paint our faces,
black mask

like we're Mad Villains.
Dressed in ghost jerseys,

we dance on aerosol petroglyphs.
Our signatures
lie upon all the silver
in this Glistening world.

Shaolin
is cedar, pine Hogan.
Thug Mansion is deer hide Tipi.
We mix these Gathering Nations
in until we all permeate
sage.

We dance to remember.
We dance until the world
is gone. Everyone is gone. The world is a ghost and everything is

silent.

So we drop the Sun
Dagger onto vinyl.

and let it sing.

Malcolm London (1993)

Grand Slam

Because the streets is a short stop:
Either you're slingin' crack rock
or you got a wicked jump shot.
—Notorious B.I.G.,
Things Done Changed

Huron St and Lavergne Ave
intersect like a baseball diamond

southeast corner

1st base
a police camera sits
like an announcer's booth.

a throne flashing blue
overseeing everything here
as if it is foul play

southwest corner

2nd base
a boarded up building

serving more coke
to more patrons
than a World Series game

fast balls black mothers into aging guitars
strung out on street corners
their own sons standing on the pitcher's mound

northwest corner

3rd basemen
uniformed in hoodies

pelle jackets and timberland boots,

are corked bats
ready to strike out
at anyone who stares

too long, walks too boldly
or throws the wrong curve
of fingers.

dreadlocks beneath fitted caps
on swivel for any woman swinging hips and batting an eye
do anything and everything illegal
just to score food on their plates

yankee mascots taunt
anyone in a brown skin jersey,
this small negro league
crackerjacked by an empire

controlled by white umpires.

             northeast corner

             since the late sixties my grandmother
             has made her living room window a bleacher
             watching america's favorite pastime

             bases loaded
             with her offspring
             who have never made it to the majors

most of us have stopped short
of coming home

safe.

Kush Thompson (1994)

this, here

This, we tiptoe.
This, we flower in euphemism.
The street has swallowed itself into border. Into railroad track.
This, where the bus line ends.
This, where little boys bike across curfew and into eulogy.
This, where board-slapped windows domino into mansions.
Runaway men into joggers.
This, where Oak Park River Forest alumni rep westside,
Redlands East Valley minstrels "Gangsta Day" during spirit week.
This, where the grass, and the quiet,
lulls mothers to sleep.
This, where your heart is not yet
a restless telephone wire shackled to the ankle
        of every one you have ever loved after sunset.
This, where the news stations tell you everything you know about
        what lives across your street, outside of your living room window,
        at the end of your driveway.
This, deliberate. This abrupt.
This sloppy stitching.

Here, you are exception,
urban, and articulate.
the black friend that let them poke pencils through your kink that one
        time
while you curled a trembling smile, pretending not to be
token or voodoo doll
Half house, half field
a Susie Carmichael or Huxtable.
The black family in a White House
ran north and bought the plantation.

This all too familiar of being someplace but not.
You were raised on "twice as good."
Mama left the westside when you were two.
you were raised into valley-girl accent.

your voice lost all of its skyline until
you went to high school through metal detectors.
You were raised on ditches and division streets.
Here, where you were born before you were conceived.

Here, where your cousin lives in the basement
Here is your first real boyfriend
the first tongue in your mouth, and first
    call from the county.
Here is the splintered wall your back will know.
Here, where you are no bourgeois success story,
just lucky enough to slip through cracks and make it
to your front door each night.
Here is where your ashes will be scattered.
Here is your home 6 years from now.
Here is your home 50 years ago.
Here is your redemption skin.
    Your corner store.
    Your corner stone.
Here is your Gramma's house and dusted porcelain
and stuffed bears on the living-room walls.
Here, where everything grows without permission.
Here, where sunflowers rise from the potholes
each and every summer.

E'mon McGee (1996)

My niece's hip-hop

Is double Dutch and twee lee lee like a bumblebee
Patty cake and tender headed girls by the radio in window seats.
It's my oohs and ahhs. Sweet chapped lips on Sunday mornings
Fresh prince of clean air. Eve's bayou on the riverside
And female niggas more like lady. Holiday Inns on south Cicero
Hip-hop is drunken master in my mom's drunken dances
It runs a lot like Chicago and SWV in my house.
I find beats in bowls of cereal and kitchen sinks
Groan with me when I'm hungry or pressed for time
When chances don't come as easily
In a home where music was my discipline.
The strongest sample of any artist made me cry.
I am the built from the beat.
I am a hip-hop root.
Walkmens always had me running
Skating on riffs and runs like CD players and fresh batteries
College Dropout and stops by my locker
Going back to Cali on Chicago corners
I won't forget
Her graces were always said in a rhyme
Always sung in a rapping song.
We grew up on raps made into prayers
Before I ate food or went to sleep.
We grew up on singing raps
I won't forget.
Endowed a literature I speak
Was once spoken to
I live a theme song
A scheme of a black girl
Being nostalgic
Being beautiful
in Nike and Jordan
A ballerina in tube socks
Foot working, shuffling power
Through her toes and tongue.

Dancing to remixes of Ali speeches

And the truth. A vibe of cursive
And curses. I know every cuss word
Every slang slanted word blended
in a conversation. I know a hip-hop
conversation. A converse I keep
At the bottom of my shoe.

Hopefully my face will be seen on MTV before my ass will.
Hopefully my face ain't too caked to be called beautiful or natural
Like Barbie before extensions or a face lift.
More like Minnie Riperton before Beyonce
30 seconds of ratchetness
We aren't classically trained
Taken through woods and wild willows.
Females daisy dukin
Cream shaking their money maker
But still broker than yesterday.

I still got hope saved in my back pockets for my niece.
She too camo faced in darkness
Too bleached to know the difference between the sunrise and her skin
Too phased in being a hot mama
Forgets her edges slicked and greased and head nets and naps
Hopefully I won't see her ass on MTV when I wake up
Won't see goodies spilling out cookie jars and glasses of milk
It's been a while since she's been harvested in a cloud
Been too busy kicking dust off her shoes
Feeling unwanted and unsatisfied in pleated pants and t shirts
She's been daisy dukin
Juking to new tunes MTV wakes her up to

Hip-hop, Please keep her
A ballerina in tube socks

Angel Pantoja (1997)

Murder Is My Name

Propelling towards death.
I am bronze as a shield,
freshly shined & cleaned for war.
Only, I don't protect life.
My copper form reflecting the sun's rays
as I push against the air.
Who
    am
        I?
To determine who should feel this
excruciating pain I bear.
My galvanized lungs
bursting with blood & air.
In a mixture as black as the skin I target.
But am I really this demented?
To fiend for the sweet,
comforting touch of burning flesh
to soothe my shrapnel corpse.
Now deformed as the bag of son I leave,
For a young mourning mother to receive.
Her once-vibrant oxblood torso,
now slumped over like a somber weeping willow.
Frail branches hankering for the son they recall.
Only to receive a young Pedro or Denzel reborn.
Haggard from gangrene halites
melting his cold, gangster exterior.
  Who
    am
        I?
To have no life myself.
Yet idolized & feared by man.
Allowed to reshape men into fallow grisly forms.
Young faces varicose from my very touch.
Sorry neutron,
Sorry DW, Sorry young Latin King.

Sorry for snatching away the breath from within
your lungs.
It's just,
sometimes I don't understand
who I am.
At least I know one thing.
I am a gyrating scream of Chicago's reality,
Propelling towards death.

Nile Lansana (1997) and Onam Lansana (1999)

Lesson one

Son,

i love you,
that's why I'm telling you this
to protect you
you're a black boy
i can only give you advice on this
i'm sorry
that I have to tell you about mirandas
instead of reading you bedtime stories.

i'm sorry
i have to read you your rights before goodnight
the police
are supposed to be
our neighborhood watch
zimmerman might have a
badge this time
not the voice
in his head saying that it's okay to

pull the trigger,

i'm only standing my ground
we watch them as they watch us
caught in a never ending staring contest
pupils with the intensity of
your finger on the trigger.

Son,

i'm gonna tell it like it is

your skin
makes you a target
the United States
is a shooting gallery
where targets aren't
red circles
but black dots

Son
you're a black dot
my black dot
in this shooting gallery
i have to keep you safe
your hand is just as close to your wallet
as theirs to their holsters

move slowly
arms
handcuffs
holster

they expect you to make a mistake
don't smile they might think you're lying
don't sweat they might think you're nervous
    nervous means guity
guity means
cuffs and miranda bedtime stories.

you have the right to remain silent.
now I lay me down to sleep
anything you say can and will be used against you
i pray the lord my soul to keep
you have the right to an attorney
and if I die before I wake
i pray the lord my soul to take

we live in a world
where the people who should be protecting us
take us off the world just as much as they keep us on it

this battle is center stage
Amadou Diallo
41 shots
innocent
Sean Bell
50 shots
innocent
Flint Farmer
16 shots
innocent

black men will always get lynched but they stop using ropes
a long time ago

Oscar Grant
1 shot
innocent
he was supposed to take his daughter to Chuck E Cheese
he was riding the train home
police pulled him and his boys off the train
and put a hole in his back

i wish you still treasured the
1st amendment like you do the second

we reppin Chicago
the center of
a shooting gallery called the United States

revolution in open caskets

i hear too many church bells
for dead bodies

arms
handcuffs
holster
arms

handcuffs
holster

Son, promise me you'll never have to dance to that beat

Ars Poeticas
&
Essays

Art, Artifice, & Artifact

I was born in 1964 in small-town Enid, Oklahoma. The youngest of six, I was immersed in Black Power politics and culture well before I learned to read. My two oldest sisters, afros like small planets, integrated the Enid High School orchestra, my brother was likely among the first Black student to play in the school band (trumpet, under the influence of Miles Davis), and another sister led Black student demonstrations. I was too young to understand most of this activity, but was informed by it, as well as the Nikki Giovanni and Amiri Baraka poems taped to the walls of my eldest sisters' room.

By third grade my best friend Zack (a full-blood Cherokee) and I were obsessed with cars, basketball, and the etymology of language. Phonemic reading strategies still fresh from first grade, we moved on to question the logic of words: Why is that thing called *chair?* Why is that a *sofa?* I was already fascinated with sound and symbol after growing up in a house filled with my siblings' music.

I was a chubby, wide-eyed Black boy wrestling with the transformative audacity of words and deeply affected by their myriad vehicles. I quoted the comedian Flip Wilson, with the plan of becoming him later in life, and by sixth grade I was on to Richard Pryor. I recited scripture and performed in holidays shows with my cousins at church. For about two years, I hung out with a dude who cursed at his parents, which I found exhilarating and stupid at the same time. Then, there was the ever-present electricity of violence in the house that made me wince, made me quiet, and made me hide in syllables and imagination.

Words and music were sanctuary and edification.

The sibling closest to me in age is the fourth girl child in the family. Four years separate us, and though this chasm is no longer significant, it was life-changing when I was twelve. My siblings were ideas and occasional visitors. I spent most of my teens alone in a house with blue-green shag weary from aged footprints.

But they left their music.

Earth, Wind & Fire is why I picked up a tenor saxophone. Stevie Wonder is why I picked up a pen. Grandmaster Flash, Kurtis Blow, and the Sugarhill Gang put it all together for me.

The first time I heard "Rapper's Delight" unexplainable changes occurred in my being that I did not fully comprehend for a decade. The Sugarhill Gang furthered/reinforced a way of seeing I was stumbling to master—the teenage-male hormonal need to string words together with a cleverness that produced laughter, swagger, or girls. Sometimes all three, though usually not in that order of import.

I was a ninth grader at Longfellow Junior High School (ironically, all of the middle schools in Enid are named after poets) when I first heard "Rapper's Delight" in 1979. Music and the ability to make others laugh, has remained, and likely will always remain, central to any relationship I forge. My best friend Russ and I still, two years later, had the *Saturday Night Fever* soundtrack on heavy rotation, in addition to our personal favorites: Russ—ABBA, Bay City Rollers and early 70s rock his older sisters inflicted on him; me—Kool & the Gang, the Spinners, and always Stevie. Later that school year a friend, the son of a university professor, would visit an older brother in California and return with a hundred albums by bands with the weirdest names he could find: Human Sexual Response, the Legendary Pink Dots, the Police, etc. His shopping excursion indelibly informed our sleepy town lives. But, for me, not quite as much as:

> I said, a hip hop the hippie to the hippie
> > To the hip, hip a hop, a you don't stop, the rock it
> To the bang, bang boogie, say up jump the boogie
> To the rhythm of the boogie, the beat
> > Now what you hear is not a test—I'm rappin' to the beat
> > And me, the groove, and my friends
> > Are gonna try to move your feet

That was it for me. Word as rhythm. Word as beat. Word in conversation with rhythm. Word as art, artifice, and artifact. We abandoned the Bee Gees very quickly.

Almost as quickly I became the hip-hop pusher for teenage white dudes drunk on 3.2 beer and curiosity. I still, to this day, have no idea what happened to my copy of the eponymous *Kurtis Blow* vinyl. But for a time I was the link to rap for a small group of middle-class white dudes who dared not venture into "The Ville" to buy records.

The literal "other side of the tracks" in Enid is called "The Ville." This is the Black side, the "hood," on Enid's south side. The kids from "The Ville" and the kids from my neighborhood attended Longfellow, which was, and is still, considered the "thug school." Enid's apartheid was palpable. Blacks could only visit the skating rink on Sunday nights, "Black Night," until the mid 1970s and my elementary school was closed due to desegregation in 1975.

I wandered from hip-hop for a portion of the 1980s in pursuit of all things political, angry, and not made in the United States. My disillusionment with the nation, its politics, and most of its culture led me to Africa, the West Indies, and Europe. Though I kept in touch with hip-hop, I was mostly elsewhere—Mutabaruka, Miriam Makeba, Two-Tone Ska bands from England. Grandmaster Flash's "The Message" and other overtly political tracks kept my attention, but I didn't feel Rap speaking to where my head was in 1984. Many tracks in that moment felt like recycled disco, but this also marked the emergence of Run DMC, Whodini, and the Treacherous Three. I just wanted emcees to say something that would make Ronald Reagan vomit and then disappear. I also wanted the music to capture my imagination.

My prayers were answered in 1986 and it was on nonstop for a long minute.

The years 1986 to 1996 represent the first significant era in my life, in terms of rap and personal growth. No way to say this better than a sampling from my discography:

King of Rock—Run-DMC, 1985

Licensed to Ill—Beastie Boys, 1986

Criminal Minded—Boogie Down Productions, 1987

Paid in Full—Eric B. & Rakim, 1987

Yo! Bum Rush the Show—Public Enemy, 1987

By All Means Necessary—Boogie Down Productions, 1988

In Full Gear—Stetsasonic, 1988

It Takes a Nation of Millions to Hold Us Back—Public Enemy, 1988

3 Feet High & Rising—De La Soul, 1989

The Cactus Album—3rd Bass, 1989

Business as Usual—EPMD, 1990

Fear of a Black Planet—Public Enemy, 1990

Step in the Arena—Gang Starr, 1991

Bizarre Ride II the Pharcyde—The Pharcyde, 1992

Can I Borrow a Dollar?—Common, 1992

93 'til Infinity—Souls of Mischief, 1993

Midnight Marauders—A Tribe Called Quest, 1993

Reachin' (A New Refutation of Time and Space)—Digable Planets, 1993

Blowout Comb—Digable Planets, 1994

Blunted on Reality—Fugees, 1994

Illmatic—Nas, 1994
Ready to Die—The Notorious B.I. G., 1994
Southernplayalisticadillacmuzik—OutKast, 1994
Do You Want More?!!!??!—The Roots, 1995
Gothic Architecture—Rubberoom, 1995
Stakes Is High—De La Soul, 1996

Certainly there are many groundbreaking albums not on this list (I hear my boy Adrian Matejka saying, "Where's the Wu, Q?"). This is simply the partial soundtrack of my movement from Oklahoma to Chicago, my transition into manhood.

Hip-hop, in 1988, helped remind me of who I was and of that in which I believed and held sacred. I moved to Chicago in 1989, leaving behind an ugly experience in broadcast journalism, and for nearly two decades felt a contempt for the state of Oklahoma only natives can truly appreciate. I was fired from my first professional gig in TV news in Oklahoma City largely because life inside Babylon's mouth involved perpetuating a conservative right wing agenda and sustaining an ill-fitting fear of African American men. My deep conviction to journalism serving as "the public's trust" was met with a battle with my own naiveté. I experienced the excitement of hearing Dan Rather voice an international news scoop I helped initiate, while being assigned the task of greeting the Grand Imperial Wizard of the state's Ku Klux Klan compound.

Chuck D sorted it out for me.

Public Enemy guided me toward self-worth, reclamation of history, and Islam. Though my belief in diversity and my background did not completely jibe with the teachings of the Honorable Elijah Muhammad or Minister Louis Farrakhan, PE led me to discipline, faith, and a community of serious Black men. I liken my years as a practicing Muslim to the military in many ways. I needed to grow up and, after being fired from Channel Nine, discover a deeper and sincere purpose for my life. *It Takes a Nation of Millions to Hold Us Back* and *Fear of a Black Planet*, along with the Holy Qur'an and the teachings of El-Hajj Malik El-Shabazz (Malcolm X) were my textbooks. I also returned to poetry, long since abandoned as I became more immersed in broadcast journalism.

One week following my twenty-fifth birthday, I arrived in Chi-town with two suitcases, a folder full of poems, and dreams of becoming a poet and cultural worker in the city that fed some of my guiding lights: Haki Madhubuti and Gwendolyn Brooks. I received the amazing blessing to have been mentored by these two giants.

Ms. Brooks possessed a guarded optimism toward hip-hop. She appreciated Rap as poetry, or at least as lyric. But, she found most of the language unoriginal and the music mostly boisterous. Ms. Brooks never employed profanity in her work. She considered swear words a reflection of a poverty of ideas, which in turn would make most Rap Fat Albert's junkyard. However, as she shared in workshop, if there is no other word that will be as precise in communicating your concept, then use that word. She believed in "exactness" and her enduring poetry bears witness to this.

Though Ms. Brooks harbored some appreciation for emcee's wordplay, her disappointment with the lack of political or social consciousness in most hip-hop affected her desire to mentor many young emcees. This is not to suggest she turned anyone away who reached out to her, as that is not the case. But Brooks and Madhubuti, unlike Mama Sonia Sanchez and Nikki Giovanni, did not actively embrace emcees and the art. The one possible exception may reside in the son of our former Chicago State University colleague and close friend, the late Dr. Donda West.

Mama Sonia's mutual admiration love fest with Yasiin Bey (Mos Def) is so pronounced they engaged in something few would ever have imagined: a car commercial. Consider one of the Black Art Movement's leading voices for human rights and, almost twenty years ago, one of the illest emcees in the game, selling Buicks. This is not a critique of their decision to do the commercial, as my respect for both of them is real and Mama Sonia's love is a phone call away every day. Moreover, it is a telling reminder of the state of Rap in the Millennium.

I consider myself, for the most part, a direct descendent of the Black Arts Movement (BAM), at least contextually. BAM doctrine supported art "for, by, and about Black people." This tenet was introduced to me via my siblings' afros in 1973. It was reaffirmed by hip-hop, furthered by my work in Chicago's public schools, and crystallized while raising four sons in what some people call a "war zone." Malcolm X said, "Pro-Black doesn't mean anti-anything."

Recently, my oldest son, Nile, and I watched the "Time Is Illmatic" documentary on the creation of Nas' masterpiece, one of my favorite records of all time. He paused the film often to ask questions about many topics: the early beefs between The Bridge and the Boogie Down, and Nas and Jay-Z; was Brooklyn that violent when we lived there in his toddler years; what happened to AZ? *Illmatic*, of course, is on his required old school listening list. Though it may have been another late night conversation for Nile, it is a moment I will cherish for many a day. This is how I feed my sons. This, to me, is hip-hop.

t'ai freedom ford

Artist Statement

Without question, I am a child of hip-hop. In 1983, you could find me beatboxing in the elementary school bathroom where the cavernous acoustics gave me life. In high school, I spent my lunch period knuckling beats and spitting rhymes. By the time I graduated in 1990, my yearbook was filled with an encouraging refrain: keep on rappin! In college, I wrote lyrics but began writing poems so that I wouldn't be confined by rhyme scheme and beats per minute. In 1993, I began performing poetry in Atlanta, where my hip-hop infused delivery served as a way to engage, educate, entertain.

Without question, my poetry has hip-hop in its DNA. Which is to say that my poetry is also inherently African, undeniably American, and unquestionably aggressive. Which is to further say that the poems are unafraid to acknowledge their culture, their history, and their political stance. Twenty years later, the poems may be a bit more studied, they may flirt with form, they may better understand prosody, but at their core they are rebellious, subversive, inspired by the hood, and rooted in hip-hop.

Michael Mlekoday

Artist Statement

Before I ever wrote a poem, I stood in a prayer circle with my friends and traded rhymes. A prayer circle, yes. Cipher-as-prayer, as witness that your words can call down thunder and resurrection if you believe in them hard enough.

For where two or three gather in my name, there am I with them.

In "Tradition and the Individual Talent," T. S. Eliot argues that, as much as literary history informs the present, the present also informs the past—that literary history moves both ways, that the tradition is always evolving. When I listen to Kendrick Lamar, I hear traces of Rakim—but when I listen to Rakim, I hear, too, what he has become.

The DJ spins two records at once. History moves back and forth with the crossfader. The poems I read in high school—well, you already know. Dead white guys.

The songs I listened to in high school, though, pierced me like hooks. I'd grown up on N.W.A., LL Cool J, Public Enemy—black dudes from the coasts. I was a white kid in the Midwest rocking a backwards hat, sorely out of my element but hungry. Then I found Atmosphere, I Self Devine, Eyedea & Abilities—kids from my own neighborhood, rapping about the streets I rode the bus down every weekend, about the winter only my city and body knew. Hey, I could do this, I thought.

Fifteen years later, and hip-hop has crossfaded me back to those old dead white guys (and girls, and folks of color, and queers) whose work lives primarily in books. In high school, Whitman never meant shit to me, but now I read "Song of Myself" and can't help but hear De La Soul's "I Am I Be" in the background. These are prayers that say *I am here. We are here.*

Hip-hop, as much or more than any other literary tradition I know, is intertextual, built of allusions and echoes that call back and forth through history. It is also a tradition that refuses to sacrifice substance for style or style for substance—hip-hop is always both sonics and politics, flash and prayer.

In my own work as a poet, I take from the hip-hop tradition this dedication to the here-and-now-and-always-was, this belief that a dope enough line can break the necks of my enemies just by making them nod their heads, that poems can riot and kill and resurrect and sweeten and gingerly hold you in hospital rooms as your father is dying in silence, and I pray that, if my own words prove too weak or quiet or stale, the next kid in the cipher will save me.

Douglas Kearney

Artist Statement

Oh hell naw! But yet it's that, too!
—Andre 3000

When I consider the impact hip-hop has had on my work, content comes to mind immediately. The concerns of much of the culture's aesthetic expression figure around presence: what does it mean to be a person—especially a person of color—in a context and how do I ensure my presence against erasure? This aspect of erasure puts pressure on presence—the wildstyle calls out at the same time that it encodes; rappers warn you about danger even when they celebrate their place in it; the breaker's body is an explosion of presence, historically in public space; the DJ marks a track via his/her intervention, both inserting the DJ's presence and suggesting the potential erasure of the track.

Yet, content seems to me too easy a "resting place" in considering hip-hop's influence. These ideas aren't particular to hip-hop alone, and a poem that mentions graf writers, MCs, breakers, DJs, etc. is not necessarily investing in the culture, exploring it, representing it (i.e., is Tony Hoagland's "America" a hip-hop poem?).

Thus, my work engages methodologies associated with hip hop as vital components of what y'all name a breakbeat poetics. Further, I'm especially interested now in leveraging techniques outside of rap to affect my writtens; the poems I've submitted make frequent use of analogues to sampling (most clearly via overt quotation), which of course requires digging (I only allow myself to use quotes I remember, not ones I would have to find online). "No Homo"—via its intentional "misquoting" of Lil Wayne/Ice-T tracks, utilizes the remix. Another production technique, "chopping," guided the writing of "Drop It Like It's Hottentot Venus.," a multitrack poem built entirely of anagrams from its title. "Quantum Spit" self-samples, samples, and chops, like Public Enemy's *It Takes a Nation of Millions to Hold Us Back*. It also attempts to represent scratching typographically. My poems' use of what I've been calling "performative typography" synthesizes some of graf's visual complexity and multiplicity, asking whether the audience is meant to read or look. At the same time, it gestures toward the relationship between an MC and a beat.

Put simply: I push toward an intersection of content and procedure in my breakbeat poetics. The subject is in danger of erasure: sometimes art endangers it; sometimes it seeks to make it indelible.

Angel Nafis

Artist Statement

When I was about nineteen years old I attended a panel at the University of Michigan in celebration of hip-hop and the publication of Jeff Chang's book *Can't Stop Won't Stop*. I remember one of the panelists completely changing the tone of the discussion and opening up the room when he said, "I'm not just hip-hop because I listen to and make the music, I'm hip-hop because of the way I lace my boots. How come I don't put the shoe-string through all the hoops? That's hip-hop." That phrase affirmed something that lived so deeply within me but had never been articulated. It freed something and helped me see myself. As a both a person and a writer, hip-hop's influence of who I am is so pervasive it's nearly immeasurable. I don't rap. I've barely ever written anything even resembling a technical verse. But when I have writer's block, I pace the long hallway of my apartment saying the last sentence I wrote over and over, head nodding up and down, until the next sentence presents itself. When I finish a first draft of a poem, I edit it first by reading it aloud multiple times and listening for where the poem comes alive, or where it falls flat, cutting out lines that don't rhythmically move the poem's meaning forward. When I go to format I rarely use punctuation, I write in clipped sentences, I brag, I metaphor, I yo mama joke my way through the poem until it looks like a song. In all these ways I feel and see the spirit of the culture embedded deep in my process and way of understanding how things should be. Hip-hop is my apparatus. The things that make me want to write, the things that inspire me, the things that feel important and holy are the historically untold stories that hip-hop has always privileged. Those are the stories I am called to and they guide me in life and in creation.

Aziza Barnes

A Locus of Control and the Erasure

"Locus of control" is a term used in psychology to define how one determines who controls her life. A person who possesses an internal locus of control is someone of the mind that she controls her own life, what happens to her, and when change can occur. The converse, a person with an external locus of control, is one who believes the world controls her life. This is a person with a mentality that "things happen to me," as opposed to "I happen to things." A fundamental aspect of Black American culture and its outlook on life in America is submitting oneself to the notion that one does not have control over one's life. Since jump ("jump" being shackles, Elmina Castle, Black bodies as cargo, the Middle Passage, etc.), there has been a cultural consensus that "things happen to me." Never do I, a Black American, happen to something. Or, if I do happen to something, the result is ineffectual or ends with my demise. This point of view is particularly acute in Black America after 1968. After an upsurge of protest following the murder of Emmett Till in 1955, Black American leaders, in a manner that was globally unprecedented, emphasized and illuminated resistance. Determined to acquire agency in their own lives, they called their generation to question the very notion of "rights." After the assassinations of Martin Luther King, Malcolm X, and countless other pillars in Black American resistance, with the 70s on the horizon and precious little to show for it, came hip-hop.

It comes as no surprise to me that in the evolution of hip-hop, Black American artists would come to question and defy their condition in the country of their birth and try to alter their locus of control. In its origin, hip-hop is defiance, a battle cry, a marking of territory. My father, a DJ in the South Bronx in '72, would come to tell me as much: that hip-hop began as "basement parties, tagging subway cars... proclaiming 'I am!' when no one seemed to care you existed." What I find compelling about hip-hop's evolution is the endeavor to not only command an internal locus of control, but to control one's world even after death.

Kendrick Lamar's song "Sing about Me, I'm Dying of Thirst," off his 2013 album *good kid, m.A.A.d city,* is emblematic of a hip-hop artist of my generation (the generation of kids who witnessed 9/11 from TVs and schoolyards—a war already happening to us—who came into the world on the heels of the crack epidemic—the dissolution of the Black home), struggling to comprehend how much control he has over his life. The chorus: "When the lights shut off/ and it's my turn/ to settle down/ my main concern/ promise that you will sing about me/ promise that you will sing about me." Lamar's lyrics describe a story of his coming up in Compton, Los Angeles, California, surrounded by gang warfare and police, both of which have a tighter grip on his life than he does. Lamar, upon the shooting of his brother, reflects, "I know exactly what happened/ you ran outside when you heard my brother cry for help/ held him like a newborn baby and made him feel/ like everything was all right/ and a fight he tried to put up/ but the type of bullet that stuck had went against his will." This particular verse ends with Lamar saying, "and if I die before your album drop, I hope—" ending with gunshots and an assumedly dead Lamar. At the end of the following verse, Lamar raps, "I'll probably live longer than you/and never fade away/ I'll never fade away/ I'll never fade away..." and the track continues, Lamar's voice fading out until he is muted completely. Even within his song Lamar cannot control his own fate, though he is obsessed with his inability to do so.

Lamar's "Sing About Me, I'm Dying of Thirst" stands in stark contrast to a hit single by a rapper from a generation prior to him, from Notorious B.I.G.'s 1994 *Ready to Die* album. The single? "Juicy." "Juicy" focuses on Christopher Wallace's coming up into the rap game from the games he played as a Black boy in Brooklyn. The text of "Juicy" is a declaration of "living life without fear" and all a man can do when in a position of control. Even in saying, "I made the change from a common thief," it is he, Christopher Wallace, who enacted a change in his life. Wallace happened to the world, after the world tried mercilessly to happen to him. The title of his album, *Ready to Die,* is also indicative of a man who has decided he will choose his moment to exit. While the two rappers' songs deal with death and control in disparate ways, what remains consistent is the notion that their words belong to them, immortalize them, eulogize them in the way a newspaper headline reflecting on the death of a Black man in America, would not.

An erasure is a style of poetry that is defined as "a form of found poetry created by erasing words from an existing text in prose or verse and then framing the result of this effort as a poem." I dig this definition. I also dig erasures. Oddly enough, this style of poem is incredibly hard to do successfully, depending on the given text. The writer must go into the text with her own objective and carve out a poem from that which is probably inherently poetic. An erasure happens to a text, and the act of creating one empowers the writer with the ability to claim what is not exactly yours. An erasure is a theft, a hijacked poetry. The two texts I've made erasures of are Notorious B.I.G.'s "Juicy" and Kendrick Lamar's "Sing About Me, I'm Dying of Thirst."

The era I have come up in the 9/11 era, the Trayvon Martin era, the stop-and-frisk era, the Obama era, a supposedly "post-racial" era, is one of heightened disillusionment. Now more than ever, Black Americans question their power and continued lack of control over their lives in a society that has announced that the era of race itself as an identifier is over. The hip-hop that speaks to me most clearly and acutely is the work of my contemporaries, who do not strive to manufacture a control over their own lives but simply comment on their lack of it. I feel that the erasure is a form of poetry most befitting my generation. It's a reclamation, ownership with the swagger of theft, a holla back to taking back.

In erasing Lamar's and Wallace's songs, a critical action occurs: I, the writer, can effectively alter the rappers' speech, intentions, and meanings. I erase what they proclaimed themselves to be. An erasure is the form of the disillusioned poet, but also that of the romantic one. In erasing "Juicy," I am likewise excavating the song, digging for any deeper meaning behind Wallace's words, looking for some unnamable talisman. The same is true of Lamar's song, which took three weeks to erase. The erasure is about demanding a truth where there isn't one or uncovering that which didn't want to be found. Writing one is a deliberate act of happening to something, a reorientation of one's locus of control.

Life Is Good: How Hip-Hop Channels Duende

When I discuss hip-hop these days, I am usually talking to my youngest brother, who was one of the most talented rappers in our hometown. Usually, it is inextricably bound up with how we grew up and how we thought our friends would not go to college or live beyond high school. Then there are those who did survive past college or thirty, and I talk to my best friend from high school who worked two part-time jobs and collected disability for partial blindness. He supported his mom and two younger siblings while we were both in school, and sometimes all we had was a head nod to a beat to sustain us. Someone telling a story that looked and sounded a little bit like us. Now, I talk to my friends who are grown and growing up, and some of them are dying. We become aware of the mortality and vulnerabilities around us when they die of high blood pressure, diabetes complications, heart problems, cancer, and substance issues: part and parcel of racism.

I recently told my brother while I was working on a thousand-piece puzzle with my mother, "I am so grateful that you made it to age thirty." He asked me, "What you mean, Tar?" I said, "You always ran up in those spots where people would get wild, and I would have nightmares that someone would shoot you." And we talked about Joe Buck, who cut kids' hair for free for the first day of school and gave free haircuts for job interviews, and how they robbed him and shot him down for the small bit of cash that was on him. My brother wrote a song for him, and it was then I knew that hip-hop was the home for elegy—but it was also dangling on the precipice of duende. So, I was rereading Lorca's *In Search of Duende* and looking for some link beyond a contemporary continuation of the blues tradition that hip-hop obviously echoes, when I read this: "Behind these poems lurks a terrible question that has no answer. Our people cross their arms in prayer, look at the stars, and wait in vain for a sign of salvation" (11).

Whenever I encounter needless and inherently systemic loss, I think of Lorca.

"The duende does not come at all unless he sees that death is possible. The duende must know beforehand that he can serenade death's house and rock those branches we all wear, branches that do not have will never have, any consolation" (58).

When I think of how death is looming and possible, it is not difficult to see how Nas's "I Gave You Power" personifies a gun, much like Organized Konfusion's "Stray Bullet," or how Notorious B.I.G. had albums with the titles *Ready to Die* and *Life after Death*. Nor was it unusual to hear MC Lyte's "Poor Georgie" or Nonchalant's "5 O'Clock in the Morning."

Then I think of what mattered to my students at Westinghouse High School on the West Side of Chicago, who loved Nas's "One Mic," and a young man named Xavier who eagerly showed me his copy of B.I.G.'s *Life after Death* as soon as it dropped. At least three students died during my time as a teaching artist there: one was in a fire with her baby, one was shot, and another was hit by a drunk driver who dragged her body for blocks before he stopped.

Then, there was one of my students at Rutgers who wrote a letter to Notorious B.I.G. based on Langston Hughes's "Theme for English B," because the Bed-Stuy legend had taught him something about writing before he came to my class. The opportunity to write about loss and trauma affirmed that they were survivors with capacity, talents, and rights to survive and thrive. Even though the affirmations in hip-hop were (and still are) reflected in material gains, I still feel that fantasy is what sustains people in their most vulnerable moments, which is why Lorde can say "I cut my teeth on wedding rings in the movies./ And I'm not proud of my address./ In the torn up town." in the song "Royals."

> The magical property of a poem is to remain possessed by duende that can baptize in dark water all who look at it, for with duende it is easier to love and understand, and one can be sure of being loved and understood. In poetry this struggle for expression and communication is sometimes fatal. (58)

But all of this brings me to Nas, the emcee who grew up in the Queensbridge projects. He had a mother who was a teacher and his father is a well-known musician named Olu Dara, but the lure of dropping out of school and making illicit money was still tempting until Nas found his pen. To me, Nas always sounded like your homeboy who you felt would eventually right himself and live a long life, if he was careful… and lucky. *Illmatic* has just reached the twenty-year mark as a hip-hop classic, but it's been something to hear him pen more confessional, grown-up work that mirrors aspects of my own life as an adult woman who has experienced the loss of love through divorce. "Life Is Good," in which he holds a version of his former wife's wedding dress, speaks to me. Then I think of what I said recently to poet Kyle Dargan: "Writing has always saved me. When friendships and relationships disappear, writing has always ensured that I have a place to land." Hip-hop has been that place for so many people, a solace trapped in the breakbeat, between headphones, on linoleum, in fluid movement, behind turntables, in the arc of aerosol spray.

When I consider duende and hip-hop, I see how this culture has become an outlet from the very systemic forces that attempt to invalidate marginalized people, a place to construct possibilities for survival. When I hear Nas deliver his lyrics in "One Mic," I am transported back to the image in the video of him standing under a bare light bulb in a dark, basement-like room. There are no fans, no bling, no swag, no preposterous posturing. There is only Nas and his voice intoning how he only needs one mic. Even as each verse escalates with a different violent act that rises in volume and intensity, when he comes back to the chorus, Nas is calmly, softly telling us that one mic is solace and balm. Lorca says: "The duende's arrival always means a radical change in forms. It brings to old planes unknown feelings of freshness, with the quality of something newly created, like a miracle, and it produces an almost religious enthusiasm" (53).

This enthusiasm that he describes sounds exactly like the outlets of hip-hop culture and its global reception, which continues to permeate popular culture. So I keep thinking life is good, and I have taken Martin Luther King saying "longevity has its place" as more than a familiar phrase. There is always this pressure to live, but to see Nas lean back as a grown man and say he is alive and financially secure while explaining how those very conditions that could have killed him made him stronger and proud—not in the sense of Horatio Alger, but as a person who is continually typecast as a criminal incapable of happiness, joy, or a nuanced, complex history. This is what I think when I look at my youngest brother or when I consider J. California Cooper's novel *Family*. In *Family*, a mother attempts to poison herself and her children to avoid the relentless trauma of slavery. She becomes a ghost who narrates the story of her children, who are unsuccessfully poisoned and eventually flung all over the world. There is joy in surviving, and the psychic weight gives them ways of expressing themselves that she never imagined. So when Chrisette Michelle sings the following hook in Nas's "Can't Forget about You," I think of my youngest brother and how proud we both are that we've made it—even though death is inevitable, and often, the very thing that impedes the lives of those we love. I'll end with this hook: "These streets hold my deepest days/

This hood taught me golden ways/ Made me, truly this is what made me/ Break me, not a thing's gonna break me/ I'm that history/ I'm that block/ I'm that lifestyle/ I'm that spot....That's my past that made me hot/ Here's my lifelong anthem/ Can't forget about you."

Works Cited

Lorca, Federico. *In Search of Duende* (New York: New Directions, 1998).

Lorde. "Royals." *Pure Heroine.* Universal Music Group, 2013.

Nas. "Can't Forget About You." *Hip Hop Is Dead.* Def Jam Recordings, 2006.

Roger Bonair-Agard

Journeying to the break: The cost of the pilgrimage

I got to go to the record store with my parents when I was nine to purchase my first record of my own. It was 1977 and we lived in Winnipeg, Canada. Disco was still strong and had not yet suffered the all-out culture attack on its existence that led to its dismantling and rebuilding into house music. I picked the album *Risque* by the group Chic, encouraged by the heady beat and strident vocals on their hit single "Good Times." I was taken in too, by the group's album-cover swagger—the beautiful, daring woman on the piano, the cool brothers standing in the background in an opulent room. That winter I stood in front of our record player and played that song over and over again, dancing until I tired myself out. I knew the song by heart, every instrumental entrance and exit, the bridge. I'd keep the cover out so I could look at them while I danced, so they could inhabit me, or I them, I guess. In that alone winter, the only black child in Greenwood Elementary, fighting in school every day, I had few friends, even though I topped most everyone else in academics, soccer, football, sprinting, and handball.

My stepfather lost his job with the Canadian government when the ruling party lost the next election and we returned to Trinidad. I had lived in Canada for a winter. We returned early in 1978. In 1979, I was about to enter secondary school. I'd passed our local elementary exit exams—the Common Entrance exams—to go to a prestigious school in the city. Everything was about to bright, new, and shiny. I rode the backseat, my mother and stepfather maneuvering the car through a mountain road, when the song from my Canadian winter came on. I recognized the beat before the first bar of music was done. I cleared my throat to join in on the opening line. Instead a fast-talking man jumped in:

I said, a hip hop the hippie to the hippie/ To the hip, hip a hop, a you don't stop the rock it/ To the bang, bang boogie, say up jump the boogie/T o the rhythm of the boogie, the beat/ Now what you hear is not a test—I'm rappin' to the beat/And me, the groove, and my friends/ Are gonna try to move your feet.

I was transfixed and transformed. I wanted to be part of whatever was going on on the radio. I talked animatedly for the rest of the ride, reaching between my parents, switching back and forth between the two stations trying to catch "Rapper's Delight" again.

That was my first introduction to the break beat—the music pulled from the top of the record and looped for a continuous beat to be emceed over. This was as much a revelation to me as the rapping itself. I had no concept of how such a thing was possible. It was like going down a cave to the place where bass lived. Someone had made such a journey possible, and the guy talking was the journey's narrator.

Art that is born in and of the African diaspora is an art that takes the scraps of a culture that has been designed to allow it nothing and repurposed those scraps into fantastical, modern inventions. African diasporic art has given us the collage of Bearden, steel orchestra music from discarded oil drums, reggae, blues, Afro-beat, the fashion of Azede Jean-Pierre, and everything ever done with a turntable and a switch in hip-hop culture. It is an intellectual property arrived at in a set-up meant to deny the sons and daughters of Africa any kind of enfranchisement in the modern Western capitalist world, which defines one's personhood by such enfranchisement and ownership. As such, this art made in the African diaspora becomes the only property of the owner—the thing worth defending with one's blood when necessary.

To consider the breadth and depth of what the break beat means, and how it can be deconstructed, is to understand first of all what it means to build and compose a music from such corridors of already existing music; what it means to build a completely new sound, a new series of tunnels down the cave to the place where bass lives. To consider the break beat, therefore, is a kind of hajj, a journey that must not be lightly undertaken. Where the break leads is a treacherous place and desperation has sent its composer there. What she has uncovered is sacred for what she has had to endure to get there. What you are witnessing is a religion that might change you forever. Indeed it must.

The break beat is also the secrets of the mask maker's wire-bending, which he will take with him to his grave. It is also Jit Samaroo's complex orchestral arrangements, locked away in his head by Alzheimer's. The break beat is everyday on the streets of the Lower East Side of NYC and South Side of Chicago and the Ninth Ward of New Orleans, where fashion heads are trolling for the innovation that will become the latest craze. It is the poems of Douglas Kearney and the collage of Krista Franklin and in the three-dimensional poem-song-sculptures of avery r. young. The break is forever chipping away new labyrinths toward the place where the human soul goes to feed when nothing else will let it eat. The break is moving. It is a shape-shifter and a trickster. I imagine the orisa Elegba guarding the gates of the break—demanding tribute to be allowed on the journey, whether as composer or witness.

The lyrics of the song from which that first break beat came begin "Good Times!" *These are the good times/ Leave your cares behind!* These are the lyrics pre-empted by Wonderman's admonition about how imperative it *was* that you "try to move your feet." This too is the work of the break beat in the African diasporic tradition. It must show one message and interrupt it with another. The break beat is a direct descendant of the Negro spiritual, the wailing of the song to cross Jordan that tells you Mama Harriet is making a trip. The break beat is our own intellectual property, but it is also about a journey to be undertaken when we know we must cover our tracks or risk death. Even the strident, celebratory tones of Chic know their message is the cover for the deep digging that is going down, for the journey that disco was before it got waylaid by whatever is always trying to tell Black art how to present itself in the world. "Leave your cares behind" is directly related to the fact that *what you hear is not a test.*

The anthology here is peopled with writers who've paid their tribute to Papa 'Legba one way or the next. They've studied and lived in the liminal space from which the break emanates. They've pledged to the tradition of the break and the pilgrimage it demands. Each is chipping away a different maze to get to where bass lives, and ensuring that his tracks can only be followed by those who pay the necessary tithes. It is why this anthology is a bible and a code-book. It is essential reading, and trickster it is—offering several doors through which you may enter, if you have a clue about what you're travelling to.

Patrick Rosal

The Art of the Mistake: Some Notes On Breaking as Making

Things—somewhere in the slim inch between a dancer's body and the ragged piece of cardboard pulled over the street—go wrong. Even if you know the trick to the suicide: the dip at the knees, loose wrists at your side, how detonation begins at the toes, up into the flip, landing not on your feet again—but on your back—even if you know you have to over-rotate just slightly so your soles and palms slap the floor to spare your spine the full force of the fall, things, inevitably, go wrong.

Let me tell you this story. One summer night, circa 1986, Boys Club, Jersey City, the cypher started on the dance floor off-center, just the dancers and a couple round-the-way honeys twirling their curls, when an uprock battle broke out between my ragtag crew and a six-pack of athletic dancers from the other side of Newark Ave. There was nothing really impressive about the battle, just the usual: poppers with no bones, windmills, backspins, hopping handspins, a couple biters here and there. Mostly, we were getting our asses whupped.

But then a friend of mine, June Jacinto, stepped into the circle in his b-boy stance, did a corny little toprock and, god bless him, bolted off his chunky size 7 ½ feet into the air and did a suicide. It was dark and the move was quick, so we couldn't see exactly how he did it, but the hard smack of his body against the floor met with a brief gasp from the crowd which detonated into "Ahhhhh shit!!" and a chorus of "Hooooo!" for the last thing we saw was June frozen on his back in b-boy mockery of the other crew; turns out, in the middle of his front flip, he slipped off his krep and, in some split second between takeoff and landing, placed the grimy shell-toe behind his head, finally laid out, reclined on his back, one leg crossed over the other, in an effortless freeze. The battle was over. The other crew, dispirited, got taken out.

It was the sickest version of that back-cracking dance move I had ever seen. I had no idea June knew how to give up his hands to catch his shoe in the middle of a suicide and place it behind his head like that. Well, evidently, neither did June. As the circle broke up, he told us that his sneaker flew off mid-air and he *happened* to catch it. Instinctively, he slipped it behind his head and landed with a smile on his face like he had planned the feat all along.

Dissonance is a kind of sense. Wonder, just another version of being lost. An artist constructs things out of what he's got, what's right in front of him: a sound, a hue, an image, some line or phrase that is whole or familiar, and then—he plays. It's all material for the making. We hope to stumble upon the unlikely ways a familiar thing might detune, fissure, impinge, or twist until—well—it breaks, hopefully, into something compelling, maybe new. "Play every note loud—especially the wrong ones," Dizzy Gillespie once said. "Si me preguntáis de dónde soy, tengo que conversar con cosas rotas," writes Pablo Neruda. ("If you ask me where I'm from, I have to speak with broken things.") A poet makes use of what's ruined, discarded, or forgotten, improbable places. All great American art, you could say, is an ode to asymmetry.

Emily Dickinson writes, "Tell all the truth but tell it slant." Not proportionate, level, and square. What if truth can be crafted out of bad angles? This, too, is the art of the accident, the moment when one abandons old notions of gravity and becomes, as a result, curious about new coefficients of friction. It is the botched dance move, the wrong note, and the truth told slant which replicate a moment in midair, a suspension, where it seems anything, terrifyingly, can happen.

I think maybe June had done hundreds of suicides before that night, when the b-boy gods cursed him with fat laces that were just a little too slack on one shoe. June didn't practice that battle-ending, shoe-catching front flip. He hadn't even imagined it until he got that move off at the Boys Club. What he did practice was risk. He paid in cuts and contusions many, many times before that glorious suicide. There were the dozens of mistakes in basements, house parties, street corner ciphers. Some mistakes you keep for good. As breakers, we believed all of them were worth the trouble.

[break!]

The *break* is the moment when everything in a song stops—except for the drums and bass or the drums alone. When Kool Herc, as we know, took two copies of the same record and spun the break back and forth, he extended the drum beat for as long as people on the floor wanted it to last. Thanks to Herc, the break wasn't just a fissure, a brief account, a short reprieve; it was the ongoing pulse, the call to what Afrika Bambaataa calls the Godself. Instead of thinking of it as a moment that comes and goes, the whole music was a sustained breaking. Herc changed the notion/ the practice/the role of the break in history. He changed history, music as intervention, dance as intervention, the ticks on the clock become the proverbial *break* o'dawn.

[break!]

When we think of a break in terms of business and industry, it's a period of time in which production stops. But on the dance floor, the break is when the crowd goes to work, movin' and groovin' and shakin' and winin'. While the work of business emphasizes efficiency, outcomes, regulation, and activity, work on the dance floor is about getting loose and getting lost.

For us young dancers the break and the breaking had to be *funky*, a word which Abdel Shakur, in his editorial introduction for the funk issue of the *Indiana Review* a few years back, traces to an African word that refers to the sweaty, musky smell of an elder, a stink which communities understand as a sign of wisdom, perfume as proof of a life lived, troubles troubled, olfactory evidence of access to the barely reachable, to the spiritual unknown.

[break!]

Poems are models for the ways that dreams intrude upon fact, mystery upon certainty, dissonance upon harmony, the grotesque upon the elegant upon the lopsided upon the mundane. They are worlds broken into one another. Think of the last stanza of Aunt Emily's famous poem "I felt a Funeral, in my brain":

> And then a Plan in Reason, broke,
> And I dropped down, and down—
> And hit a World, at every plunge,
> And Finished knowing—then—

When we arrive at the end of knowing, where do we end up? Here:
"___"

"—," a visual representation of the end of "knowing," the end of received logic, a subversion of rigid reason. The poem (and the knowing) end with "—." That is, we arrive at the break itself.

[break!]

In "The Stretching of the Belly," poet Etheridge Knight takes Dickinson's "—," her typographical representation of the limit of knowledge and reason, and makes it funky:

> Markings are / not to / be mocked
> Markings are medicants
> Markings / are / signs
> Along the hi / way

Scars are / not
Marking scars do / not / come from stars
Or the moon Scars come from wars
From war / men who plunge

Knight's callback to Dickinson is remarkable. He takes her break in reason, "—", and breaks it with "/". In other words, he breaks the break.

Herc finds a way to do on vinyl what Knight is doing on the page and in the air—a way to perpetuate the break, a way for the music to break itself. I have often heard white readers of Knight refer to his "markings" as self-indulgent and gimmicky. In fact, Knight's slash mark honors the "—" of Dickinson's lyric while, at the same time, making it its own. It is arbitrary. It is a legit diacritic mark. The root of the word *diacritic* (*krinein*, cf. *crisis*), in fact, comes from the Greek word meaning *to separate*. "Markings / are / signs."

Check out how Dickinson's "—" splits Heaven from earth or Heaven from hell. Knight's "/," on the other hand, points to both simultaneously. Dickinson tells us the truth "slant," Knight shows it.

You might even, for a moment, imagine the diacritic mark of each poet as a dancer. Then Dickinson's "—" is June's body mid-suicide or a ballet dancer's perfectly horizontal jeté. Knight's "/" touches stratosphere and dirt at the same time. So while a conventional break might mark a chasm or gap, it is also the site of contact, of touch itself.

[break!]

Call it mystery or the numinous; some might call it the Holy Spirit or God itself. It is the very subject of the question that marks art and science as kin: it is the how-so and what-if. John Keats urged, in the idiom of his time and place, that we should write poems we have no business or talent to write. Effort—fueled by surprise. And to be open to surprise is to yield some portion of one's will to what one does not know for certain by logic alone (negative capability).

[break!]

A poet is one who—sometimes by the peculiar wit of stick-up kid, trickster, aswang, b-boy, duende—*breaks into* language, i.e., puts himself at risk. And an artist breaks only by being vulnerable to his own breaking.

[break!]

Flaws and fractures are the substance of the imagination. Breaking is making. Risk and mistake, conceived in the slim inch of the crossfade or cut, between trapezius and concrete, when one has dared to leave his feet, bruised and busted up with regular abandon, when one has tested the air, without knowing how things might fly off. You can get to Heaven by ascent, but what the American traditions teach us is: you can't get up unless you know how to break it on down.

Blueprint for BreakBeat Writing

I was born in 1989, at the end of hip-hop's infancy. By the time I dropped into being, hip-hop had a Grammy and platinum records. Reagan had already wreaked his brand of havoc on the American underclasses and crack was well integrated into our communities. By the time I came of age, much of the cultural context for hip-hop was already in motion—drug war, mass incarceration, neoliberalism, post–civil rights respectability politics, urban divestment and subsequent repatriating gentrification, zero-tolerance schooling and policing. I don't have a particular moment when I "discovered" hip-hop or saw it take over the world. For folks of my age bracket (late '80s to early '90s), hip-hop was a central part of the zeitgeist; the rapper was just as viable a musical star as the singer. I was a child when hip-hop surpassed country as America's biggest-selling musical genre. The centrality of hip-hop to cultural identity isn't an argument to me so much as it's the up that is sky.

Hip-hop is an imperfect culture, reflective of an imperfect people. Hip-hop, like the dominant worldwide culture, is cis-male-hetero dominated. This is wack. This is a vital point to start with and one that I will return to later, and that we all must return to in every conversation.

Hip-hop music is an ecosystem. Hip-hop speaks to multiple artistic media and an entire shifting coda of language, dress, attitude, and political thought. Hip-hop music also falls at the intersection of musical form and political/poetic speech because much of the music is especially text-heavy. Hip-hop is as much about what is being said as it is about how it sounds. In traditional poetry we express this spectrum as lyric versus narrative. While we recognize some rappers as important because of their sonic genius rather than deep content (Missy Elliot or Biz Markie), we recognize others as vital because of what they had to say despite a limited sonic or rhythmic range (Tupac or Chuck D). Each rapper carries elements of both properties, but it is important to point this out for critics who might question the level of artistic value in some of hip-hop's more textually simplistic figures.

But the central question of my work as an editor and poet remains: what does any of this hip-hop shit have to do with poetry? The answer is, quite simply, everything. W. E. B. Du Bois, when he writes his early masterpiece, *The Souls of Black Folk*, takes up the task of theorizing how black folks got over, how they made it to his early twentieth-century present day. His first answer and recurring refrain is music. He positions the sorrow songs as central to the culture of Black folks through and rising out of slavery and he points out the direct tie between Black America's artistic value and their ability to educate themselves (e.g, the Fisk Jubilee Singers as the foundational fundraising arm of Fisk University).

Du Bois writes, "The problem of the twentieth century is the problem of the color-line." He posits that now after the broken promise of Reconstruction, the quandary of what to do with this new, semi-free, Black class of Americans would be the central question for the country to answer. America answered. America's answer to Du Bois,' "problem of the color-line" was death. Economic, civil, sexual, psychic, and physical death were the strategies employed in that century through sharecropping and debt peonage, ghettoizing and redlining, lynching and rape, over-sexualizing and asexualizing, mass incarceration and police brutality, poll tax and offender disenfranchisement, suburbanization and gentrification, etc.

However, the conversation between power and the disempowered does not end with America's answer. Black folks responded artistically and politically by asserting the importance of their lives. This assertion of life is present in every major Back artistic movement from the Harlem Renaissance to the Black Arts Movement to the current movement of BreakBeat Poetics. This assertion of life is maybe best articulated in Lucille Clifton's masterwork, "won't you celebrate with me," in which she says, "come celebrate/ with me that everyday/ something has tried to kill me/ and has failed." For Clifton, celebration is central as a nonwhite, nonmale person who defies the odds by continuing to draw breath. This declaration of living and the resolve to celebrate that life is in direct opposition to the dominant American agenda.

Hip-hop would pick up this mantle in full almost immediately because of its genesis as a party music of the divested urban underclass. The Notorious B.I.G. insightfully raises this exact point when he borrows the ending of the Last Poets' important composition "When the Revolution Comes" to serve as the centerpiece of his early solo track "Party and Bullshit." In this song, Biggie describes the before, during, and after of a hypothetical party scene as a means to contemplate his own mortality and the mortality of his peers. Biggie's potential violence in this record is not senseless; it's a strategy to preserve his life and the lives of those he loves. The listener looking to dismiss this song as shallow is not listening.

The writers we present in these pages are the offspring of Clifton and Biggie. We are the offspring of Nathaniel Mackey and Missy Elliot.

Phyllis Wheatley and Lil' Kim. Pablo Neruda and Rakim. Carl Sandburg and Common. Frank Marshall Davis and Melle Mel. Essex Hemphill and Queen Latifah. The Dark Room Collective and the Wu-Tang Clan. Carl Phillips and MF Doom. James Baldwin and Tupac Shakur. Nikki Giovanni and Kendrick Lamar. Li-Young Lee and MC Lyte. The Native Tongues and the Nuyoricans. We are many.

We write to assert the existence of our selves, to assert our right to our own lives and bodies. These considerations influence not only the subject matter but also the aesthetic approach to making poems. I understand this influence to manifest itself in a number of ways:

1. We believe in the necessity for poems to live in multiple media (page, performance, video, audio, various multigenre presentational forms).

2. We believe in work rooted in a democratic cypher of ideas rather than privileging high intellectual or artistic pedigree. For us everything is on the table and equally valid until proven wack.

3. We believe in a foundational canon that is multicultural and multiethnic by definition and that celebrates and elevates the art and lives of people of color.

4. We believe in art that speaks to people's lived personal and political experience.

5. We believe in art that invites, acknowledges, and celebrates the voices of poor people and other disenfranchised people.

6. We believe in art that samples, steals, and borrows to create the most compelling and important work possible.

7. We believe in Alice Fulton's charge to "make it new" and/or Andre 3000's revelation that "you only funky as your last cut."

This list is not perfect, but it is intended to gesture toward the foundational ethics that I've observed in my generation of makers born directly into hip-hop. The poems we have worked to compile are not perfect. Hip-hop is an imperfect culture, reflective of an imperfect people. *The BreakBeat Poets* is an anthology edited by three cisgender, hetero men who claim Chicago as their personal artistic capital. I think it is important to name. I hope that by doing so we can continue the conversation and encourage others to add to the incomplete cypher we've set forth. That is, for me, the ethic of hip-hop. The most primary rule is that the cypher must expand and must stay current. Hip-hop is shark art; when it stops moving it dies. I aim for this anthology to add to the conversation about hip-hop and literature and life. Most of all, I aim for this anthology to be an expansive invitation for all.

Alfaro, Ben. "What the Eyes Saw." *Uncommon Core: Contemporary Poems for Learning and Living.* Red Beard Press, 2013.

Andersen, Lemon. "The future." *County of Kings.* 2009.

Asghar, Fatimah. "Unemployment Poem #2." *Word Riot.* 2013.

Asghar, Fatimah. "When Tip Drill Comes on at the Frat Party Or, When Refusing to Twerk Is a Radical Form of Self-Love." *Courage: Daring Poems for Gutsy Girls.* Write Bloody Publishing, 2014.

Barnes, Aziza. "Juicy (an erasure)." *me Aunt Jemima and the nailgun.* Button Poetry, 2013.

Betts, Tara. "Switch." *Arc & Hue.* Aquarius Press/Willow Books, 2009.

Blake, Sarah. "Adventures." *Mr. West.* Wesleyan University Press, 2014.

Blake, Sarah. "Ha Ha Hum." *Mr. West.* Wesleyan University Press, 2014.

Brown, Jericho. "Motherland." *The New Testament.* Copper Canyon Press, 2014.

Choi, Franny. "PUSSY MONSTER." *Floating, Brilliant, Gone: Poems.* Write Bloody Publishing, 2014.

Cirelli, Michael. "The Message." *Lobster with Ol' Dirty Bastard.* Hanging Loose Press, 2008.

Cirelli, Michael. "Astronomy (8th Light)." *Vacations on the Black Star Line.* Hanging Loose Press, 2010.

Coval, Kevin. "the crossover." *L-vis Lives! Racemusic Poems.* Haymarket Books, 2011.

Coval, Kevin. "jewtown." *Schtick: These Are The Poems, People.* Haymarket Books, 2013.

Diggs, LaTasha N. Nevada. "damn right it's betta than yours." *TwERK.* Belladonna, 2013.

Diggs, LaTasha N. Nevada. "gamin' gabby." *TwERK.* Belladonna, 2013.

Diggs, LaTasha N. Nevada. "who you callin' a jynx? (after mista popo)." *TwERK.* Belladonna, 2013.

Douglas, Mitchell L. H. "HOOD." *Blak al-fe Bet: Poems.* Persea Books, 2013.

Faizullah, Tarfia. "NOCTURNE IN NEED OF A BITCH." *Blackbird.* 2012.

Faizullah, Tarfia. "SELF-PORTRAIT AS SLINKY." *Ninth Letter.* 2013.

Faizullah, Tarfia. "BLOSSOMS IN THE DARK." *jubilat.* 2014.

Faizullah, Tarfia. "100 BELLS." *Poetry.* 2015.

Felix, Camonghne. "Police." *Bayou.* 2014.

Girmay, Aracelis. "BREAK." *Kingdom Animalia: Poems.* BOA Editions, 2011.

Girmay, Aracelis. "ELEGY IN GOLD." *Kingdom Animalia: Poems.* BOA Editions, 2011.

Goodwin, Idris. "Old ladies and dope boys." *These Are the Breaks.* Write Bloody Publishing, 2011.

Goodwin, Idris. "Say my name." *These Are the Breaks.* Write Bloody

Publishing, 2011.

Goodwin, Idris. "These are the breaks." *These Are the Breaks*. Write Bloody Publishing, 2011.

Hammad, Suheir. "break (embargo)." *Breaking Poems*. Cypher Books, 2008.

Hammad, Suheir. "break (rebirth)." *Breaking Poems*. Cypher Books, 2008.

Hammad, Suheir. "break (sister)." *Breaking Poems*. Cypher Books, 2008.

Hodge, Chinaka. "Small Poems for Big." *Toss the Earth: Poems that Move Us: A Penmanship Anthology*. Penmanship Books, 2012.

Kearney, Douglas. "Quantum Spit." *Quantum Spit: A Poem*. Corollary Press, 2010.

Kearney, Douglas. "Drop It Like It's Hottentot Venus." *SkinMag*. A5/Deadly Chaps, 2012.

Kearney, Douglas. "No Homo." *SkinMag*. A5/Deadly Chaps, 2012.

Lansana, Quraysh Ali. "seventy-first & king drive." *Southside Rain*. Third World Press, 1999.

Lansana, Quraysh Ali. "crack house." *Mystic Turf: Poems*. Willow Books, 2012.

Lansana, Quraysh Ali. "mascot." *Mystic Turf: Poems*. Willow Books, 2012.

Marshall, Nate. "prelude." *Anti-*. 2013.

Marshall, Nate. "juke." *Indiana Review*. 2014.

Matejka, Adrian. "Beat Boxing." *Copper Nickel*. 2010.

Matejka, Adrian. "Robot Music." *Copper Nickel*. 2010.

McConnell, Marty. "The World tells how the world ends." *Medulla Review*. 2012.

McConnell, Marty. "object." *Lavender Review*. 2013.

Medina, Tony. "Everything You Wanted to Know about Hip Hop But Were Afraid to Be Hipped for Fear of Being Hopped." *An Onion of Wars*. Third World Press, 2012.

Medina, Tony. "The Keepin' It Real Awards." *An Onion of Wars*. Third World Press, 2012.

Miller, Ciara. "In Search of Black Birds." *Muzzle*. 2015.

Mlekoday, Michael. "Self Portrait from the Other Side." *The Dead Eat Everything*. Kent State University Press, 2014.

Mlekoday, Michael. "Self Portrait with Gunshot Vernacular." *The Dead Eat Everything*. Kent State University Press, 2014.

Mlekoday, Michael. "Thaumaturgy." *The Dead Eat Everything*. Kent State University Press, 2014.

Morris, Tracie. "Untitled." *Rhyme Scheme*. Zasterle Press, 2012.

Murillo, John. "1989." *Up Jump the Boogie: Poems*. Cypher Books, 2010.

Murillo, John. "Ode to the Crossfader." *Up Jump the Boogie: Poems*. Cypher Books, 2010.

Murillo, John. "Renegades of Funk." *Up Jump the Boogie: Poems*. Cypher Books, 2010.

Nafis, Angel. "Conspiracy: a Suite." *BlackGirl Mansion*. Red Beard Press, 2012.

Nafis, Angel. "Ghazal for My Sister." *BlackGirl Mansion*. Red Beard Press, 2012.

Nafis, Angel. "Gravity." *BlackGirl Mansion*. Red Beard Press, 2012.

Nafis, Angel. "Legend." *BlackGirl Mansion*. Red Beard Press, 2012.

Olivarez, Jose. "Ode to the First White Girl I Ever Loved." *Uncommon Core: Contemporary Poems for Learning and Living*. Red Beard Press, 2013.

Olivarez, Jose. "Home Court." *Home Court*. Red Beard Press, 2014.

Perdomo, Willie. "Shit To Write About." *Smoking Lovely*. Rattapallax Press, 2003.

Perdomo, Willie. "Word to Everything I Love." *Smoking Lovely*. Rattapallax Press, 2003.

Perdomo, Willie. "Writing about What You Know." *Smoking Lovely*. Rattapallax Press, 2003.

Priest, Joy. "No Country for Black Boys." *Black Space*. 2013.

Rosal, Patrick. "B-Boy Infinitives." *Uprock Headspin Scramble and Dive: Poems*. Persea Books, 2003.

Rosal, Patrick. "Kundiman Ending on a Theme from T La Rock." *My American Kundiman: Poems*. Persea Books, 2006.

Saenz, Jacob. "Evolution of My Block." *Poetry*. 2010.

Saenz, Jacob. "GTA: San Andreas (Or, 'Grove Street, bitch!')." *Poetry*. 2012.

Saenz, Jacob. "Evolution of My Profile." *Jet Fuel Review*. 2013.

Shockley, Evie. "duck, duck, redux." *The New Black*. Wesleyan University Press, 2011.

Shockley, Evie. "post-white." *The New Black*. Wesleyan University Press, 2011.

Smith, Danez. "cue the gangsta rap when my knees bend." *RHINO*. 2014.

Smith, Danez. "Dinosaurs In The Hood." *Poetry*. 2014.

Smith, Danez. "Dear White America." *HEArt Online*. 2014.

Tallie, Mariahadessa Ekere. "Global Warming Blues." *Women's Studies Quarterly*. 2014.

Tallie, Mariahadessa Ekere. "Paper Bag Poems." *Black Renaissance Noire*. 2014.

Tallie, Mariahadessa Ekere. "Sunday." *Minerva Rising*. 2014.

Thornhill, Samantha. "Elegy for a Trojan." *Spaces Between Us: Poetry, Prose and Art on HIV/AIDS*. Third World Press, 2010.

Thornhill, Samantha. "Ode to a Killer Whale." *Cimarron Review*. 2010.

Thornhill, Samantha. "Ode to a Star Fig." *Hedgebrook Cookbook: Celebrating Radical Hospitality*. She Writes Press, 2013.

Vuong, Ocean. "Prayer for the Newly Damned." *American Poetry Review*. 2012.

Vuong, Ocean. "Self-Portrait as Exit Wounds." *Assaracus*. 2012.

Vuong, Ocean. "Always & Forever." *Quarterly West*. 2013.

Vuong, Ocean. "Daily Bread." *Crab Orchard Review*. 2013.

Wicker, Marcus. "Ars Poetica in the Mode of J-Live." *Maybe the Saddest Thing: Poems*. Harper Perennial, 2012.

Wicker, Marcus. "Bonita Applebum." *Maybe the Saddest Thing: Poems*. Harper Perennial, 2012.

Wicker, Marcus. "Stakes Is High." *Maybe the Saddest Thing: Poems*. Harper Perennial, 2012.

Wicker, Marcus. "When I'm alone in my room sometimes I stare at the wall, and in the back of my mind I hear my conscience call." *Maybe the Saddest Thing: Poems*. Harper Perennial, 2012.

salutes: Nate & Quraysh, two of the illest and smartest writers i know, what a privilege it is to build and create with y'all. Idris Goodwin, for the title and ideas thrown around on the damn near daily, all that shit and shit-talk saves me. all the staff at Haymarket Books for their grind and dedication to the word(s) / word. Anthony and Julie for continuing to believe in me and all these books. Hebru Brantley, and his manager Pia, for the cover art and making the city/ country/ world a fresher place to be. all the poets in the book, y'all crazy with it, and nice and nice with it, thank you for the privilege of sharing your work. all the staff at Young Chicago Authors for giving me the space to make, for supporting and believing and living the work and the word. Rebecca Hunter for the all support and building. all the Louder Than A Bomb poets who continue to courage in public and spit that raw and that real. all the hip-hop artists who inspire and inspired me, all the folks who create the fresh shit and next shit and could give a fuck. keep it coming. keep it funky.   **—Kevin Coval**

This book, in so many ways, represents how I see, think and move through the universe. Love to Kevin for the vision and Nate for nurturing concept to reality. We did it, fellas.

Big thanks to Julie Fain, Rachel Cohen, Tamara Nopper, and the outstanding crew of humans at Haymarket Books for guidance, patience and understanding. I am proud to join your impressive book list. Love to all the poets and artists who live in this book and make this book live. Thanks to Mama Sonia Sanchez and Bob Holman for ageless wisdom and support. Special thanks to my teenage sons, Nile and Onam, the youngest contributors to this book, and the most important.   **—Quraysh Ali Lansana**

Shoutout to Kevin & Q for building this beast of a book with me and for trusting me to be young and to show and prove. Shoutout to Julie, Rachel, Tamara, and the whole posse at Haymarket for their commitment to this project. Shoutout to all the poets in this book for your words and your belief. Shoutout to my grandma (RIP) for taking me to my first hip-hop jam when I was a shorty and hanging out as an old lady in a room full of MCs, breakers, graf writers, and other ne'er-do-well dreaming kids. Shoutout to my mom for playing Lauryn Hill, Too $hort, Kurtis Blow, and so much of the canon in the crib. Shoutout to Mr. Muhammad for letting us write raps for vocabulary extra credit. Shoutout to Mark Jarman for letting me play Dead Prez and argue with you in Vanderbilt's English Department once a week. Shoutout to my whole Chicago hip-hop community for being the best poetry workshops. Special shoutout to JusLove, SCP, Defcee, Wizard Jenkins, Jyroscope, ADD-2, FM Supreme, Green Slime, and Vic Mensa for rocking with a young MC.   **—Nate Marshall**

Biographies

Editors

Kevin Coval is the author of *Schtick, L-vis Lives!: Racemusic Poems, Everyday People, Slingshots: A Hip-Hop Poetica*, and *More Shit Chief Keef Don't Like*. Coval is the founder of Louder Than A Bomb: The Chicago Youth Poetry Festival and artistic director of Young Chicago Authors. Coval won a New Voices/New Visions award from the Kennedy Center for a play coauthored with Idris Goodwin about graffiti writers called *This is Modern Art*, which premiered at Steppenwolf Theater.

Quraysh Ali Lansana is the author of eight poetry books, three textbooks, and a children's book, the editor of eight anthologies, and the coauthor of a book of pedagogy. He is a faculty member of the Creative Writing Program of the School of the Art Institute and the Red Earth MFA Creative Writing Program at Oklahoma City University. He is also a former faculty member of the Drama Division of the Juilliard School. Lansana served as director of the Gwendolyn Brooks Center for Black Literature and Creative Writing at Chicago State University from 2002 to 2011, where he was also associate professor of english/creative writing. *Our Difficult Sunlight: A Guide to Poetry, Literacy and Social Justice in Classroom & Community* (with Georgia A. Popoff) was published in March 2011 by Teachers & Writers Collaborative and was a 2012 NAACP Image Award nominee. His most recent books include *The Walmart Republic,* with Christopher Stewart (Mongrel Empire Press, September 2014), and *reluctant minivan* (Living Arts Press, May 2014).

Nate Marshall is from the South Side of Chicago. His first book, *Wild Hundreds*, won the Agnes Lynch Starrett Prize and is forthcoming from the University of Pittsburgh Press. He received his MFA from the Helen Zell Writers' Center at the University of Michigan and is a Cave Canem Fellow. His work has appeared in *Poetry,* the *New Republic*, and elsewhere. Nate won the 2014 Hurston/Wright Founding Members Award and the 2013 Gwendolyn Brooks Open Mic Award. He is a founding member of the poetry collective Dark Noise. He is also a rapper.

Benjamin Alfaro is a Detroit-based writer and teaching artist. He is the coauthor of a collaborative poetry collection, *Home Court* (Red Beard Press, 2014) and has been published widely. He is a writer in residence and youth leadership coordinator with the InsideOut Literary Arts Project, serving area high schools and community centers.

Lemon Andersen is a Brooklyn-based playwright, television writer, brand creative, and Tony Award–winning poet. He has been interviewed and profiled by National Public Radio, the *New York Times*, NBC, and the *Wall Street Journal* and published in the *Nation* magazine. His engaged YouTube audience totals upwards of one million viewers.

Fatimah Asghar is a poet, scholar, and performer. Her work appears in the *Paris-American, Drunken Boat, Word Riot*, and elsewhere. She created Bosnia and Herzegovina's first spoken-word poetry group, REFLEKS, while on a Fulbright studying theater in post-violent contexts. Her chapbook *Rewind/Play* is forthcoming from YesYes Books in summer 2015.

Aziza Barnes is twenty-two, blk & alive. Her first chapbook, *me Aunt Jemima and the nailgun*, won the first Exploding Pinecone Prize. Her work appears in *PANK, PLUCK!*, and *Callaloo*. She is a poetry editor at *Kinfolks Quarterly*, a *Callaloo* fellow, and a graduate of NYU's Tisch School of the Arts.

Joshua Bennett is a Princeton University doctoral candidate and has received fellowships from the Ford Foundation and Callaloo Creative Writing Workshop. Joshua's wirk has won the Lucille Clifton Poetry Prize, and is published in *Anti-, Callaloo,* and the *Collagist*. He is also founding editor of *Kinfolks: A journal of black expression*.

Tara Betts is author of *Arc & Hue* and *THE GREATEST!: An Homage to Muhammad Ali*. A Ph.D. candidate and a Cave Canem fellow, she is coeditor of *Bop, Strut, and Dance*. During the 1990s, Tara wrote as a hip-hop journalist for several publications, including *XXL* and the *Source*.

Sarah Blake is the founder of the online writing tool Submittrs, an editor at Saturnalia Books, and a recipient of an NEA Literature Fellowship. Her first book, *Mr. West*, is an unauthorized lyric biography of Kanye West published by Wesleyan University Press. She lives outside Philadelphia, Pennsylvania.

Reed Adair Bobroff is To'dich'íínii Diné from New Mexico and a student at Yale University. Primarily a spoken-word artist, he has been featured on HBO's *Brave New Voices* and performed in numerous cities. Reed is the founder of Spoken Roots, which teaches poetry in underserved and Native American communities.

Roger Bonair-Agard was born in Trinidad and Tobago. His collections of poetry include *Tarnish and Masquerade*, *Gully*, and *Bury My Clothes* (long-list finalist for a National Book Award). He is a two-time National Poetry Slam champion and a Cave Canem fellow and teaches poetry at a juvenile detention facility in Chicago.

Jericho Brown is the recipient of fellowships from Harvard University and the NEA. His first book, *Please*, won the American Book Award and his second book, *The New Testament*, was published by Copper Canyon Press. He is an assistant professor in the creative writing program at Emory University in Atlanta.

Mahogany L. Browne is the author of *Swag* and *Dear Twitter: Love Letters Hashed Out On-line*. She has released five LPs and her journalism is published in *XXL* and the *Source*. She is an Urban Word NYC mentor, publisher of Penmanship Books, and director of poetry at Nuyorican Poets Cafe.

Jason Carney is an award-winning poet, writer, and educator from Dallas, Texas. A four-time National Poetry Slam Finalist, he appeared on three seasons of HBO's *Def Poetry Jam*. He is a graduate of Wilkes University MFA program for creative writing and an adjunct instructor at Brookhaven College and Parker University.

Franny Choi is the author of *Floating, Brilliant, Gone* (Write Bloody Publishing). A recipient of the Frederick Bock Prize, she has been a finalist at all three major national poetry slams. She is a VONA Fellow, a Project VOICE teaching artist, and a member of the Dark Noise Collective.

Michael Cirelli is author of four poetry collections, most recently *The Grind* (Best Book of 2014 from Amazon Editors' Favorites). He is executive director of Urban Word and teaches at New York University. The follow-up to his award-winning curriculum, *Hip-Hop Poetry & the Classics*, is forthcoming from Street Smart Press.

Kristiana Colón is a poet, playwright, actor, educator, activist, and Cave Canem Fellow. Her play *Octagon* is the winner of Arizona Theater Company's 2014 National Latino Playwriting Award and Polarity Ensemble Theater's Dionysos Festival of New Work. Kristiana appeared on season 5 of HBO's *Def Poetry Jam*.

Kyle Dargan is the author of *Honest Engine, Logorrhea Dementia, Bouquet of Hungers,* and *The Listening.* He has received the Cave Canem Poetry Prize and the Hurston/Wright Legacy Award. He is an associate professor and director of creative writing at American University and also editor of *POST NO ILLS* magazine.

Mayda Del Valle was a contributing writer and original cast member of the Tony Award–winning *Def Poetry Jam* on Broadway. She has been featured in *Latina,* the *Source,* and the *New York Times.* She is currently a teaching artist with the youth organization Street Poets in Los Angeles.

Denizen Kane was a poet from Tree City. He wrote a heap of poems and wandered around for a long time. But he's gone now.

Joel Dias-Porter (aka DJ Renegade) is a former professional DJ, Cave Canem fellow, and father. He has been a Haiku Slam Champion and Individual Finalist in the National Poetry Slam. His poetry appears in *Best American Poetry 2014* and *TIME.* His CD of jazz and poetry is *Libation Song.*

LaTasha N. Nevada Diggs is a writer, vocalist, and sound artist living in Harlem. The author of *TwERK* and cofounder and coeditor of *Coon Bidness, yoYO,* and *SO4,* her performances have been featured at the Museum of Modern Art, the Whitney Museum of American Art, and the Walker Art Center.

Mitchell L. H. Douglas is a cofounder of the Affrilachian Poets and associate professor of English and director of creative writing at IUPUI. His second poetry collection, *blak\ \al-fa-bet_* (Persea Books), was a winner of the 2011 Lexi Rudnitsky/Editor's Choice Award. He is a native of Louisville, Kentucky.

Safia Elhillo is Sudanese by way of Washington, D.C., currently living in New York City. A Cave Canem fellow and a poetry editor for *Kinfolks Quarterly*, she is pursuing an MFA at the New School. Her work appears in *As/Us magazine, Vinyl Poetry, Bird's Thumb*, and TV1's *Verses & Flow*.

Thomas Sayers Ellis is the author of *The Maverick Room* and *Skin, Inc.* His poems have appeared in *Poetry, Tin House*, the *Nation*, the *Paris Review*, and *Best American Poetry*. Ellis has recently been a visiting writer at Wesleyan University, the University of San Francisco, and the University of Montana.

Eve Ewing is a Chicago-born writer, teacher, scholar, and artist. Her poems and essays have appeared in *Bird's Thumb, joINT, Union Station, Blackberry, In These Times, AREA Chicago, Newcity*, and the *Chicago Weekly*. She is managing editor of *Kinfolks: A journal of black expression* and cochair of the *Harvard Educational Review*.

Tarfia Faizullah was born in Brooklyn and raised in West Texas. She is the author of *Seam* (SIU 2014). Her poems appear in *jubilat, Poetry Magazine, Kenyon Review, New England Review, Ploughshares, Best New Poets 2013*, and elsewhere. She is a visiting professor of poetry at the University of Michigan.

Adam Falkner is a writer, educator, and scholar. He is the founder and the executive director of the Dialogue Arts Project. He is also a Zankel Fellow at Columbia University's Teachers College, where he is currently a Ph.D. candidate and instructor of english education.

Camonghne Felix is an MFA candidate at the Milton Avery Graduate School of the Arts at Bard College, a Pushcart Prize nominee, and the 2013 recipient of the Cora Craig Award for Young Women. You can find her work in various publications including *Union Station, No Dear*, and elsewhere.

t'ai freedom ford is a New York City high-school English teacher and reformed "slam" poet. A Cave Canem fellow, she received her MFA in fiction from Brooklyn College. Her poetry has appeared or is forthcoming in *Drunken Boat, Velvet Park, Sinister Wisdom, Union Station, Wilde*, and *T/OUR Magazine*.

Krista Franklin is an interdisciplinary artist whose work floats between the literary and the visual with a focus on personal narrative, African diasporic cultures, and the interiority of women of color, folklore, and spiritualism. Willow Books published her chapbook *Study of Love & Black Body* in 2012.

Aracelis Girmay is the author of *Teeth* (GLCA New Writers Award) and *Kingdom Animalia* (Isabella Gardner Poetry Award and finalist for the National Book Critics Circle Award). Girmay is a faculty member of Hampshire College's School for Interdisciplinary Arts and also teaches poetry for Drew University's low-residency MFA program.

Idris Goodwin is a breakbeat poet, playwright, and essayist. He is the author of the Pushcart-nominated essay collection *These Are The Breaks* (Write Bloody, 2011) and the award-winning, widely produced play *How We Got On* (Playscripts, 2013) He has performed on HBO, *Sesame Street*, and the Discovery Channel.

Suheir Hammad is the author of *breaking poems* and recipient of a 2009 American Book Award and the Arab American Book Award for Poetry 2009. Her work has been widely anthologized and also adapted for theater. She featured in the Tony-winning *Russell Simmons Presents Def Poetry Jam* on Broadway.

Aleshea Harris is a playwright and performer who received an MFA in writing for performance from California Institute of the Arts. Her work has been shown many places including: the Edinburgh Fringe Festival, the Costume Shop at A.C.T., and L'École de la Comèdie de Saint-Étienne. She currently teaches at CalArts.

Alysia Nicole Harris is a poet, teaching-artist, and former member of the Strivers Row performance poetry collective. She is currently pursuing her Ph.D. in linguistics at Yale University and her MFA in poetry at New York University. She hails from Alexandria, Virginia, and currently lives in New Haven, Connecticut.

francine j. harris is a Cave Canem fellow and teaches at Interlochen Center for the Arts. Her first collection, *allegiance*, was a finalist for the 2013 Kate Tufts Discovery and the PEN Open Book Award. Her work has appeared or is forthcoming in *Poetry, Boston Review, Rattle, Ninth Letter*, and *Ploughshares*.

Chinaka Hodge received The 2014 San Francisco Foundation's Community Leadership Award, has been a Sundance Feature Film Lab Fellow, and was visiting editor for the *California Sunday Magazine*. She serves on the board of directors for Headlands Center for the Arts and is playwright in residence at SF Playwrights Foundation.

Randall Horton is the recipient of the Gwendolyn Brooks Poetry Award, the Bea Gonzalez Poetry Award, and most recently a National Endowment of the Arts Fellowship in Literature, and an assistant professor of English at the University of New Haven. Triquarterly/Northwestern University Press published Randall's latest poetry collection *Pitch Dark Anarchy*.

Paolo Javier is the former Queens poet laureate (2010–14) and author of four full-length poetry collections, including *Court of the Dragon*, forthcoming from Nightboat Books.

Britteney Black Rose Kapri is a Chicago teaching artist, writer, performance poet, and playwright. A former ensemble member for Kuumba Lynx, she is an alumna turned teaching artist of Young Chicago Authors. She is a member of the Not Enough Mics. Britteney's chapbook, *Winona and Winthrop*, was published in 2014.

Douglas Kearney is a poet/performer/librettist and author of *Patter* and the National Poetry Series selection *The Black Automaton*. He has received residencies/fellowships from Cave Canem, the Rauschenberg Foundation, and others. His work has appeared in journals such as *Poetry, nocturnes, Pleiades,* the *Boston Review,* and *Callaloo.* He teaches at CalArts.

Nile Lansana attends Jones College Preparatory High School in Chicago and is a member of the Rebirth Poetry Ensemble, which was among the city's top teams and participated in the 2014 Brave New Voices festival, placing among the top sixteen youth poetry teams in the world.

Onam Lansana attends Jones College Preparatory High School in Chicago and is a member of the Rebirth Poetry Ensemble. He is the youngest storyteller ever to feature at the National Association of Black Storytellers Conference. Onam has also participated in a variety of programs, including Young Chicago Authors.

Malcolm London is a young Chicago poet, performer, activist, and educator. Called the Gil Scott-Heron of this generation by Cornel West, he appeared on PBS for the first TED Talk television program with John Legend, Bill Gates, and Geoffrey Canada. London is a former Louder Than A Bomb champion.

Mario is a Chicago poet, educator, activist, and radio chat-show host who has been performing in the Chicagoland area and the United States for over twenty years. He currently hosts *News from the Service Entrance* on WHPK in Chicago and is a contributor to Chicago Public Radio's WBEZ.

Adrian Matejka is the author of *The Devil's Garden* (winner of New York/New England Award) and *Mixology* (a winner of 2008 National Poetry Series). His poetry collection, *The Big Smoke*, won the 2014 Anisfield-Wolf Book Award and was a finalist for the 2013 National Book Award and 2014 Pulitzer Prize.

Marty McConnell lives in Chicago, Illinois, and received her MFA from Sarah Lawrence College. Her work has recently appeared in *Best American Poetry 2014*, *Southern Humanities Review*, *Gulf Coast*, and *Indiana Review*. Her first full-length collection, *wine for a shotgun*, was published in 2012 by EM Press.

E'mon McGee is a senior at Austin Career Academy in Chicago and a member of Kuumba Lynx Performance Ensemble. She was a recipient of the 2014 Guthman Internship at Young Chicago Authors. She is a two-time Louder Than a Bomb poetry slam champion and a Brave New Voices participant.

Tony Medina is author of *Broke Baroque*, *An Onion of Wars*, and *My Old Man Was Always on the Lam*. A professor of creative writing at Howard University, Medina has received the Paterson Prize for Books for Young People, the Langston Hughes Society Award, and the African Voices Literary Award.

Ciara Miller is a poetry MFA candidate and an African American/African diaspora studies MA candidate at Indiana University. She has published poems and scholarly essays in *Callaloo*, *SLC Review*, *Alice Walker: Critical Insights*, *PLUCK*, *Chorus*, *Toegood Poetry*, *Cave Canem Anthology XII*, *African American Review*, *Muzzle*, and *Blackberry*.

Michael Mlekoday is a poet and performer whose first book, *The Dead Eat Everything*, was chosen by Dorianne Laux as winner of the 2012 Stan and Tom Wick Poetry Prize. Mlekoday serves as editor and publisher of Button Poetry / Exploding Pinecone Press and is a National Poetry Slam champion.

jessica Care moore is CEO of Moore Black Press, executive producer of Black WOMEN Rock!, and founder of the Jess Care Moore Foundation. The author of several works, her first recording project, *Black Tea—The Legend of Jessi James* is being released in 2015 by Talib Kweli's Javotti Media label.

Tracie Morris is a poet and multimedia performer whose most recent collection, *Rhyme Scheme*, includes a sound poetry CD. She holds an MFA from Hunter College, has studied classical British acting technique at the Royal Academy of Dramatic Art, and holds a Ph.D. in performance studies from New York University.

John Murillo teaches creative writing at New York University and is also an assistant professor of creative writing and African-American literary arts at Hampshire College. His first poetry collection *Up Jump the Boogie* was a finalist for both the 2011 Kate Tufts Discovery Award and the PEN Open Book Award.

Angel Nafis is an Ann Arbor, Michigan, native and a Cave Canem Fellow. She is the author of *BlackGirl Mansion* and her work has appeared in *Union Station, MUZZLE,* and *Mosaic.* She is an Urban Word NYC mentor and the founder of the quarterly Greenlight Bookstore Poetry Salon reading series.

José Olivarez is a nationally recognized poet, educator, and activist from Calumet City, Illinois, and author of the book *Home Court.* The son of Mexican immigrants, his work has been published in the *Acentos Review, Specter, Luna Luna,* and other places.

Angel Pantoja is a young poet who was born in Fresno, California, and raised in the Chicago Lawn neighborhood on Chicago's Southwest Side. He has one brother and two sisters. This is his first publication.

Morgan Parker is the author of *Other People's Comfort Keeps Me Up at Night*, selected by Eileen Myles for the 2013 Gatewood Prize, and *There Are More Beautiful Things than Beyoncé*. A Cave Canem fellow and poetry editor for *Coconut*, she lives in Brooklyn.

Willie Perdomo is the author of *The Essential Hits of Shorty Bon Bon*, a finalist for the National Book Critics Circle Award, *Smoking Lovely*, winner of the PEN Beyond Margins Award, and *Where a Nickel Costs a Dime*, a finalist for the Poetry Society of America's Norma Farber First Book Award. He is founder/publisher of Cypher Books, a core member of the VONA/Voices faculty and is currently an Instructor in English at Phillips Exeter Academy.

Paul Martinez Pompa is the author of *Pepper Spray* and *My Kill Adore Him*, which was awarded the Andres Montoya Poetry Prize. He is also a recent recipient of an Illinois Arts Council award.

Joy Priest was born and raised in Louisville, Kentucky. She has received grants from the Kentucky Arts Council and Bread Loaf Writers' Conference. A member of the Affrilachian Poets, her poems appear in *pluck! Journal of Affrilachian Arts & Culture, Solstice, Drunken Boat*, and *Best New Poets 2014*.

Lynne Procope is a Cave Canem fellow and a former National Poetry Slam champion. Her work has been widely published in journals and anthologies. She is curator of the Gaslight Salon Series, cofounder and managing editor of *Union Station* and executive director of the louderARTS Project.

John Rodriguez was a poet-writer-scholar. His work has appeared in *Phati'tude, One Word, Home Girls Make Some Noise, HOKUM, Days I Moved through Ordinary Sounds*, and *Bum Rush the Page.* He held a Ph.D. in English from the CUNY Graduate Center. John transitioned in 2013. Rest In Power.

Patrick Rosal has authored four poetry books, most recently *Brooklyn Antediluvian.* His essays and poems appear in *Grantland*, the *New York Times, Tin House, Gulf Coast, Harvard Review*, and *Best American Poetry.* A faculty member of the Rutgers-Camden MFA program, he is founding co-editor of *Some Call It Ballin'.*

Jacob Saenz is a CantoMundo fellow whose poetry has been published in *Poetry, TriQuarterly, Pinwheel*, and other journals. He has been the recipient of a Letras Latinas Residency and a Ruth Lilly Poetry Fellowship. He currently serves as an associate editor for RHINO.

Aaron Samuels is a Cave Canem Fellow and nationally acclaimed performer. His work has been nominated for a Pushcart Prize, featured on TV One's *Verses & Flow*, and published in *Crab Orchard Review, Muzzle*, and elsewhere. His debut collection of poetry, *Yarmulkes & Fitted Caps*, was released in 2013.

Evie Shockley is the author of *a half-red sea, the new black* (winner of the 2012 Hurston/Wright Legacy Award in Poetry), and *Renegade Poetics: Black Aesthetics and Formal Innovation in African American Poetry*. The creative writing editor for *Feminist Studies*, Shockley is an associate professor of English at Rutgers University.

Danez Smith is the winner of a 2014 Ruth Lilly/ Dorothy Sargent Rosenberg Fellowship from the Poetry Foundation. He is the author of *[insert] boy* (YesYes Books, 2014). He is a Cave Canem, VONA, and McKnight Foundation Fellow. He lives in Minneapolis, Minnesota. Ludacris was his favorite rapper for years.

Nadia Sulayman is an artist and activist from Chicago. She earned an MA in international studies with a research emphasis on poetry, hip-hop, and visual art as resistance by women in the Palestine liberation movement. She has worked in education and as a community organizer for ten years.

Enzo Silon Surin is a Haitian-born poet and social advocate. His poetry has appeared in numerous publications and he is the author of *HIGHER GROUND* (Finishing Line Press, 2006). He holds an MFA in creative writing and currently serves as an assistant professor of English at Bunker Hill Community College.

Mariahadessa Ekere Tallie is poetry editor of *African Voices* literary magazine. Her first book of poetry, *Karma's Footsteps*, was published in 2011. She earned an MFA from Mills College and has taught at Medgar Evers College and York College. She is one half of the recording duo the Quiet Onez.

Kush Thompson is an emerging teaching artist for Young Chicago Authors. In Fall 2014, she joined, as a German consulate, the Berlin-based Wort.Word.Lich collaboration for its first-ever bilingual showcase tour. Her debut chapbook, *A Church Beneath the Bulldozer*, was recently published with New School Poetics.

Samantha Thornhill performs her work across the United States, Europe, Africa, and the Caribbean. She holds her MFA in poetry from the University of Virginia and, for the past decade, she has taught poetry to actors at the Juilliard School. She is the founding curator of Poets in Unexpected Places.

Ocean Vuong is the author of *Night Sky With Exit Wounds* (Copper Canyon Press, 2016). His poems appear in the *New Yorker, Poetry,* the *Nation, Boston Review, Guernica, Best New Poets 2014,* and *American Poetry Review*, which awarded him the 2012 Stanley Kunitz Prize for Younger Poets.

Marcus Wicker is the author of *Maybe the Saddest Thing*. He has received the 2011 Ruth Lilly Fellowship and Pushcart Prize and fellowships from Cave Canem and the Fine Arts Work Center. Marcus is an assistant professor of English at the University of Southern Indiana and poetry editor of *Southern Indiana Review*.

Steven Willis was born and raised in Chicago. He attends Manhattanville College on a full scholarship. He began doing poetry at the age of fifteen as a participant in Louder Than a Bomb and prides himself on telling stories.

Jamila Woods is a poet, singer, and teaching artist from Chicago, Illinois. She is the associate artistic director of Young Chicago Authors and a member of the Dark Noise Collective. Jamila is also the front-woman of the soul-duo band M&O and has been featured in *OkayPlayer, JET,* and *Ebony.*

avery r. young is a writer, performer, and visual artist. He is a Cave Canem alum and his work appears in several publications. As artist in residence at The University of Chicago, young completed a collection of sound designs to be featured in his first full-length album *booker t. soltreyne: a race rekkid.*